SHORTLINE RAILROADS OF ARKANSAS

SHORTLINE RAILROADS OF ARKANSAS

CLIFTON E. HULL

UCA PRESS
Conway, Arkansas

UCA Press

Box S
Conway, Arkansas 72032

Printed in the United States of America

British Cataloging in Publication Information Available

Distributed by arrangement with
University Publishing Associates, Inc.

4720 Boston Way
Lanham, MD 20706

3 Henrietta Street
London WC2E 8LU England

Library of Congress Cataloging-in-Publication Data

Hull, Clifton E.
Shortline railroads of Arkansas.

Bibliography: p.
Includes index.
1. Railroads—Arkansas. I. Title.
TF24.A8H85 1987 385'.09767 87-30080
ISBN 0-944436-00-5 (pbk. : alk. paper)

All UCA Press books are produced on acid-free paper which exceeds the minimum standards set by the National Historical Publications and Records Commission.

To the many men who financed, built, and operated the little shortlines through the hills, valleys, forests, and swamps of Arkansas, a belated "thank you"

PREFACE

THE STORY OF AMERICAN RAILROADS has been told many times, and the ramifications of their growth have been explored by masters in the art of history and storytelling. The flamboyant romance of our great rail systems has been extolled by learned authors and motion picture studios.

But one aspect of America's rail lore has been neglected like a country cousin, and that is exactly what it is: the realm of the shortline country railroads. The very nature of the little pikes makes them unique in contrast to the coldly efficient transcontinental systems.

The story of the shortline railroads needs to be told before it is too late. Our little country-cousin roads are quickly disappearing even while the large, sophisticated systems are struggling for existence.

This volume is an attempt to preserve the identity of a few of the little pikes which flourished in the hills and forests of

Arkansas. Their story is an intimate one, and I have endeavored to present the more personal side of their existence. The dull statistics of corporate structures have been recorded in many sources, but the daily life of the little streak of rust winding through the dense forests and precipitous hills of Arkansas exists mainly in the memory of men who are all too quickly passing away from the scenes of their days on the railroads.

This is their story.

CLIFTON E. HULL

North Little Rock, Arkansas
June, 1968

ACKNOWLEDGMENTS

THE STORY OF SHORTLINE RAILROADING, being essentially personal, can be told best through recollections of the people who worked on them, the people who were served by them and who loved the comings and goings of the Lilliputian trains, and through the efforts of many others who have an interest in the preservation of their history. I am therefore deeply indebted to the following people, for without their taking the time from busy daily schedules to tell me of railroad experiences in their younger years, I could never have written this book.

E. R. (Ever Ready) Braswell of Harrison, the grand old man of the Missouri & Arkansas, is a walking fountain of information on this troublesome road. Commodore Kirk, Elmer Swope, and Troy Bouyear of Beaver recalled many stories of their days on the rails. L. R. Parmelee, civil engineer at Helena; W. N. Deramus, president of the Kansas City Southern; Charles E. Winters; and the late Sam Leath, historian at Eureka Springs for half a century, were all very helpful. Don Goforth, enterprising young editor of the *Rogers Daily News,* preserved much history of the little pikes in the northwest corner of Arkansas. Marion Bayles of Fayetteville was well acquainted with the rails to St. Paul and Pettigrew.

My thanks go to E. D. Callan, general manager of the Dardanelle & Russellville; H. M. Braswell, J. B. White, and Austin Temple, vice president, chief engineer, and president, respectively, of the Ashley, Drew & Northern; and W. E. Hirst of Prescott. It was pure pleasure listening to Joe Wilson, civil engineer at Texarkana, recall the building of the Memphis, Paris & Gulf. Al Fred Backus, general superintendent of the Graysonia, Nashville & Ashdown; Reece Jones, former hogger on the Little Rock, Maumelle & Western; Dr. Fred Henker of Little Rock; Harry E. Hammer, Public Relations Department, Missouri Pacific; and Nan Peters and Carol Devore at the secretary of state's office were helpful in many ways.

T. W. M. Long, president and general manager of the Reader, and Sallye Moseley, agent at Reader, provided much valuable information, as did hogger Nat Turner, fireman C. A. Wheelington, conductor V. F. "Happy" Walker, and brakie C. O. Sykes, all of Reader.

Dr. John Ferguson, director, and Mrs. Jones and Mrs. Bowles, clerks at the Arkansas History Commission, along with Bob May, Arkansas Commerce Commission, made my work easier. Mrs. Frances Jackson, research librarian at the Little Rock Public Library, was of invaluable assistance during my two years of microfilm reading. David Bizzell, clerk and historian at the Pulaski County Courthouse; David Morgan, editor of *Trains* magazine; and Earl Saunders, professional photographer of Little Rock, proved invaluable in time of need.

For much moral support and enduring patience through the long months of research and interviews and for assistance in reading miles of microfilm, my wife is due a small halo.

CLIFTON E. HULL

CONTENTS

ILLUSTRATIONS

Antoine Valley
Caddo & Choctaw
Graysonia, Nashville & Ashdown
Murfreesboro & Nashville
San Augustine County Lumber Company
Reader
Little Rock, Maumelle & Western
Malvern & Freeo Valley
Ozan-Graysonia Lumber Company
Arkansas Central
Ft. Smith, Subiaco & Rock Island
Fayetteville & Little Rock
St. Louis, El Reno & Western
Ft. Smith & Western
Prescott & Northwestern
Gould Southwestern
Arkansas Railroad
Warren, Johnsville & Saline River
Warren & Saline River
Warren & Ouachita Valley
Jonesboro, Lake City & Eastern
Blytheville, Leachville & Arkansas Southern
Bradley Lumber Company
De Queen & Eastern
Dierks Forests, Inc.
Dierks Lumber & Coal
Texas, Oklahoma & Eastern
Doniphan, Kensett & Searcy
Ozark & Cherokee Central
Fordyce & Princeton
Bauxite & Northern

MAPS

SHORTLINE RAILROADS OF ARKANSAS

MISSISSIPPI, OUACHITA & RED RIVER

1

IT SEEMS QUITE PROPER to begin this account of Arkansas short-line railroads with the story of the first railroad in the state to receive a charter. It was granted on August 12, 1852. While it is true that the Memphis & Little Rock operated the first locomotive in the state, its charter was not granted until January 10, 1853.

In the early 1850's, there was a great deal of talk and planning for the construction of a transcontinental railroad beginning at the port city of Charleston, South Carolina, and extending by way of the most direct and convenient route to a terminus at San Francisco. During the heyday of railroad building in America, there was a marvelous display of great and grandiose dreams. Great plans can always be scaled down, but small plans usually remain small.

When word of the grand scheme made its way across the muddy waters of the Mississippi River, it was joyously received by the people of southern Arkansas. They could see no reason why the railroad should not pass through their section of the state on its way to the Pacific.

At the same time, considerable planning was being done on the Cairo & Fulton, which was coming out of Missouri from near St. Louis, passing through Little Rock, and extending southwestward to Fulton on the Red River. Two branches were proposed: one from Little Rock to Fort Smith on the border between Arkansas and Indian Territory, the other from Little Rock to a point on the Mississippi River opposite Memphis. But this system would leave southern and southeastern Arkansas isolated.

With transcontinental rails approaching from the east, it was deemed far more feasible and practicable to build in Arkansas a road which would become a link in the continent-spanning route. People came to the conclusion that the proper line should begin on the west bank of the Mississippi, about forty miles downstream from the mouth of the Arkansas River, at a place known as Gaines Landing. From here it would extend westward to the vicinity of the popular steamboat landing town of Fulton on the Red River, thence the few remaining miles to the Texas border.

If dreams and plans were to bear fruit, determined action would be required. A bill was introduced in the 1851 session of the Arkansas General Assembly requesting that a charter be granted for the construction of the Mississippi, Ouachita & Red River Railroad, the name deriving from the three major streams to be encountered. During the early years of the eighteenth century, people tended to settle relatively near navigable streams because they were depended upon as the only arteries of transportation. A railroad was the only means by which the interior areas could be opened to settlement. If the rails were laid, the settlers would come, the land would be developed, and much business would be generated. This sequence of events seemed to be the normal one. The acquisition of a railroad would guarantee prosperity for all.

In only a few months, much interest was generated among Arkansans who lived along the proposed route. On December 22, 1851, a "railroad convention" was held in Camden, on the Ouachita River. The meeting was arranged so that people could discuss the multitude of problems connected with the task of building and operating a railroad. It was an undertaking completely foreign to them; many—in fact, most—had never seen a train.

One saving factor was the presence of two gentlemen possessing the necessary knowledge and integrity. It was they who had promoted the idea of building a railroad to develop the latent wealth of the land. Colonel John Dockery, a citizen of Lafayette, was the prime moving force behind the project. He eloquently addressed the convention, presenting facts and figures to show that the pioneer road was a necessity and to prove conclusively that it could be built and operated at a profit to stockholders. Peter K. Rounsaville also spoke at length, giving listeners the benefit of his generous and varied experiences as an agent for a number of railroad enterprises in North Carolina. The people were shown the potential for such an enterprise, and they were convinced of their ability to provide the means for its construction.

From among those attending the meeting, nine prominent gentlemen were selected to formulate a message to be presented to the people of southern Arkansas. The honor of this task was given to Dockery, Rounsaville, Peter McCollum, N. S. Graves, James A. Warner, George Gallagher, Abner A. Stith, Isaac Strain, and James A. Jones. These men took time from their businesses and farms to talk personally with any and all who would listen. Glowing accounts appeared in newspapers, and enthusiasm grew.

An added incentive to proponents of the railroad was a bill passed by Congress on September 4, 1841. On this date, Arkansas was given ownership of 500,000 acres of government-owned public lands for the purpose of making specified internal improvements, such as roads, railways, bridges, canals, river projects, and swamp drainage. And on September 28, 1850, Congress gave Arkansas all swamps and overflowed lands within its boundaries as an aid to the construction of levees and drainage systems necessary to reclaim such land and make it productive.

August 12, 1852, was a typically hot and humid summer day

in Arkansas, but it was a day of joy and high hopes in the southern counties. The General Assembly granted a charter to the Mississippi, Ouachita & Red River Railroad. The road was given permission to issue capital stock in the amount of $1,500,000, represented by 15,000 shares valued at $100 each. Provision was also made for the state to subscribe to the company's stock.

During the 1854 session of the General Assembly, Governor Elias N. Conway proposed that the state grant a portion of the internal-improvement lands to the new railroad. The method of making the grant was rather involved. It was finally decided to grant alternate sections of land extending a distance of six miles on either side of the final surveyed route. This method would give the company ownership of land in a checkerboard pattern, with the government retaining possession of the alternate sections.

Lloyd Tilghman was hired as chief engineer to supervise surveying of the most feasible route and to oversee construction of the road. A man of indisputable character, Tilghman had an enviable record as a railroad builder.

Before beginning the survey work, he covered the general area of the road on horseback, making notes and sketches. Returning to his headquarters at Camden, he carefully studied the results of his trip and decided to separate the route into "eastern" and "western" divisions.

The eastern terminal was established at Ferguson's Point on the Mississippi, instead of Gaines Landing, as was originally planned. Tilghman had the responsibility of obtaining land for right-of-way from the citizens through whose property the road would pass. He and the owner of the Gaines Landing area could not reach an agreement on the price of land required for a station, warehouse facilities, and a terminal yard. Tilghman refused to pay what he thought was an exorbitant price and began looking for an alternate location.

Just a few miles away was an equally suitable place; there was deep water for riverboat traffic and plenty of high ground for a rail terminal. When the owner, a Mr. Ferguson, heard of the controversy, he hastily arranged a meeting with Tilghman. Ferguson realized the potential of increased business for his landing facilities on the river if a railroad terminal was available, and there were even greater possibilities if this fledgling enterprise became part of a great transcontinental rail system.

As a result, Tilghman obtained possession of sixty acres of land with a half-mile frontage on the west bank of the Mississippi. This would be sufficient for all the requirements of the railroad, and there would be plenty of land left over upon which to begin a small town. Soon after writing a few letters, Tilghman had several inquiries from people in Memphis, Columbia, and the surrounding area concerning purchase of lots on which to build homes or places of business. The income from these sales would yield sufficient revenue to pay for all the clearing and grading between the Mississippi and the Saline rivers.

From Ferguson's Point, in the approximate area of the present town of Arkansas City, the preliminary survey was extended nearly due west along a ridge through a dense canebrake, which required an embankment of only two and one-half feet, uninterrupted by even one culvert for a distance of a mile.

Proceeding westward about six miles, the line passed near the present site of McGehee, then headed northwest. Leaving the swamplands of the Mississippi River and crossing serpentine Bartholomew Bayou, the route passed through terrain which became a series of rolling swells of gravelly clay, ideally suited for embankment construction. A sharply rising ridge, forming the main watershed divide between Bartholomew Bayou and the Saline River, was crossed by way of a natural gap just a couple of miles south of the town of Monticello. From the south edge of the Arkansas Agricultural and Mechanical College campus at Monticello, one can see a faint trace of the old roadbed.

Crossing the Saline River, the crew laid out a chalkline-straight route to Moro Bayou. They reached this little stream early in the month of August, 1854, and were forced to abandon their work because of excessive heat.

Later that fall, the western-division survey began at Camden, on the Ouachita River (labeled "Washita" on some early maps). Approaching the river from the east, the party had the choice of two crossings. One missed Camden completely, while the other was right in the middle of town.

This situation was resolved to the satisfaction of all concerned when a Major Bradley came to Tilghman and proposed to donate 150 acres of the most desirable land in town if the railroad would come that way. It was decided that the city route was best. The land donated by Major Bradley was described as "a beautiful situation for an extensive depot, together with an abundance of room for warehouses, stores, and some most beautiful locations for private dwellings." It was anticipated that the land would yield $10,000, even with the railroad retaining possession of a large part of it.

The railroad was to cross the Ouachita by means of a steel bridge span that would offer no interference with barge traffic on the river. The party proceeded westward, with slight variations, passing near Lamartine, Jenkin's Mill, and Bell's Summit. From a point two miles south of Lewisville, the party fought its way through the swampland of the Red River to a point known as Dooley's Ferry. It was chosen as the western terminal instead of the town of Fulton, inasmuch as it met the requirements of the charter, was less expensive, and was a suitable place to construct a moderately priced bridge to afford a connection with a proposed extension through Texas.

With the route fairly well established, the time for construction was at hand. Contracts for grading, building culverts and bridges, and placing ties and rails were let—at most advantageous bids—to highly responsible parties.

The twenty miles of the road's eastern end were contracted to J. W. Martin of Warren with the understanding that subcontracts would go to plantation owners Ferguson and McDermot. Ferguson was assigned the area between the Mississippi River and Clay Bayou, while McDermot chose a four-mile section extending eastward from the west boundary of Chicot County. The two men agreed to accept payments from the company every three months, 60 per cent of which would be in cash and 40 per cent in company stock.

In August, 1854, chief engineer Tilghman executed a contract with B. A. Osgood for the construction of all trestles and bridges on the eastern division. Osgood was known personally to Tilghman, who said he was worthy of the company's confidence in every respect. Osgood readily agreed to accept 20 per cent of his payment in stock. Like Ferguson and McDermot, he was eager to become part-owner of the railroad. Osgood recruited a large force of workers and placed J. H. Williamson in charge of them. Williamson had earned for himself an enviable reputation in Illinois.

In the early fall of 1854, the swamplands near the Mississippi River were the scene of frenzied activity. Brawny men of the bayou country attacked the dense forest with brute force. Vast wildernesses of canebrakes were cleared. Lusty, cursing mule skinners moved the heavy black earth with their Fresno scrapers to build up embankments across wide stretches of stinking, stagnant swamps. The enveloping, humid heat set man and beast alike to sweating until all were dripping wet and crusted with salt. Huge, smokelike clouds of mosquitoes made life hell on earth for all living creatures. The stings of these bloodsucking insects were a continuous torment, for men and mules were unable to defend themselves against the voracious attacks of their tormentors.

To anyone unfamiliar with the swamp mosquito, it is impossible to describe the vicious assaults of which they are capable. They totally clogged the nostrils of defenseless mules during the night. These animals, dead from strangulation, were buried in the swamp. Many of the men were debilitated from the dreadful malarial chills and fever brought on by mosquito bites. Several died from the rigors of the fever. Along with the poor beasts of burden, they gave their lives for the little twin ribbons of iron marching slowly through the mucky swampland.

Where possible, contractors would hire local men to clear the forest and grub out the stumps. In this way, every dollar spent for building the road was kept in the country, so that all the people felt its benefits.

Clearing and construction of the western division were accomplished through the combined efforts of J. D. Hill, D. W. and D. P. Lear, William Cleaver, Tyra Hill, N. Miller, J. Byrne, T. P. Dockery, and N. Clifton. These gentlemen accepted about 35 per cent of their pay in stock. The cost for clearing, grubbing, earthwork, and bridges was $71,368.52 for the eastern division, $61,423.10 for the western. By the end of November, 1854, the entire route had been cleared and grubbed, and a four-mile strip from the Mississippi was graded and ready for rails.

The MO & RR was to serve an area with a great potential of on-line business. The newly developing Red River region offered some of the finest cotton land to be found anywhere, and there were 1,500,000 acres of virgin land waiting to be developed.

Two men from the neighboring state of Tennessee came to Camden in the latter part of 1854 and traveled extensively in the area. Their prospecting resulted in the discovery of a vein of coal which measured six feet thick and extended along the Ouachita River a distance of seven miles. Mr. Wyatt and Mr. Watson assured people the coal was of high quality and existed in great quantity. They brought samples to Lloyd Tilghman for testing, knowing the local populace would rely upon his opinion.

He placed some of the coal on the grate of a woodburning fireplace and kindled it with a little wood. It burned with an intense heat, emitting a clear, white flame. Another sample was placed in a sheet-iron retort having a half-inch opening at the neck, and the retort was set on an ordinary wood fire. Soon coal gas was being discharged so freely that, on opening the mouth of the retort and applying a lighted candle to it, the gas burned with an exceedingly bright flame, equal to the brilliance of two candles in the room.

Wyatt and Watson bought quite a bit of property in the coal

field around the town of Camden. They made arrangements to deliver twenty thousand bushels of coal every week at the mouth of the Red River—when there was sufficient water to float a barge. Tilghman was confident the coal would be riding the rails by the following ycar.

Work moved along with aggravating slowness. The little road was beset by the devils of adversity. Sickness struck down men in the work crews; frequently the Angel of Death made visits to the camps; floodwaters destroyed portions of the new roadbed. Another stumbling block was the financial panic of 1857. At that time, there was no money available for building railroads.

The depression slowly passed away, and the little road's future began to take on a rosy hue. Then came that tragedy of all tragedies, the Civil War, which completely halted construction for several years. The forest reclaimed the rough-graded roadbed, and the completed portions soon deteriorated through neglect.

The war waxed and waned, then the days of carnage were over. On July 31, 1868, Governor Powell Clayton signed a bill granting $10,000 per mile in state bonds to railroads which needed assistance. The bonds were to be paid out in thirty years, bearing interest of 7 per cent a year. Any railroad which had not previously received federal land grants would be given state bonds at the rate of $15,000 per mile.

To qualify for such aid, each railroad had to issue a map of its proposed route showing the territory to be covered and the terminal points, an affidavit from the president and chief engineer showing the estimated cost of grading the first one hundred miles, a similar affidavit to the effect that ten consecutive miles had been graded and set up for actual use, and to furnish the governor other information as he might require. The bill had been approved by a vote of five to one.

The Mississippi, Ouachita & Red River received a windfall of $1,950,000, a real shot in the arm for this struggling little road—and it was certainly needed. Crops had not been anywhere near normal, and the people of southern Arkansas were in crippled condition as far as local financial resources were concerned. All this made it almost impossible for them to meet their obligations toward the company. By no means had their interest lessened, however. One plantation owner living near the road had a slave woman who bore quadruplets. The infants were promptly named "Mississippi," "Ouachita," "Red River," and "Railroad"!

No. ______ 400 Shares.

MISSISSIPPI, OUACHITA AND Red River Railroad Company.

This Certifies That The State of Arkansas is the owner of Four Hundred Shares in the Capital Stock of the Mississippi, Ouachita and Red River Railroad Company, transferable on the Books of the Company upon the surrender of this Certificate.

Dated Oct 11th 1873

J. E. Sickels, Secretary.

President.

SHARES $100 EACH.

Old Man Trouble seemed to have passed by, but he had only gone to the back door to come in. The various roads receiving state bonds dumped them on the market at the same time. Their value immediately dropped until they were not worth the paper they were printed on. This was the deciding factor in the annihilation of the Mississippi, Ouachita & Red River.

There were several miles of light rails winding through the swamp, and there is some dispute concerning the service provided. It was reported that nothing larger than a handcar was ever operated. As late as May, 1871, contemporary newspaper accounts state that one locomotive and several cars were operating over eighteen miles of completed road and that sixty-eight miles had been graded. One local investor who had been led to anticipate the snorting of the iron horse along the road expressed his views in a letter to the editor of a newspaper: "The iron horse was snorting, but in the stable. His provender came from the pocketbooks of the stockholders, while the road still remained in too bad a condition for him to travel on."

The southern section of Arkansas depended heavily upon the completion of this road. When it failed, the favors of state government and enterprising citizens shifted toward the northern section. If the rails had joined the Mississippi and Red rivers, Arkansas' cities, colleges, and highways might have been earlier and more evenly distributed between the northern and southern sections of the state.

In 1875, the defunct MO & RR was included in the reorganization of a road extending from near Ferguson's Point to Pine Bluff: the Little Rock, Pine Bluff & New Orleans. The reorganized company was known as the Little Rock, Mississippi River & Texas. In later years, a portion of the MO & RR was put into actual operation and was known as the Warren & Ouachita Valley. Thus the first railroad chartered in Arkansas died young.

AUGUSTA TRAMWAY & TRANSFER–AUGUSTA RAILROAD

2

In the mid–1880's, the St. Louis & Iron Mountain was eagerly laying rails from the west bank of the Mississippi River opposite the port city of Memphis, Tennessee. Climbing from the swampy overflow lands, which extended several miles from the bank of the "Father of Waters," the rails crossed Crowley's Ridge, whence was obtained the ideal clay and gravel material to construct the roadbed upon which the light iron rails were laid.

Heading for a connection with the main line of the Iron Mountain at Bald Knob, the construction crew was nearing the swift-flowing White River. Sitting on the eastern bank of the river was the little town of Augusta.

One morning, the chief engineer for the Iron Mountain crew saddled his horse and rode the couple of miles into town. After a brief look around and after making a few inquiries, he asked for an interview with the city fathers. Introducing himself, he proceeded to impress upon them the many advantages that would be theirs if the rails of the great Iron Mountain spanned the White River at the fine little town of Augusta.

These august gentlemen listened politely and took the proposition under advisement. They would study it, ascertain what the townspeople thought about it, and let him know their decision in a day or two.

Upon his return visit, the chief engineer was informed that Augustans could see no real advantage in the railroad's bisecting their town. Generally, when a railroad entered a town, there was an influx of quite a few undesirable people who would be only a source of annoyance and trouble. The great hustle and bustle of a railroad would tend to disturb, if not destroy, the pleasant tranquility of the town. Any amount of import or export of goods and passengers the town required was adequately provided by boat and barge on the White River, which was navigable for several miles farther upstream (when there was enough water to float a barge).

The Iron Mountain's chief engineer was very disappointed, for most towns were eager for rails to be laid through their corporate limits. Then they would have connection with the outside world, they would be situated on an artery of commerce, and prosperity was practically guaranteed. In fact, they were so eager that the right-of-way land for the depot and yards was nearly always donated. In addition, a generous subscription of cash was usually offered to those responsible for selecting the location of the line. Possibly, the company was technically unaware of the exchange of cash. This would be further inducement for the locating engineers to route the rails through towns where there was a possibility of receiving freight revenue.

The St. Louis & Iron Mountain's emissary mounted his horse and indignantly took his departure, angrily shaking the dust of the streets from his feet. It took very little engineering calculation to determine that a crossing of the White River could be accomplished elsewhere. This was done forthwith, and the rails were rapidly extended westward. Augusta was left sitting on the river-bank.

Traffic on the railroad flourished, while traffic on the river began to dwindle. There were no wagon roads through the area.

All of this soon became painfully evident to the good folks of Augusta-on-the-White. A committee of citizens went to St. Louis, headquarters of the Iron Mountain, to confess their sin of arrogance, but it all was in vain. Mr. Jackson, chief engineer for the railroad, said that if the people had even treated him to an elaborate banquet, he could have diverted the rails to enter the town. Instead, he said, Augustans had treated him as if he were "a nobody, had paid no attention to him at all," and he had had his revenge.

When the delegates returned home and reported to their fellow citizens, a decision was reached to the effect that Augusta must have a connection with the railroad if it was to survive. The world was passing them by in a steady stream—just a mile away, on the railroad. They could no longer depend on the river to provide the transportation necessary for their well-being.

The St. Louis & Iron Mountain was not disposed to construct a spur line to Augusta. The town would be forced to build its own railroad to connect with the lifestream of commerce flowing near by, yet so far away.

So it came to pass in 1887 that the people of Augusta, Arkansas, constructed their own little railroad, one mile long, and called it the Augusta Tramway & Transfer Company. Its construction was not quite up to the specifications of the Iron Mountain, but it was their very own and had cost only $4,500. The rolling stock and motive power were rather unorthodox and left a lot to be desired, but they served the purpose and allowed operations to begin.

For the transportation of passengers, there was provided a de-luxe model of a standard-gauge streetcar. The vehicle had for many years traveled the boulevards and avenues of St. Louis, that mighty metropolis on the Mississippi. To demonstrate the great civic pride in Augusta's regal passenger vehicle, the little car received a heavy coat of gleaming, canary-yellow paint, while the interior was varnished until the wood fairly glistened. Long wooden seats were placed against, and parallel with, the walls of the car. The back of these seats were finely upholstered.

The freight cars were rather mundane and nondescript—mostly boxes with four wheels. Later, when business had shown a heartening increase, regular freight-car interchange was made with the Iron Mountain at New Augusta, which was the name applied to the southern terminus of the tramway.

The motive power might best be described as being an 0-4-0 hayburner, commonly known as a mule. There was no fuel problem, and no damage suits resulted from roadside fires set by sparks from the stack. However, there was somewhat of an inconvenience during the wet season: the "engine" got stuck in the mud of the unballasted roadbed. All traffic came to a halt when the rains came. And if the "engineer" was a little slow in applying the car brakes on a downgrade, the train usually ran into and crippled the engine.

Such fine equipment permitted the company to operate at a profit, and it wasn't long until the treasury allowed the purchase of a real, honest-to-goodness "iron-horse" engine. It seems to have been a little 0-4-0 "T" Porter job from a plantation in Alabama, although this cannot be verified. It was acquired in 1900, and soon after this the company bought a couple of 0-4-4 "T" Forney-type slide-valve engines with enclosed cabs. The Augusta Tramway & Transfer Company was nothing but first class, and it commanded respect from the entire community.

By 1903, the passenger business had increased until the canary-yellow streetcar bobber was inadequate. There was a rumor floating around to the effect that a very fine full-size passenger coach was available from the near-by Searcy & West Point Railroad (about which more later). It was purchased in 1904 and brought to Augusta. The little mule car was discontinued and placed in the yard of J. G. Landers, one of Augusta's citizens. Here it stood for several years, slowly succumbing to the effects of time and weather.

The great portion of the passenger business was in meeting the three or four trains of the Iron Mountain at New Augusta. For several years the road used a little gasoline motorcar to meet night trains. This service was discontinued when conductor Wilkins struck a match to look for a gasoline leak. After this fiasco, a horse-drawn bus was operated at night until passenger service was terminated about the time of World War I.

In 1900, John Short came to work for the AT & T. In 1907, he was promoted to the position of conductor, serving in this capacity until 1912, when he became an engineer.

Short was very much pleased when the road bought the passenger coach from the Searcy & West Point. John was born and raised just ten miles north of Searcy. When he was eight years old, the Searcy and West Point discontinued "mulepower" and bought an engine and a passenger coach. John came to Searcy with his father soon afterward and finally got up enough courage to ask the agent what the fare was to Kensett. When he learned it would cost him a quarter, he hesitated for a little while, then decided to live recklessly. He purchased a ticket and climbed aboard. It was his first train ride.

It brought back fond memories to Short when the AT & T bought the coach and he had the opportunity to pull it behind his engine. It could seat ten passengers comfortably, and the fare was only fifteen cents from Augusta to the Iron Mountain depot.

Dame Fortune smiled on the little one-miler for several years. In 1897, the road paid a 16 per cent dividend, and twenty-two stockholders shared the benefits of $20,000 worth of capital stock. In 1916, business was very good and good men were rather scarce. Engineer John Short's son, Earl, was placed on the payroll. Earl's days of railroading were rather brief—he died in 1922. Later, in 1934, a third generation of the Short family was working for the road, though only occasionally and in a nonpaid status. Earl Short's thirteen-year-old daughter, Joyce, who was in the seventh grade, divided her time between her studies and helping her grandfather. With great enthusiasm and with complete disregard for the size of the task, she shoveled coal, helped with repairs around the shops, and even ran the engine on Saturdays. As soon as school was out, Joyce, to the dismay of her grandmother (with whom she lived), would head for the shops.

Business continued to boom during the years of World War I. During one night in 1916, $100,000 worth of cotton was shipped over the rails of the Augusta Tramway & Transfer Company. The trip was made at night because of the increased humidity of the night air, which lessened the danger of sparks from the locomotive setting fire to the cotton.

By 1917, the little road had come upon hard times. On December 14, the AT & T was offered to the highest bidder at the Woodruff County Courthouse. The assets and franchises were sold for $30,000 to the newly formed Augusta Railroad.

The Augusta Railroad Company was incorporated on April 4, 1918, by eleven men of the community: J. C. McDonald, R. H. Winfield, F. H. Kittrell, T. J. Stacy, H. P. Dale, T. E. Bonner, E. G. Thompson, W. N. Gregory, J. H. Dale, C. L. Adamson, and R. T. Harville. Mr. Harville was appointed as receiver of the road by a decree of Woodruff County Chancery Court for the Northern District until the new company was granted a charter by the state and had subscribed to sufficient capital stock to assume the $30,000 mortgage with which the little pike was saddled and could not retire.

At the time the Augusta Railroad Company assumed control, the line of rails extended from the foot of Locust Street at its intersection with Front Street in Augusta, running east along the streets of the town, thence proceeding south to the depot of the Missouri Pacific at New Augusta (the St. Louis, Iron Mountain & Southern had merged with the Missouri Pacific in 1917).

Business gradually declined over the years. There were sporadic periods of prosperity, but they were few, far between, and short lived. The excitement of the early days was missing.

Early in the morning of July 3, 1907, D. C. Brogden, a traveling salesman, climbed the stairs to his room on the second floor of the hotel. He had been up all night, arriving aboard the passenger coach, and was in need of a few hours' sleep. He undressed, and as he was ready to retire, he picked up the pillow, fluffed it up, and saw a man's purse where it had been lying under the pillow.

Opening it, he discovered $250 in cash and several pearls, later valued at more than $3,000. There were also some papers which helped to establish the owner's identity. The purse had been left under the pillow the night before by T. P. Umsted of Newport, a pearl buyer who was making a boat trip up the White River.

The money, pearls, and papers were returned to their rightful owner. I hate to think of what would happen to such items if they were left in a motel for someone to find today.

The little Augusta Railroad became known indirectly throughout the South. During the early 1900's, it was the subject of a song, popular among the Negroes of the Delta country, entitled "Little Dummy Line." It had an almost limitless number of verses, but the best known was this one:

Some folks say de Dummy don't run,
Come an' lemme tell you what de Dummy done done;
She lef' St. Louis at half-pas' one,
And she rolled into Memphis at de settin' of de sun.

Quite a feat for a one-mile railroad on the bank of the White River in Arkansas! Later, the song came to mean any dinky railroad upon which black people might find themselves riding or working.

In the 1940's, a local "artist" was commissioned to letter on the tank of the locomotive the message that the Augusta was the "World's Shortest Railroad." He mixed up his adjectives, and the message proclaimed it as the "World's Smallest Railroad."

At about the same time, Lucius Beebe, prolific author of railroad lore, visited Augusta. The bill of fare at one of the local restaurants did not impress him favorably, and he opined that the chief engineer of the old St. Louis & Iron Mountain was probably justified in bypassing the town. Perhaps Augusta was equally impressed with Beebe's well-known cynicism.

The little road continued its slow but steady decline. E. T. King, who became general freight agent and traffic manager in 1946, said the locomotive was fired up only three times during the month of March, 1958. The shipment of cotton had dropped from 7,600 bales in 1952 to 1,114 bales in 1957. A. W. "Ace" Taylor, the engineer since 1949, remarked that local merchants, and especially members of the lumber industry, preferred to patronize truck lines. Besides Taylor, the only employee in the last days was Paul Thomas, a part-time fireman and brakeman.

In March, 1958, the Augusta Railroad applied to the Interstate Commerce Commission for permission to abandon service. Joining many hundreds of other little streaks of rust throughout the country, it has steamed its way into history.

HOT SPRINGS RAILROAD

3

THE FIRST WHITE MAN to drink the healing waters of the many hot springs found in a long and narrow valley of the Ouachita Mountains in western Arkansas was Hernando de Soto. Soldier of fortune and gallant gentleman, De Soto was born in Spain about 1500. As did some other adventurers, he came to the New World searching for a mystic fountain. Those who drank from it would remain forever young. The aches and pains which are the lot of the human race as the rapidly advancing years take their toll would never come to the fortunate one who drank of the magic waters.

Long before De Soto found his way southward from the village of Coligoa in the mountains of northwest Arkansas to the province of Cayas, the Indians had gathered in the valley of vapors to rest their weary bodies and to drink and bathe in the hot waters flowing from the depths of the earth. To them, this lovely place was sacred and must forever be a land of peace. No form of violence was to desecrate the valley.

When the stranger appeared in their valley, they were careful not to divulge to him the secret of the curative powers of the steaming springs. De Soto and his men stayed in the valley of springs for a month while their horses fattened and thrived on the abundant supply of maize and leaves, and here they all drank from a lake of water very hot and rather brackish. This was in the autumn of 1541.

The gentleman from Spain continued his wanderings through the strange and wonderful New World. Soon after his visit to the valley of hot waters he was stricken with a fierce swamp fever and gave up the ghost on the banks of the mighty river which flowed to the southern sea.

The red man made visits to the valley of springs for many years, but such a secret as the many health-sustaining springs and the lake of very hot water could not remain a secret forever. The invading white man was spreading across the land, ever westward. It was inevitable that he should discover the place.

The first white man to come to the valley to stay was one Manuel Prudhomme, who built a crude cabin there in 1807. Gradually, others came, one and two at a time. News of the hot springs' restorative powers was carried throughout the land. Others came: the sick, the halt, and the lame. Word spread; still more came. Finally, the red man was completely removed. The white man reigned supreme.

The white man's tribe was seemingly numberless. One member of it was born in New York State in 1819. As a very young fellow, he helped his brother peddle ginger cookies at any sort of gathering. He began his commercial career at the age of seventeen: he bought a few head of cattle and, after fattening them and having them butchered, peddled the meat. He was a schoolteacher for a few terms, then purchased a flour mill, which proved to be a very good investment—but he soon traded it for a tannery. While working with the flour mill and tannery, he learned much about wheat and hides.

This industrious young man was destined to become one of many white men to make a long and arduous trip to Arkansas' great valley of springs. His name was Joseph Reynolds.

In 1856, he moved his tannery business to Chicago, where he formed a close acquaintance with Phillip D. Armour, an industrious meat packer. By 1862, Reynolds had four boats making their way up and down the Mississippi River, busily collecting hides and grain at every port from St. Paul to St. Louis. It was in this trade that he earned for himself a nickname that was to survive down through the years until the present time.

> It was when I was a comparatively young man—about a hundred years ago—and I had been in the tannery business back east. I came to Chicago to engage in the business of trading in pelts. One spring I was on a trip into the Northwest and when I bought furs and skins I packed them in boxes and just at random made a rough diamond on the outside and signed with J. R. The next day I found that another young fellow also was using J. R., so I changed my R to an O just because it was the easiest way to do it. I did a great deal of business and people began calling me "Diamond Jo." When I built my line of Mississippi River steamers I named it the "Diamond Jo" line.

One day a passenger aboard one of Reynolds' ships, the *Mary Morton*, named for his wife, stopped to chat for a while with a carpenter who was repairing a window sash. Before leaving the ship, the passenger complimented the captain on the character of his employees and mentioned his pleasant surprise at finding such intelligence, courtesy, and wealth of information as possessed by the handyman. "Yes, he is right sharp," the captain replied. "Most any trip you'll find him puttering around with his kit of tools, the most unassuming person aboard. He is Jo Reynolds and he owns this ship as well as a half-dozen more just like it."

Early in 1874, the southbound passenger train of the St. Louis,

Iron Mountain & Southern rolled to a clanking, jerky stop at the unpretentious depot at the little town of Malvern, Arkansas. As the travelers climbed down from the open-vestibule coaches, it was noticed that most of them were in varying stages of physical disability. Several were being lifted down on stretchers.

Among those who were still able to make their own way was a tall, slender man, moving gingerly away from the train. He was carefully favoring his legs as he moved slowly along, his back slightly stooped. His hair and well-trimmed beard were well sprinkled with gray. The suit he wore was dusty and wrinkled from traveling, but stylish and very well cut. In the bosom of his white shirt front was a single large white diamond.

"Diamond Jo" Reynolds, suffering from painful attacks of rheumatism and arthritis, had made his way to the valley of hot springs at the Hot Springs Reservation in Arkansas. If only he could bathe in the magic waters and drink from the many free-flowing fountains, he thought, he would be made whole and free from the torment of pain which accompanied every waking moment.

Inquiring about accommodations, he was informed that a stagecoach would provide transportation over the remaining twenty-five miles. Eight of the weary, pain-bedeviled travelers climbed into the heavy, cumbersome coach of the El Paso Stage Company. Thus began the tortuous ride through the Ouachita Mountains. It was far from comfortable at the very best.

Somewhere in the mountain wilderness, the stage broke down. The passengers could offer no assistance in repairing it and the driver was unable to do so alone. Rather than remain stranded in the mountains all night, the passengers were compelled to walk the rest of the way into town. In their condition, it was not a pleasant journey.

Reynolds informed the stage company people that he thought they could offer a better system of travel for invalids seeking health at the hot springs. He was told in rather forceful language that if he didn't like the service he might try something better. His normal combative spirit was aroused, and he began a study of how to provide better transportation. If a sick man could withstand the stage journey and still get well, he, Reynolds, could build up quite a good business for himself if he could devise a comfortable means of travel.

Over a period of several months, Reynolds' health gradually improved. Pressing business needs compelled him to return to Chicago, so he again made the stage trip through the mountains.

Arriving at the depot at Malvern, he looked back toward those forbidding pine-clad hills. "I must come this way again, but never will I ride that thing," he said.

"What're you gonna' do, ride a mule?" the driver asked.

"No," he snapped, "I'll build me a railroad!"

Diamond Jo Reynolds kept his promise. He built his railroad from Malvern through the forested mountains of the Ouachita Range; construction began in the spring of 1875. Jo Reynolds came to Malvern to live while he supervised the building of his railroad, which was typical of him. He directed all his enterprises personally; he knew exactly what was going on. While in Malvern, he found lodging in the home of Professor Thomas Morse. When the time came to begin laying rail, the honor of driving the first spike—a golden one provided by Reynolds—was accorded to the three daughters of Professor Morse—Fannie, Susie, and Sophie.

The decision was made to build the road as a 36-inch narrow gauge. Perhaps we should be of the same mind as Linwood Moody in his chronicle of the little two-footer roads in Maine. He said 24-inch gauge was normal for a railroad; all others were WIDE gauge. Be that as it may, the three-footer was less expensive for the initial cost of construction, and it could more easily negotiate the sharp curves which were necessary to reduce expensive cuts and fills through the mountains.

Even at that, Reynolds sank practically his entire fortune in building his railroad. By July 3, 1875, the grading and trestle work was completed on the first six miles out of Malvern. On July 27, Colonel R. A. Thornton was awarded the contract for construction of all the depots between Malvern and Hot Springs. The equipment and materials were the very best available, for whatever Reynolds did, he did it first class. He took great pride in the little road and spared no expense in seeing it finished.

As the rails gradually pushed their way into the rough mountain country, the stage line was shortened by just that much. Probably Reynolds was afforded a bit of inner satisfaction when, on October 28, 1875, the El Paso Stage Company discontinued its service between Malvern and Hot Springs. On January 25, 1876, the narrow-gauge Hot Springs Railroad was completed. Here are a few of its statistics:

Maximum grade: 106 feet per mile, or 2 per cent.
Sharpest curve: 20 degrees, or 288-foot radius.
Weight of rail: 35 pounds to the yard.
Weight of engines: 15.5 tons.
Average cost of road and equipment per mile: $15,000.
Equipment: 2 locomotives, 3 passenger cars, 1 baggage and express, 22 freight cars.
Financial statement: Capital stock authorized, $250,000; amount paid in, $250,000.
President: Joseph Reynolds, Hot Springs, Arkansas.
Chief Engineer: G. D. C. Rumbaugh, Little Rock, Arkansas.

The little Hot Springs Railroad was indeed a thing of beauty to behold in action. The eleven-car trains ran twice a day: eight freight cars, one baggage and express combined, and two fine passenger coaches. They rolled briskly along behind a beautiful little 2–4–0 locomotive with a diamond stack, an oil-burning headlight nearly as large in diameter as the front of the smoke box, and a long wooden pilot (cow-catcher). Reynolds wanted silk curtains in the windows of the engines—just like those in the passenger coaches—but the engine crews almost rebelled and he finally relented: draperies in the cabs were linen.

On the engines there were quite a few brass fittings, which were kept brightly burnished with beeswax that was furnished to all firemen. The little teakettle engines were equipped with wood-carrying tenders which had to be supplied from the piles of cordwood stacked beside the rails at Cove Creek, eighteen miles southeast of Hot Springs. Many times when the hogger spotted the tender at the woodpile, several of the passengers would climb down from the Lilliputian varnished cars to lend the crew a hand in "wooding up"—they would get where they were going that much quicker.

Frequently, there were some familiar faces among the auxiliary "wood passers": Charles A. Dana, the well-known journalist who became managing editor of the *New York Tribune*, was assistant secretary of war under President Lincoln, and later became editor of the *New York Sun;* Admiral George Dewey, who sank, burned, or captured every Spanish ship in the Battle of Manila Bay; John L. Sullivan and James J. Corbett, gentlemen of the fight ring; Billy Sunday, who was a member of the glamorous White Stockings baseball team in Chicago; James G. Blaine, speaker of the House of Representatives in Washington and senator from the state of Maine; Phillip Armour, meat-packing tycoon from Chicago; and Jay Gould, master railroad manipulator.

Looking on from the cool shade of a large tree, one might have recognized Mrs. George Pullman, wife of the sleeping-car magnate from Chicago; Emma Abbott, the "American Canary," a dramatic soprano; or Helen Gould, wife of Jay Gould.

Most of the notable figures on the American scene eventually made their way south to ride the Hot Springs Railroad, known, of course, as the "Diamond Jo Line." They all paid the magnificent fare of ten cents a mile, or $2.50 to ride the steam cars from Malvern to the spa, which seemed rather inexpensive when compared with the six-dollar fare which had been charged by the El Paso Stage Company. But the fickle public soon forgot the high fare and rough riding of the cumbersome stage and began complaining that the railroad had a monopoly on transportation.

The fare was reduced to two dollars for a one-way ticket. Ere long, there began a barrage of requests for free passes. To meet the situation, Reynolds came up with the idea of printing a supply of facsimile two-dollar bills, standard currency at that time. On

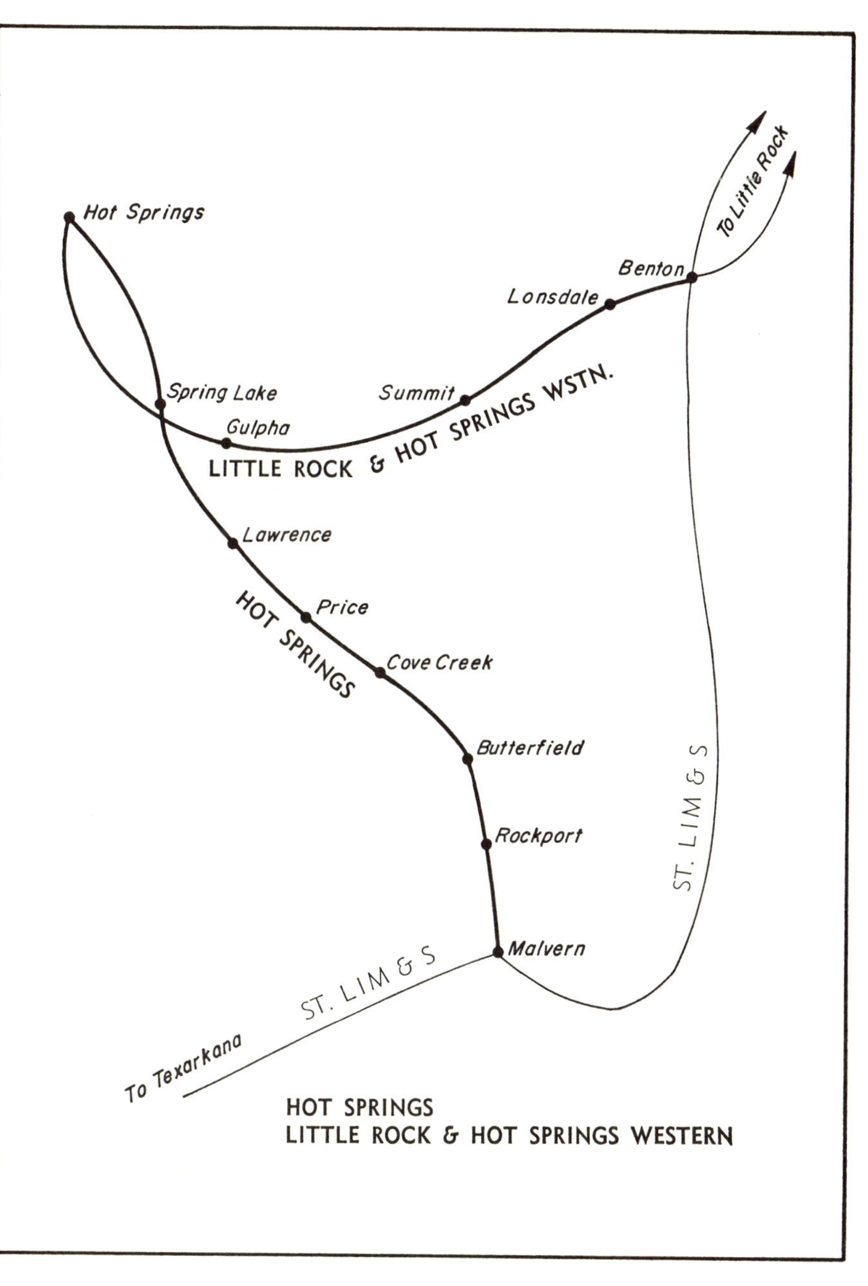

HOT SPRINGS
LITTLE ROCK & HOT SPRINGS WESTERN

the face of each was printed this statement: "The Hot Springs Railroad bank will pay to the bearer two dollars if presented to the auditor of said railroad at Hot Springs, Arkansas, by any train conductor in the employ of the Hot Springs Railroad Company. (Signed) Jo Reynolds, President." The bills became collector's items and today are very rare.

No bonds were issued during the construction of the Diamond Jo Line. Reynolds used, and almost depleted, his personal fortune in pushing the rails through the mountains. He soon realized that he was going to need some operating capital. Boarding the Iron Mountain train at Malvern, he headed for Chicago.

A couple of days later, he walked into the office of his good friend, Phil Armour. The latter knew him fairly well and was able to guess what was on his mind. With a bit of droll humor which his face did not reveal, Armour said: "Jo Reynolds! You're just th' man I want to see. Can you let me have $50,000?"

"Why, that's just what I was going to ask you. I never needed money so badly in all my life," Reynolds replied.

"How much do you need?" asked Armour.

"Two hundred thousand dollars," said Reynolds in his matter-of-fact way.

Phil smiled and reached for his checkbook. "All right, I'll let you have it."

Reynolds dropped a bundle of stock certificates on the desk. "Here, you hold these till I can repay you," he said.

The certificates represented the entire value of the Diamond Jo Line. Phil refused to take them and insisted they be returned to the safe deposit vault from whence they came. A friend in need!

One man, more than any other, enjoyed the "fun" side of the Diamond Jo Line: Billy Sunday. Before he became famous as a revival minister, he was a professional baseball player, a member of the Chicago White Stockings. It was through his influence that the White Stockings became the first big-league team to hold spring training down south—they rode the Diamond Jo to Hot Springs.

After quite a bit of planning, the decision was made to build a permanent meeting hall for the Hot Springs Business Men's League, the forerunner of the present-day Chamber of Commerce. The amount of money which would be required for such a project seemed an insurmountable obstacle, but the White Stockings came to the rescue. At the height of the spring training season, the team held several exhibition games, the proceeds going to the building fund. It was sufficient to swing the deal.

Early one spring, the team left cold, blustery Chicago and headed south. The fellows were in a jubilant mood. Reaching Malvern on the Iron Mountain, they boarded the narrow-gauge cars of the Hot Springs road in the gray dawn hours.

Up ahead in the engine cab, hogger John Ryan notched his throttle back and soon had the little cars reeling on the sharp reverse curves through the many cuts and rumbling across the frequent trestles.

John dropped the reverse lever down and drew out another couple of notches on the throttle. He was approaching a short but steep hill grade with a fairly sharp curve at the top. The barking exhaust lifted a few sparks, even through the baffles of the diamond stack. The little 2–4–0 bucked and snorted her way up the hill and lurched into a cut as she took the curve.

As the pilot emerged from the cut and the track became tangent, John saw a dull red glow where a pile trestle should have been. In a split second which seemed as endless as eternity, he remembered hearing old-timers from the engine cab tell of similar situations. He had always considered these stories with a wee bit of reservation. Now the decision was his and time had run out. At the speed he was running, it was impossible to stop. The shining brass brake valve was just beneath his hand on the throttle. He could wipe the clock and try to join the birds. The passengers would have to take whatever came.

In reflex action, John jerked the throttle wide open. The little teakettle engine surged onto the burning skeleton of the trestle. The piling had burned from under it, the rails had sagged but were held together with bolts and fishplates. The little hog canted to one side, righted herself, and slewed the other way. The short wheelbase let her ride the sagging rails without hanging up. She staggered up onto solid footing and heaved the two reeling coaches across. John's trembling hand wiped the clock.

The startled and shaken passengers stumbled from the coaches. Walking back nearly three hundred feet, they stared at the smoldering ruins of the trestle. Like disappointed angels of death, wreaths of smoke slowly drifted away through the forest.

Billy Sunday said, years later, that although the incident did not persuade him to enter the ministry, it did make a profound impression on him. He kept wondering: "What does God still have for us on this train to do?"

During the heyday of railroading in the 1880's and 1890's, Jay Gould was gobbling up independent lines to form his giant St. Louis, Iron Mountain & Southern system. He and Reynolds arrived at an agreement that Gould would not attempt to confiscate the Diamond Jo if Reynolds would maintain facilities and schedules to accommodate all the traffic the Iron Mountain would bring to the interchange at Malvern. This arrangement worked smoothly until 1889. Gould said he felt business had increased to such an extent that through train service was necessary, for it was very difficult for many physically handicapped passengers to change cars at Malvern. Gould thought the Diamond Jo should be made standard gauge like the Iron Mountain, so the rails were widened.

There was much speculation concerning just how much Gould really cared about the welfare of his passengers. Immediately after the gauge was changed, there was a great influx of railroad tycoons' private cars into the "City of Vapors." Jay Gould's was prominently present. In those days, the movement of private cars was a courtesy arrangement; no charge was made.

The little Diamond Jo kept a haze of wood smoke from the stacks of its locomotives lingering in the mountains. As business increased, additional engines were acquired until there were five iron horses in the stable. Two of them were named *John Ryan* and *John Mann,* names of the hoggers to whom they were assigned. These were the motive power for the mixed trains running between Hot Springs and Malvern. The other engines were used on work trains and switching duties.

Engineer Ryan was one of the picturesque characters of the Diamond Jo. He came to Malvern from Illinois in 1877 and married Ella Kilpatrick; they later moved to Hot Springs. John was a hogger on the Diamond Jo and its successor, the Rock Island, for forty-five years.

Another notable character on the narrow-gauge pike was Fred Greeno, who moved to Arkansas with his father from Travis City, Michigan, at about the same time Ryan arrived. Fred's father was one of the earlier employees on the road. When Fred was eighteen years old in 1885, he fired an engine for hogger McMillan; skipper Cox was in charge of the train. Later, he worked the mixed trains as a baggage "smasher" under conductor John Hensley of Malvern.

Fred recalled that once a year Jo Reynolds would dispatch two freight cars from Chicago to Hot Springs. Freight charges were paid by Diamond Jo's employees. The cars were opened and the contents distributed equally among all the employees. One car contained potatoes; the other, flour.

As a fireman, it was Fred's duty to see that his engine was as clean as wiping could get it. Whenever the little hog was run into the roundhouse, Fred would wipe her down from drivers to diamond stack. He polished the wide bands of brass encircling the Russian iron-boiler shell and shined the big brass bell. With special care he rubbed up the hogger's name, which decorated the side of the cab just below the window. Then he climbed into the cab and cleaned all the brass fittings. (The master mechanic had a habit of casually running his hands over an engine any time he passed it.) Woe unto the fireman assigned to an engine on which any evidence of dirt or grease was found!

In 1888, Fred suffered a crushed leg in an accident and was off work for a little more than two years. He returned to work in 1890 and remained until he was retired in 1895.

During the 1880's, Jo Reynolds acquired some interest in copper mines in Arizona and accumulated a personal fortune of twelve million dollars. In the summer of 1891, he was in Arizona looking after one of his mines when he suddenly became ill. Jo was staying in a crude shack at the mine; he died there during the night.

At Reynolds' death, the Diamond Jo became the property of his widow and E. M. Dickey, one of the administrators of Reynolds' estate, who was made president of the line, with an office in Chicago. No change was made in the staff of officers, which included L. D. Richardson, general superintendent; M. N. Pierce, auditor and local treasurer; Robert M. Smith, ticket agent; Fred W. Gregory, freight agent; and E. B. Brown, express agent, all of whom were in Hot Springs. Rounding out the staff were J. A. Hanglin, master mechanic; C. W. Turner, road mechanic; and J. W. Williams, agent for the Diamond Jo and the St. Louis, Iron Mountain & Southern at Malvern.

Pierce had been in ill health for several years and asked for his retirement in June, 1893. Fred A. Bill, who had been in service with Diamond Jo steamers for twenty years, was selected by Mrs. Reynolds and Dickey to fill the vacancy. Everything concerning the railroad was new to Bill, but one thing in particular was different from his work in Chicago: many of the people in and around Hot Springs, including the employees, shared a feeling of animosity toward the railroad.

Bill was in the habit of going about his work in a cheerful mood, and he whistled quite a bit. One day he came into the office and was whistling a happy tune. "You mustn't whistle like that, Fred," warned one of the officials.

Bill, quite dismayed, asked: "Why? Is it forbidden?"

"No, but you always must have a long face. If you smile or

whistle, people will think the road is making money, and they must not know that."

Many times at social gatherings, local people would deliberately snub folks connected with the railroad. The reasons behind this feeling of enmity were never determined.

Almost immediately after Fred Bill came to the City of Vapors, there occurred an incident which provided him with the first bit of real excitement since he left Chicago.

It was a warm spring day in 1893 and young Jim Reamy was taking full advantage of it. Reamy was an assistant to Smith, the ticket agent, and was also chief clerk to superintendent Richardson. At the time in question, Reamy was outside enjoying the balmy day. He was sitting on a wooden ramp used in loading or unloading baggage cars. The sound of a shot rang out, and a bullet entered his shoulder from behind. The wound proved to be more painful than dangerous. No one was known to have a grudge against the boy, so it was presumed that the shot was not intended for him.

With the opening of the tourist season of 1895, the Diamond Jo was doing a land-office business. All available passenger equipment was in use, and extra trains were running, one right behind the other.

Soon a few cases of smallpox were discovered in Malvern. The town authorities decided to keep it quiet for fear the season would be spoiled if the presence of the disease became known. Presently, it did become known, and the number of cases was greatly exaggerated. Visitors, unable to find out just how many cases there were and what part of town was affected, became panic stricken and began leaving town as fast as trains could be run to Malvern. Pandemonium reigned for a few days.

Then the town of Malvern set up a quarantine against traffic from Hot Springs except for the one through train to and from St. Louis. This train was not allowed to discharge passengers at Malvern on the trip from Hot Springs.

It became necessary to operate the twenty-five-mile Diamond Jo in two divisions. Officials arranged a daily schedule so that a light engine would leave Hot Springs in time to meet the incoming train at Price, about nine miles out. This engine would pick up the train and bring it into Hot Springs. In the afternoon, the train was delivered to Price, where the Malvern engine was waiting. The train was thus delivered to Malvern, from which it left for St. Louis on schedule. On the outgoing train, Richardson or Bill would go along and collect fares, relieving the "eastern division" conductor from contact with the passengers and so comply with the Malvern quarantine regulations. The conductor out of Malvern collected all incoming fares. Freight was exchanged in the same manner.

After the initial onslaught of fear had abated, the excitement gradually decreased, even while the disease was rapidly spreading. The situation slowly returned to normal, and the quarantine was lifted March 31, 1895, after being in effect for about five weeks.

In spite of the seriousness of the occasion, there was a humorous incident worth mentioning. Early in the beginning of the trouble, orders were given for compulsory vaccination. Many people did not look favorably upon this turn of events, mostly because of fear and ignorance.

Pat Barry, young and brawny physician, was one of the doctors detailed to see that vaccinations were given. A young man was brought into Dr. Pat's office by a police officer. The fellow was strenuously protesting the entire procedure. Things were in a hectic mess and there was no time for argument or persuasion, so Pat landed a heavy right to the jaw of the malcontent. When the young man became aware of the world around him again, he had the makings of three most elegant scars on his left arm.

As a result of all the turmoil, the tourist season of 1895 was ruined and business fell off drastically. The Diamond Jo made special efforts with favorable advertising and reduced rates, all to no avail. Not immediately, that is. The season of 1896, the next year, was the best ever.

The Diamond Jo helped to save the financial life of a bank in Hot Springs. About the first of May, 1896, the institution known as the "Hogaboom Bank" failed to open its doors one morning. Soon after it was known for sure the bank would not open again, the president of the Arkansas National Bank, Charles N. Rix, hurried to the office of the Diamond Jo Railroad. His was the only other bank in town, and he knew his depositors soon would be calling on him for reassurance. Rix approached Fred Bill. "Fred," he pleaded, "I need every dollar in currency that I can get. I'm afraid I won't have enough to hold out against the withdrawals until I can get a shipment of cash from Little Rock late this evening."

There wasn't much cash on hand at the railroad office, but Bill said he would do anything he could to help. He devised a scheme which he felt might do the trick. He called for the freight and ticket offices to send in all the cash they had on hand just as soon as possible. A few minutes after nine o'clock, chief clerk Billy Woods made his way to the bank with a small deposit. There was a long line of customers, all making withdrawals as fast as the bank clerks could count out the money. Billy was forced to join the long line, which grew longer all the time, and it was quite a while before he came back to the office.

When Billy reported the situation at the bank, Fred decided to take a hand himself. He gathered up a small remittance from the freight office and made his way uptown to the bank. Instead of taking his place at the end of the line as Billy had done, however, Fred went directly to the teller's window, guarded with fancy iron scrollwork. There was an immediate angry response: "Get back in line where you belong! Everybody's gonna' take his own chance here!"

"Oh, I'm not takin' anything out. I want to make a deposit," Fred remarked.

"If he wants to put something in, give 'im a chance," someone chimed in.

The clerk quickly and gratefully took the small deposit. As Fred was leaving, he heard one man in the line say to the chap in front of him: "Who is that feller?"

"Why, that's the treasurer of th' Hot Springs Railroad," the second man replied.

"Well," said the first, "if this here bank's good enough fer th' railroad, it's sure good enough for me."

He was seen to drop out of line. Others immediately followed suit.

During the day, Fred Bill made several deposits, and each had its effect. Even so, there were many people who were afraid they would be left standing in line when the bank's regular closing time came. Rix assured them they had no cause for fear, that the doors would remain open until all had been served. This assurance caused a lull in the uproar, and soon the line of waiting patrons began to disintegrate. The Diamond Jo had saved the bank.

One of the more enthusiastic persons who "had it in" for the railroad was the manager of a grocery store which was a branch of a St. Louis firm. He went to a great deal of trouble and not a small amount of expense to demonstrate his antagonism for the Diamond Jo and its iron horse, and he managed to procure a certain amount of advertising for his store at the same time. He made arrangements to hire several of Bob Murray's freight wagons, complete with teams of mules, and had a great deal of freight hauled through the mountains from the Iron Mountain at Malvern. This venture proved rather expensive and was very short lived. The expense killed the courage of his convictions.

The Diamond Jo continued to prosper. The road operated its own express agency until March, 1900, when a contract was signed with the Pacific Express Company to handle this phase of the business. The Diamond Jo also leased the wires paralleling its rails to the Western Union Telegraph Company. Nationally known businesses were being introduced to Hot Springs through the auspices of the little railroad.

The first hint of competition in the form of iron rails came in 1893. The invader was from the Lone Star State, and his name was Uriah Lott. He came into the territory of the Diamond Jo advocating the building of a competing road to be known as the Little Rock, Hot Springs & Texas Railroad. He was received with great rejoicing and open arms by those who were antagonistic toward the little road which had rescued them from the high rates charged by the freight lines and the old El Paso Stage Company.

Lott's plans got under way quickly, and on December 12, 1893, the new road received its charter. "Brother Lott," as he was often called, was an exacting capitalist. He informed the residents of Hot Springs and Little Rock that he would expect $55,000 from each town to defray the cost of terminal facilities and right-of-way within the city limits. Lott also proposed to connect with the Iron Mountain at Benton, which lessened the enthusiasm of many of his backers in Hot Springs. "What advantage will it be to us to have two railroads if both of them are branches from the Iron Mountain?" they asked. Nor were many people in favor of giving a $55,000 bonus. They felt that a railroad, like any other respectable business, should be built and operated on its own merit.

Time marched on, and by March, 1894, not even one shovelful of dirt had been turned. After much agitation and with a concerted effort to raise the cash bonus at Little Rock, a roadbed of sorts was begun. It soon became evident that sufficient money would not be made available. A newspaper reporter confronted Brother Lott, who said the price of land at Little Rock had risen unreasonably in the past few days.

The grocery-store operator who had hired the freight wagons to transport his merchandise from Malvern approached Bill McGuigan for a contribution toward raising the bonus for Brother Lott. When Mac seemed a little on the lukewarm side, the grocer waxed most eloquent over the fine results which could be expected when the competing road was built. "Why, within two years after this new road's built, I sure do expect to see the rails of the Hot Springs road pulled up," he opined.

Mac gave this a little thought before he answered, "Well, now, I can't rightly see the benefit of tearing up one railroad to build another one."

Since all of Mac's property, upon which he raised a fine herd of blooded horses, lay along the route of the Diamond Jo, he allowed he would stick with the old line.

Iron Mountain officials assured the people of Hot Springs that no traffic arrangements had been made with Lott, nor were any contemplated. When the fervor of his backers waned even more, Brother Lott and the cash silently faded away.

The treasurer of the Diamond Jo Line was directly responsible for the formation of the Business Men's League. Early in the 1890's, the Iron Mountain was doing quite a lot of advertising for the resort area of Hot Springs and the Diamond Jo was paying an agreed-upon portion of the cost. The Arlington, Eastman, and Park hotels were also doing a good job of advertising, and there was even some by the smaller hotels and the individual bathhouses. In the attempt to cover the entire United States, the ads were spread rather thin.

Many of the smaller establishments performed no advertising work at all, but they reaped a proportionate share of profit from that done by others. Finally, Fred Bill took the matter up with H. C. Townsend, Iron Mountain general agent. They approached the three big hotels and then the people generally on a plan of placing one bureau in charge of all advertising for Hot Springs. The railroads offered to put up one dollar for every dollar contributed by the citizens of Hot Springs. After a few meetings, an organization was formed, with S. H. Stitt of the Arlington as president; A. R. Smith of the Avenue as vice president; Charles N. Rix, president of the Arkansas National Bank, as treasurer; and Herbert Durand of St. Louis as secretary. Nearly all establishments joined the movement, and it was a success from the very beginning.

As is the case even today, there were many lawyers looking for suits against the railroads, and they found them. Since it was little trouble to obtain a judgment against a railroad, such cases were rather lucrative for the lawyers.

Colonel J. M. Moore of Little Rock was general attorney for the Diamond Jo. He was an unusual man of outstanding ability —a real, old-time Southern gentleman—who thought every case should be tried on its merits. Moore always fought the railroad's cases as hard as he could, not expecting to secure a verdict in his favor, but to reduce the amount of damages against the road as much as possible. The local attorney for the Diamond Jo was C. V. Teague of Hot Springs, a young man with a pleasing personality and somewhat of a politician. These two made quite a team.

One day some boys were playing around the turntable at Hot Springs. The section foreman chased them away several times, but they always came back. Finally, one of them injured his foot while turning the table, but said nothing about it. Some years later, a suit was filed against the railroad. The foreman could not be positive that he had warned this particular boy to leave the company's property. The law stated that a turntable must be locked when not in use. The Diamond Jo had always used a fifty-pound "dog" latch between the rails, but the jury decided that "locked" meant secured by lock and key, and the railroad paid the penalty.

One day a very prominent attorney, Colonel Jube Rector, came into the Diamond Jo office and said he had been retained to bring suit against the road. Colonel Rector said it was his custom to attempt to settle all his cases out of court if possible. He stated his case, the railroad readily agreed, and a settlement was made— the only case ever settled out of court by the Diamond Jo.

In 1899, the shadows of evening began to grow long for the Diamond Jo. On July 18 of that year, a charter was granted to the Little Rock & Hot Springs Western Railroad, headed by Colonel Sam W. Fordyce, a former resident of Hot Springs and builder of the Cotton Belt. He felt that a new route to the Springs would be an asset. His company bought the old roadbed abandoned by Uriah Lott and extended it from Benton to a connection with the Choctaw, Oklahoma & Gulf at the south edge of Little Rock.

The Diamond Jo prepared to meet this competition by making some changes and improvements and by cutting expenses. It lost one employee to the new road: freight agent Fred W. Gregory. Everything seemed to be going along smoothly. Hot Springs had two railroads competing with each other for what business they could win. In April, 1900, the first train entered Hot Springs over the new line, which almost immediately became known as the "Hot Western."

Everyone was working hard during 1900, and there was scarcely enough business to keep both roads going. Trainmaster John Cox said he would like to have a vacation, a feeling shared by ticket agent Bob Smith. Cox and his wife, with four children and a niece, accompanied by Smith, his wife, and four children, left for Galveston. Soon after their arrival, the island was devastated by a terrible storm and tidal waves. The two families were completely wiped out, and gloomy sadness pervaded the Diamond Jo.

Early in 1901, rumors were heard that the Iron Mountain was getting control of the Hot Western. One day it was discovered that rates from Little Rock to Hot Springs were the same by way of Benton as by Malvern. Soon passengers were being routed by way of Benton over the Iron Mountain, and not long after that the sleepers from St. Louis were taken off the Diamond Jo and routed by way of Benton.

In July, 1901, the Choctaw, Oklahoma & Gulf bought that portion of the Hot Western between Little Rock and Benton, and on November 22, 1909, the Iron Mountain purchased the link from Benton to Hot Springs. This meant the end of the Diamond Jo. On May 1, 1902, the Choctaw, Oklahoma & Gulf bought it and assumed management. The first CO & G train entered Hot Springs on May 13, 1902. Every employee of the Diamond Jo was retained on the payroll. The 25-mile road had a 26-year life of troubles, trials, and tribulations. In April, 1902, the Choctaw, Oklahoma & Gulf was purchased by the Rock Island.

On Saturday, September 22, 1951, the last passenger train rolled out of the depot at Hot Springs. The 81-year-old station was demolished in November, 1961, to make way for a civic auditorium and convention hall. Just as the Diamond Jo's trains had succeeded the El Paso Stage Company's coaches, so, too, did automobiles and buses replace passenger trains into Hot Springs.

EUREKA SPRINGS RAILWAY—ST. LOUIS & NORTH ARKANSAS—MISSOURI & NORTH ARKANSAS—MISSOURI & ARKANSAS—HELENA & NORTHWESTERN—COTTON PLANT-FARGO—ARKANSAS & OZARKS

4

The Missouri & North Arkansas is by far the most controversial railroad in the history of Arkansas. It was an enigma: its 359 miles of rail stretched from "nowhere" to "nowhere," a bridge road with no traffic from its connecting roads and without sufficient on-line freight to sustain it. It was doomed to a lingering death almost from the moment of its birth. It never really lived, but neither has it completely died. The Missouri & North Arkansas Railroad was a tragic misfortune—for its builders as well as the people who depended upon its service.

The rugged Ozark Mountain country of northern Arkansas for many hundreds of years had known only infrequent human invasion. It had fallen into ownership by France from 1682 until the area was ceded to Spain in 1762. Spanish rule lasted until 1800, when France again took control until 1803, the year in which the United States gained the territory as part of the Louisiana Purchase.

Settlement of the mountainous region was very slow during the years of French and Spanish control. Government permission was required before anyone could settle there permanently, and then only under the strictest regulations. The Osage Indians called the hills their hunting grounds for quite a few years. When the United States laid claim to the land, it was opened to settlement by a rapidly expanding people.

They came quickly by the tens and twenties from the overcrowded states of the East. Especially did immigrants from the more mountainous states find it to their liking: the region reminded them so very much of the homelands they had deserted. The early settlers were inspired with the zeal of what constitutes the basic idea of freedom. The Ozark Mountain people are said to have the purest strain of Anglo-Saxon blood of any group of people in the world. It is very seldom that a foreign accent is heard, and no foreign-language publication has ever appeared from the Ozark region. A fierce and wonderful spirit of rugged individualism has reigned supreme since the mountains were first settled. However, this characteristic was to prove a detriment to the people during the strike of the operating employees of the M & NA in 1921–22.

Hidden deep in the recesses of the mountains were great springs from which flowed pure waters said to be endowed with magic powers to restore health and vigor to any who drank from their bountiful supply. The legends of these springs were known to the Osage Indians, who roamed northern Arkansas and southern Missouri. And the Cherokees also knew of the wonderful flowing fountains of health far to the west of the Great River.

Legend tells of a large party of Sioux who had set out on a long journey to the South in an effort to save the lives of those who had survived the devastation of a severe winter in the far North. They finally halted and set up camp at the forks of a great river where game abounded in the forest.

The people were very happy in their new home, the only matter of discontent being that a daughter of their chief was almost blind. One day the chief heard of a stream of water which flowed through giant beds of stone to emerge into a natural basin. This water was endowed with powers to renew the human body. The chief persuaded the medicine man to take the little girl to the springs, about a two-day journey to the south. Here the two remained for six moons. When they returned to camp, the girl's vision was equal to that of the forest animals.

White Hair, chief of the Osages in the 1840's, knew of a remarkable spring where any Indian could be cured of sore eyes just by washing and bathing in its waters during a full moon. The basin at the spring had been scooped out by Black Dog, an Osage chief, about 1775.

During the Civil War, Dr. Alvah Jackson established a hospital at the spring; it was patronized mostly by disabled Confederate soldiers. The good doctor took hogsheads (capacity: about 140 gallons) and cut them in half for bathtubs. His patients bathed in and drank of the sweet waters till they could hold no more.

The reputation of the place spread like a prairie fire before the wind. Health seekers came from the four points of the compass. The lame, the halt, the blind—they came by the hundreds. From any direction, the way in was through forest-clad mountains, steep and rugged. People came on horseback, in covered wagons, on foot. By July 1, 1879, twenty families were living near the spring.

Everywhere a structure of any kind could be erected, whether a frame house or a canvas tent, dwellings covered the hills, hanging from precipitous slopes or perching on jutting ridges. Within a year, five thousand people inhabited the hills around the spring. On July 4, 1879, the place was named Eureka Springs.

It wasn't long until the former governor of Arkansas, Powell Clayton, came to town with ideas of grandeur: the area should be developed as a nationally known health resort. In short order, he had attracted several men of considerable wealth to associate themselves with his effort. Soon the chaos which had run rampant gave way to order and discipline. A town was born, a town of permanence, even as the mountains which enclosed it.

If thousands of people would make their way through the roadless mountains, how many more would make the journey if they could come in comfort and ease? This question plagued the people until it became an obsession. The only conveyance that could handle the rapidly growing crowds of immigrants was a railroad.

It was in 1880 that prospects for a connection with the outside world began to grow brighter. The St. Louis & San Francisco Railway (Frisco) had been casting a wishful eye toward the northern border of Arkansas. A line of rails extending through the Boston Range of the Ozarks would cross the Little Rock & Ft. Smith at Van Buren, a good source of interchange business. From there, it was only about 170 miles across Indian Territory to Paris, Texas.

During 1881, the Frisco penetrated Arkansas to reach the town of the fountain of knowledge, Fayetteville. At the same time, the Frisco's builders heard the clamor from across the mountains for a railroad to Eureka Springs. The call was heeded, and the Missouri & Arkansas Railroad was formed by the Frisco. A charter was granted on February 27, 1882, to build from Seligman, Missouri, to Beaver, Arkansas, a distance of thirteen miles.

The most feasible route was finally located, and the task of construction began. The surrounding mountains resounded with the booming blast of black powder, the shouts and curses of mule skinners, and the ringing of spike mauls. The route generally followed the courses of Butler Creek, Leatherwood Creek, and White River. The invasion of the Ozarks had begun in earnest.

In those days of limited finances, the thirteen-mile mountain railroad was costing a great deal more than had been anticipated. In order to bring the rails all the way into Eureka Springs, a new company had to be formed. In June, 1882, a charter was granted by the state to the Eureka Springs Railway to build from the end of the Missouri & Arkansas rails at the settlement of Beaver, on the banks of the White River, the remaining six miles to the valley of healing waters. The guidance and direction of this venture were entrusted to Powell Clayton, M. W. Benjamin, O. A.

Hadley, James Torrans, John C. Peay, John D. Adams, George W. Dale, James Mitchell, and J. T. Brown, Jr. The cost of the road was set at $600,000.

Former Governor and former U.S. Senator Powell Clayton had been the prime moving force behind the project from the beginning. Many of the investors who were financing the road soon lost interest when they saw what it cost to build through those tough limestone mountains. Eastern capitalists could not be convinced that there would be sufficient travelers attracted to a place in such a mountainous wilderness to make railroad venture profitable. Finally, R. C. Kerens of St. Louis and Logan H. Roots agreed to furnish two-thirds of the money required. The remaining one-third was provided by Powell Clayton; B. Baer, a Fort Smith banker; E. W. Taylor, a banker from Jefferson, Texas; and Morgan Jones, a successful railroad contractor.

On April 26, 1882, the stockholders of the little six-mile-long railroad converged on the Southern Hotel at Eureka Springs. At ten o'clock that Wednesday morning, they heard their board of directors propose a consolidation of the Eureka Springs Railway and the Missouri & Arkansas Railroad. The plan met with enthusiastic approval, and the nineteen-mile road became the Eureka Springs Railway.

All during the summer and winter of 1882, the road was laboriously pushed through the mountains. Stone and earth gave way before the onslaught by crews of Jones & Cowen, railroad contractors from Texas. As they crossed White River at Beaver, workers encountered a high but narrow limestone ridge. Too narrow for a tunnel, it was divided by a notch just wide enough for the rails to be laid. The cut became known throughout the area as "The Narrows."

Below the cut, White River made a graceful, sweeping curve, leaving the little settlement of Beaver on a peninsula. The iron truss bridge spanning the river was manufactured and erected by the Delaware Bridge Company. A combination freight and passenger depot was built near the end of the bridge. From there, the rails ran alongside the tumbling waters of Leatherwood Creek to Eureka Springs—seven miles of beauty. A contemporary newspaper article stated that the scenery along the route was unexcelled anywhere. It compared favorably with the Sierra Nevadas in California and with other mountain scenery of the West.

The morning of February 1, 1883, dawned wet, cold, and rather miserable, but this did not dampen the spirits of the folks at Eureka Springs. The rails of their very own railroad had entered the city limits and they were in physical contact with the outside world. Business was begun with two locomotives, one passenger car, one baggage car, and six platform cars (flatcars). The locomotives were numbered 1 and 2. No. 1 was a 2–8–0 built by Pittsburgh Locomotive Works of Pittsburgh, Pennsylvania, in December, 1882. She had builder's number 631, 44-inch drivers and 18x24-inch cylinders. Engine No. 2 was a 4–4–0 from the Rogers Locomotive Works at Paterson, New Jersey, built in September, 1883, with builder's number 3361, having been named "Powell Clayton." A turntable was built to accommodate the locomotives because there was insufficient room to construct a turning wye in the narrow valley.

A beautiful station was built at Eureka Springs from fine-grade native materials. This structure also housed the company's general offices. Near by were a freight depot, roundhouse, shops, and coal sheds. One large free-flowing spring provided ample water for the roundhouse, machine shops, fire plugs, locomotives, toilets and wash basins in the station, plus irrigation for the station grounds and all other uses of the company.

A passenger arriving at Eureka Springs found himself surrounded by confusion: a congestion of hacks and buses and the cries of many hotel "drummers." The weary traveler entered one of the conveyances and began the journey up the canyon to the town on the higher levels of the mountain.

Business was encouraging after rails reached the mountain resort town. When passenger traffic warranted, extra cars were rented from the Frisco. During 1883, 23,500 passengers rode the steam cars to Eureka. Also arriving were 583 cars of lumber, 550 bales of cotton, 700 barrels of flour, 2,985 barrels of salt, and many carloads of cattle, hogs, coal, and fence posts. The Eureka Springs knew it was a real railroad when it had to pay out $214.50 for livestock killed or injured by its trains in 1883. Its property steadily advanced in valuation from $46,428 in 1884 to $90,617 in 1888. During 1887, total operation costs amounted to $23,376, while total income was $136,724.

Soon there was a clamor for the rails to be extended through the heart of the Ozark Mountains toward the town of Harrison. The vice president of the Frisco was friendly in his dealings with the Eureka Springs Railway and had agreed to a most generous interchange of traffic. Under such favorable circumstances, a contract was negotiated for the eastward extension of the rails. Then misfortune paid a visit to the little road, a visit which seemed to be repeated down through the years at more or less frequent intervals, sometimes in rather extended fashion: the vice president of the Frisco died. The hopes of the Eureka Springs Railway for pushing through the hills and valleys to the east also died because the new head of Frisco was indisposed toward any such agreement.

The line continued to bring health seekers to the springs. Freight traffic, while never existing in large amounts, remained about the same. But the expense of operating a mountain railroad was exceeding expectations of the road's officials. The flood waters of adversity were rising.

In spite of this, or perhaps in ignorance of the situation, the pioneer citizens who were laboriously struggling to wrest a living from the valleys and mountainsides of Carroll, Boone, and Searcy counties continued pleading for the railroad to be extended. They felt the mountains were an immovable wall between them and the outside world. If the railroad would penetrate these barriers, their lives would be made much easier.

In the spring of 1899, they had the promise of an answer to their fervent prayers: the railroad was coming.

Capitalists in Little Rock, St. Louis, and New York decided they would tackle the job; nothing ventured, nothing gained. On May 17, 1899, a charter was granted by the Arkansas Railroad Commission to the St. Louis & North Arkansas Railroad, whose ambition was to build east as far as Harrison, the seat of commerce in Boone County.

The St. Louis & North Arkansas was the first railroad to apply for a charter after the formation of the Arkansas Railroad Commission. The governor, attorney general, state auditor, secretary of state, state treasurer, commissioner of agriculture, and commissioner of state lands were appointed as a state board of railroad incorporation. When articles for a railroad corporation were filed at the office of the secretary of state, the Railroad Commission was required to meet at his office to determine whether the railroad would be in the interest of the public and to decide whether a charter should be granted. If it were granted a charter, the company was required to proceed with expedition to carry out the contracts with the public and to build the road according to the preliminary survey. Failure to complete one-fifth of it within three years was cause for forfeiture of its charter. Failure to complete the entire road within six years resulted in the forfeiture of the uncompleted portion. If the commission felt it would be in the best interest of the public, an extension of time could be granted for completion of a particular road.

Again the booming roar of exploding black powder echoed through the mountains. The shouts and curses of the mule skinners rose above the tumult of the crews laying ties and spiking down the rails. A few miles east of Eureka Springs, a hole was blasted through a mountain to permit the passage of the twin ribbons of iron. A little farther on, a branch line was run south two and one-half miles to give the town of Berryville an outlet. Then came Green Forest and Alpena.

On March 22, 1901, the track-laying crew spiked down the last rail at Harrison, county seat of Boone County and center of all commerce in the mountain region. A fine welcoming crowd had gathered, some traveling many miles from the remote hill country. They came by wagon, on horseback, and on foot, for this was the most momentous occasion yet to grace the lives of these hardy but lonely souls, derisively called Arkansas hillbillies. The North Arkansas would be the salvation for which they had waited and prayed so earnestly for so many years.

With a tumultuous shout, they greeted the arrival of flag-draped St. Louis & North Arkansas 4–6–0 No. 3. She had been built just the year before by Dickson Locomotive Works. Coupled to her pilot were a pair of flatcars loaded with raw, hand-hewn crossties. From her straight stack billowed clouds of smoke, stinging onlookers' nostrils with the pungent odor of burning bituminous coal. Nevertheless, they cheered as she ground to a clattering halt. Then the engineer leaned from the cab window of No. 3 and greeted the close-packed crowd with what had become a tradition in the realm of railroading, thereby causing the usual pandemonium associated with the event: "Watch out, everybody, I'm gonna' turn 'er around!" The railroad had officially arrived.

The St. Louis & North Arkansas was a peculiar railroad. It didn't belong to the officials who were responsible for its corporate being; neither did it belong to the crews who operated its trains, however heroic they were esteemed to be; it belonged to the thousands of people who lived in the area it served.

The railroad had been built for them, and they had taken a personal interest in it from the very beginning. They had pleaded for it, prayed for it, worked for it, paid for it. They owned no stock in it, they had bought no bonds; instead, they had made what cash donations they could afford, however meager these may have been, and when the rails crossed a hillside farm or valley meadow owned by one of these struggling men of the hill country, right-of-way was freely given. Each man gave as much as he was able.

This jealous sense of possession was an admirable thing to behold. It gave the desperately struggling hill people incentive for further efforts. Nothing could stop them now; they were connected with the outside world, their existence was assured. They were a part of world commerce, yet protected from its depleting influence by the rugged mountains surrounding them. Unfortunately, however, their pride in proprietorship was to prove detrimental in the dark years ahead.

The rails had scarcely been spiked to the ties when the bells of misfortune and dismay began to toll. The echoes were faint for a while, but were soon resounding loud and clear. The hill folk were being introduced to the hard, cold facts of the financial world: you may build a railroad through the Ozarks, but it is a very different story when you try to operate trains over it *at a profit.* Locomotives cannot lift a string of high cars over 2 per cent grades on sentiment, and those serpentine curves certainly put a strain on the budget.

In 1906, the St. Louis & North Arkansas had several locomotives on its roster of motive power, as well as five combination cars, four passenger coaches, and twenty-six freight cars. The auditor was using too darn much red ink on his ledger books! He came up with a deficit of more than thirty thousand dollars for the year. By mid-summer, it was painfully evident that something had to be done. There were two alternatives: the officials could throw a derail under the bobtail railroad and call it quits, or they could fling the lantern in an arrogant highball in the darkening night of adversity. They chose the latter course.

On the fourth day of August, 1906, the St. Louis & North Arkansas ceased to exist. In its place emerged the reorganized Missouri & North Arkansas, a new venture under the direction of John Scullin, Charles Gilbert, George L. Sands, H. W. Scullin, Powell Clayton, C. J. Crump and J. W. Freeman. The officials responsible for the operation of the new pike were John Scullin, president; George L. Sands, vice president; W. S. Roberts, secretary; and N. W. McMillan, treasurer.

The new organization immediately negotiated a contract with the Allegheny Improvement Company to construct an extension south from Harrison through the mountains to Searcy at the edge of the foothills, then across the prairie and swampy overflow country to Helena, a steamboat town on the Mississippi River. Also included in the contract was the 32-mile stretch from Wayne to Neosho, two towns in Missouri.

The M & NA had a trackage agreement whereby it could use the Frisco's rails for 9.4 miles from Seligman, Missouri, to Wayne. It could also run trains over Kansas City Southern track from Neosho into Joplin, Missouri, 19.8 miles away.

This combination yielded a direct connection from Kansas City and Joplin to Helena, where a railroad ferry across the Mississippi afforded a connection with New Orleans by way of the Yazoo & Mississippi Valley (acquired by the Illinois Central in 1946). The two larger roads could use the Missouri & North Arkansas as a bridge route to New Orleans. There would be ample traffic, both freight and passenger, over the 368-mile system.

Retained as consulting engineer was S. W. Lee, who appointed W. S. Dawley as chief engineer in charge of locating the best route from Wayne to Neosho and from Leslie to Helena. Leslie, Arkansas, had been the southern terminus since 1903.

Late in August, 1906, engineers Dawley and Lee went to Helena to investigate the town's potential for use as a railroad terminal. The Business Men's League proposed to donate the right-of-way for nearly fifty miles of track between Helena and Cotton Plant. In addition, it would make a gift of sufficient land for terminal facilities. Securing another railroad, especially one of such importance, was a matter of real concern to the people of Helena.

Their proposition was attractive enough to induce the railroad officials to file a mortgage of $11,500,000 on 129 miles of the M & NA from Seligman to Leslie. The St. Louis Trust Company was underwriter for the mortgage, and the road issued 11,500 first-mortgage gold bonds bearing coupons at 4 per cent interest.

Early in October of 1906, engineer S. W. Burchard completed a preliminary route survey into Helena, then went to St. Louis to have a talk with the owners. He proposed that the company

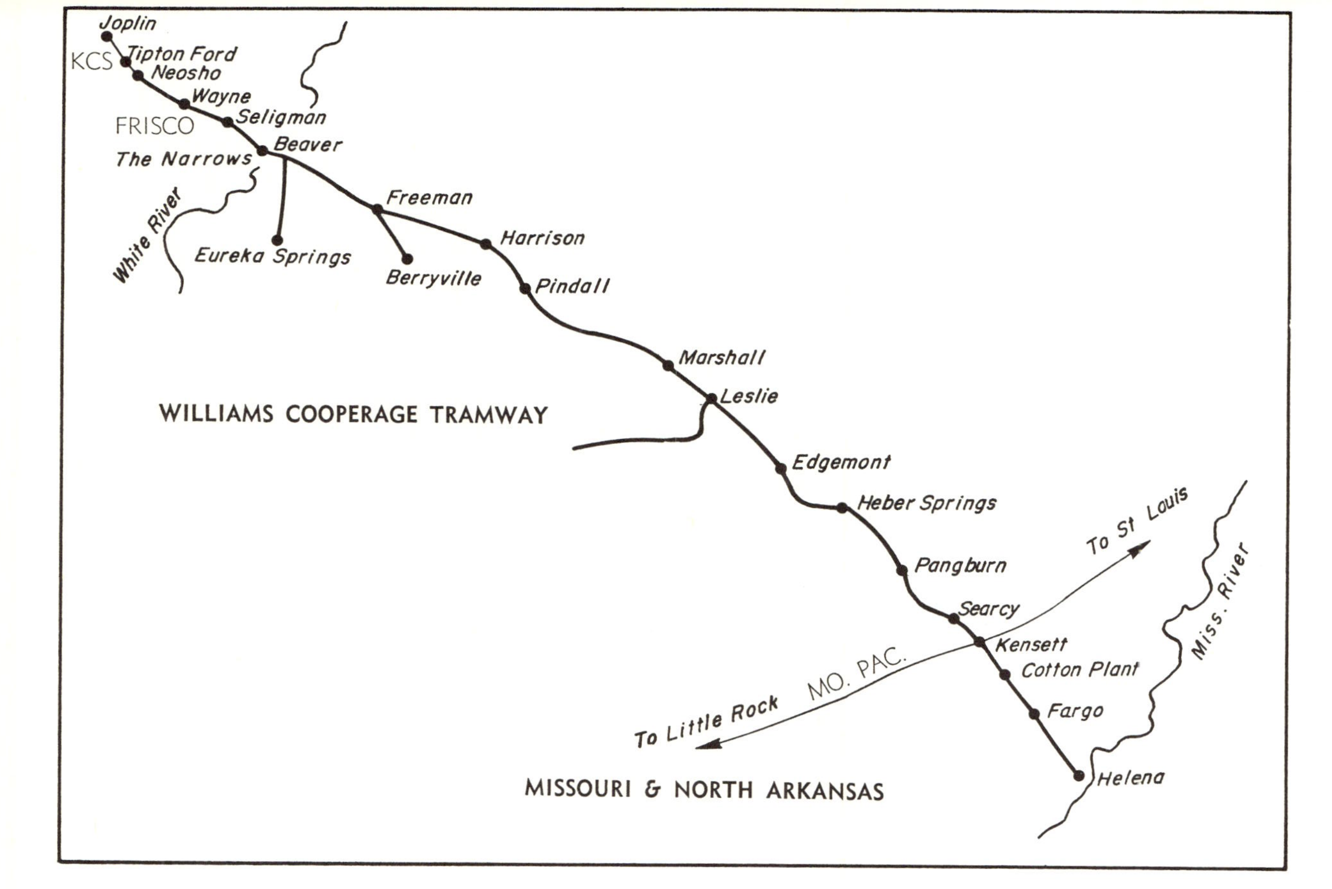

Joplin
KCS
Tipton Ford
Neosho
Wayne
Seligman
FRISCO
Beaver
The Narrows
White River
Eureka Springs
Freeman
Berryville
Harrison
Pindall
Marshall
Leslie
WILLIAMS COOPERAGE TRAMWAY
Edgemont
Heber Springs
To St Louis
Pangburn
Miss. River
Searcy
Kensett
MO. PAC.
Cotton Plant
To Little Rock
Fargo
Helena
MISSOURI & NORTH ARKANSAS

bend its track eastward and head for Memphis. This still would provide a connection to New Orleans over the Illinois Central and would eliminate several miles of construction. The idea did not find favor, so Helena remained the objective.

On October 12, the company announced that the road was to be extended seventy-five miles from Leslie to Pangburn, about ten miles east of Heber Springs. There were plenty of rails lying in the yards at Leslie to complete fifteen miles of track, and another sixty-five miles were to be delivered in January and February.

The Missouri & Southeastern Construction Company was formed to build the road into Pangburn. A contract was negotiated on October 20, and the firm was given eighteen months to complete one-tenth of the construction. About two or three months later, a contract was to be let for the remainder of the road from Pangburn to Helena.

The sense of ownership and loyalty which prevailed among the people along the northern end of the road was sadly lacking in the foothills area. Folks were not disposed to donate right-of-way, and the company was forced to begin buying land in order to expedite construction of the road.

When the rails penetrated the rough mountain country, industries were developed or transplanted. One such establishment was the H. D. Williams Cooperage Company near Leslie, where abundant hardwood timber in the area was converted into barrels, large and small. It was here that misfortune raised its ugly head one October day.

C. M. Hudson, a young man of 28, lived at Leslie. The founding of the cooperage had given him a chance for employment which he had never had before. On the day in question, he was standing atop a car which he was loading with barrel staves. He made a misstep and fell from the car, striking his side severely as he hit the ground. The local doctor determined Hudson had suffered an intestinal stricture and would require major surgery. He had no equipment to perform such an extensive operation, so Hudson would have to be taken to St. Louis.

Hudson was placed aboard the next northbound passenger train to speed him toward Joplin and a connection with a Frisco train to St. Louis. The top speed allowed, even for passenger trains, was twenty-five miles per hour, which was pretty good at that time. But even a hundred miles an hour would have been too slow. Just eighteen miles east of Eureka Springs, the young man died on a cot in the baggage car.

There also occurred another incident concerning the cooperage, and it narrowly missed being a real tragedy. As the hardwood trees were cut from the forest, it soon became evident that ox teams were inadequate for hauling logs to the mill. It was decided that a railroad was the most satisfactory answer, so one was built. As the supply of trees dwindled, the rails were extended over the mountains west of Leslie to penetrate deeper into the forest.

Two Shay engines and a little rod-type hog were purchased. Flatcars with link-and-pin couplers and equipped only with hand brakes were used to haul the logs across the mountain into the mill at Leslie, where a connection was made with the M & NA. The cooperage line crossed the M & NA and proceeded a short distance to Barrel Plant No. 1.

One day a man named Wilhelm applied at the mill for a job. He said he had been bucking the engineer's extra board out of Leslie on the North Arkansas and needed a more regular job. H. D. Williams hired him and sent him out the next morning with the regular crew on the log train. Dave Nelson was hogger on the dinkey and tallow pot George Binder had the job of keeping a head of steam in the boiler. Clyde Boyd was in charge of lifting coupling pins and manipulating the hand brakes on the flatcars.

Leaving town, they climbed the mountain west of Leslie, rolled smoothly down the other side, and stopped at the logging camp, where their train of six empty flats was set out on the spur track and loaded. Dropping the last pin through its link, brakie Clyde climbed up into the cab of the engine, which was more comfortable than riding a bouncing log car. The hogger turned the throttle over to Wilhelm to let him get the feel of it. With the exhaust barking from the diamond stack, the dinkey lifted her load to the top of the mountain.

When they reached the top of the mountain, the hogger told Wilhelm to stop while Clyde went back to club down the binders on the loaded flats so they would hold on their way down. With arrogance acquired from his days of main-line running, the new man said he could hold them with the steam jam brake on the engine. So he let the little hog drop over the summit and roll along smartly.

Reaching for the steam valve, Wilhelm set the jam to apply the shoes against the drivers. The engine hesitated, the slack in the link couplers ran in, and the six loaded flats hit her in the rear with a wallop. The dinkey started chasing her pilot down the mountain, gaining speed as she went, the side rods on her small drivers becoming only a blur.

The hogger suddenly lost his bravado and frantically opened the steam valve wide putting the full boiler pressure into the cylinder of the jam brake. At the same time, he opened the sander valve and let a steady stream of grit pour onto the rails ahead of the now sliding drivers. The abrasive sand didn't even slow the engine's headlong race. She had the bit in her teeth and was running free!

The four men decided the bucking and lurching cab was suddenly overcrowded. Scrambling out the gangway, they joined the birds. Just before he jumped, Wilhelm tied the whistle cord down.

The six cars of logs obeyed the law of gravity, as all decent log cars should, and merrily shoved the feebly protesting engine ahead of them. Down the mountain they went. Soon logs began to fly from the bouncing flatcars. The engine and six cars rode the rails around the curves and reached the foot of the mountain. With whistle screeching like a banshee, the wild maverick roared across the M & NA track, where a passenger train had passed less than five minutes before. The stampede ended at a track barrier at Barrel Plant No. 1. The twenty-ton engine instantly became a battered wreck and the six flatcars were completely demolished. Luckily, no one was injured.

The mill hands heard the incessant wail of the whistle and, running outside, saw the runaway train roaring down the mountain. They scattered in all directions. The embarrassed crew came limping into the mill after a while, looking rather sheepish but not badly hurt; Wilhelm assumed full responsibility for the wreck. It was his last run. He joined the boomer crowd and went looking for a healthier climate.

November 28, 1909, came on Sunday and H. M. Foley, who was secretary of the cooperage firm, invited two young ladies from Missouri who were visiting in Leslie to accompany him on a picnic in the forest along the company's tramway. The trees were decked in flaming fall colors—a perfect day for a picnic. Edith Wilson of St. Louis and Ruby Duncan of Poplar Bluff eagerly accepted the invitation.

Foley had appropriated one of the company's gasoline motorcars, and up the steep mountain grade they climbed. The well-filled picnic basket was tied securely to the side of the car, and the young ladies tucked voluminous skirts about their ankles. Chugging along, they slowly climbed the winding track, crested the mountain, and rolled easily around sharp curves, admiring the ever changing brilliant display of color.

The fine fall day was spent most enjoyably, and as the sun sent shadows creeping eastward, Foley and the young women boarded the car. They sputtered through the woods, again crested the mountain, and began the steep, winding descent toward Leslie. It was a rather hair-raising grade, and many times hoggers on the log trains had vigorously objected to being compelled to drop heavy trains down the mountain.

The motorcar soon was rolling along at a fair clip, and Foley began bearing down on the hand brake. He shut off the ignition and used the engine's compression to help hold the car back on the grade. But neither this nor the hand brake was a match for the pull of gravity. By then the car was rolling too fast for its passengers to jump from it, or at least they thought it was.

Suddenly, on a sharp curve, the wheels climbed over the outside rail, and both car and passengers flew through the air. The young ladies were thrown a considerable distance. Miss Duncan was bruised and shaken up pretty badly, while Miss Wilson was more scared than hurt. Foley was pinned beneath the overturned car. Miss Wilson ran frantically down the hill to the plant for help. When the rescuers arrived, they quickly lifted the car off Foley and placed it back on the rails to take him to town, but they were too late. He was dead. The mountain had claimed its victim.

On Saturday morning, November 24, 1906, the stockholders of the Missouri & Southeastern Construction Company, a subcontractor, met in Little Rock at the office of W. B. Smith, attorney for the M & NA. They proposed to alter the route south of Leslie and build into Little Rock. The citizens of the capital city were most enthusiastic about the idea.

No agreement could be made with the controlling interests of the railroad. They said the large roads with terminals at Little Rock were not friendly toward the M & NA and any division of rates with these lines would not be satisfactory. Moreover, the roads to the north, with whom the traffic routing arrangement had been made, would frown on a Little Rock terminal. When the disagreement could not be resolved, the Missouri & Southeastern sold its contract, charter, franchise, and property to the M & NA, leaving the railroad in charge of its own construction.

Early in December, 1906, an innovation was begun to expedite the delivery of mail between Eureka Springs and Seligman. A standard automobile equipped with flanged wheels was placed in charge of superintendent Nicholas and electrician Lauderback. Since it brought the mail into Eureka Springs five hours ahead of the regular train, everyone was well pleased with the arrangement.

To prepare for the time when M & NA rails would reach the Mississippi, an order was issued in December for $100,000 worth of equipment, including five new locomotives at $15,000 each and two new passenger coaches at $4,500 each. The coaches were to be delivered in March, the engines about June 1. At the time the order was made, the road owned eight boxcars, three of which were leased to the cooperage plant at Leslie. The other was used in the construction train. And there were a precious few flatcars on the equipment register.

To encourage the early extension of the rails through the foothills, the people of Searcy gave the company $6,500 in cash and plenty of land for the construction of a depot, plus all right-of-way through town. This came late in February, 1907, just before work began in earnest. By April 11, fifteen hundred men were at work grading various portions of the roadbed between Leslie and Searcy, and another one thousand would soon be required.

In 1944, L. R. Parmelee, civil engineer at Helena, recorded his experiences in helping to locate the line of the M & NA. His comments are typical of several accounts:

> The time was March 1907. As levelman, I had just joined the party of engineers who were locating the Missouri and North Arkansas Railroad from Helena northwest to Searcy. The line had been located from northwest (Eureka Springs) to Searcy. John R. Wilbanks, now of Wilbanks & Pierce, dredging contractors, was the locating engineer, chief of the party, and the late W. S. Dawley, a noble character of the profession, was the chief engineer of the Allegheny Improvement Company, a company of St. Louis financiers who had organized to do this project. In February or March of 1907 we picked up our stationing at the intersection of Louisiana and St. Francis Streets in Helena and started northwest by running first south around Crowley's Ridge.
>
> The year 1907 was a rainy one. Through water in creeks and bayous we waded and swam all during March and April, and finally reached Cotton Plant about the first of May, at least three weeks behind our schedule. Here we were delayed another two weeks waiting for the water to recede out of the White and Cache River bottoms. Finally, by moving a light outfit—that is, reducing our normal moving camp load for the 16 to 18 men of the party—we reached Peach Orchard Bluff. It took us two days to move

across about 10 miles of the bottoms. A good part of the time our wagons were flooded and floating. We moved back to old Moro in the latter part of July to make the final location. Because of malaria we came out of the bottoms with a debilitated crew. Two men died of this disease—one of them in Cotton Plant a day or so after we came out. In this party were E. E. Mashburn, a principal engineer of the State Highway Department, and Maxie Daggett, prominent druggist of Marianna. In fact, several civil engineers of later prominence in the state started on the M & NA Railroad.

In August 1907 I was ordered back to Helena as resident engineer in charge of construction of the first 20 miles of roadbed out of Helena. Our headquarters were set up in the old Clopton farm house in West Helena for the winter season of 1907–08. We had a congenial group of boys and spent a pleasant time along with our duties. In the party was Bogan Gist, present assessor of Phillips County, and with his guns and dogs we were kept pretty well supplied with game—principally birds. Also well remembered is Bush Binley, insurance man of Little Rock at the present time and a member of the Corporation Commission, who served our party as rear chain man. By relieving him of carrying the transit on one of our long muddy hikes one day, I won his everlasting gratitude. Bush had the honor of being the Helenian to ride the first train on the M & NA into Phillips County. He was standing at the Lee-Phillips County line when the steel laying gangs and work train crossed the line. Just before crossing Bush hopped on a flat car of the train and rode across.

At the time, and before our sojourn at the old Clopton Place, it was generally reported that Helena was intended to be only a division point for the M & NA, that the road was to be projected across the Mississippi River and on to Pensacola. The fact is that the late E. C. Horner, banker of Helena, with the late C. H. Purvis, engineer, made a trip to Pensacola in 1907 and obtained options on waterfront rights and options on railroads in the affected area through Mississippi between Helena and Pensacola. The 1907 and 1908 depression, with other causes, prevented the scheme from consummation, and incidentally made the M & NA a stunted child in the family of railroads.

. . . Big names among bankers, financiers and construction men of the Middle West were in the Allegheny Improvement Company. Among them were David R. Francis, George Sands, Festus J. Wade, Powell Clayton, Mr. Sullins and others. The day final inspection was made prior to turning the project over to operations was a big day for me. It was my first responsible charge. I met the inspection train, which contained some of the notables named above, at Moro and rode with them over my residency to Helena and a big dinner.

By the latter part of May, 1908, 30.5 miles of road were under construction between Woodruff and Neosho, Missouri. The grading and bridges were under contract to Scott & Sons of St. Louis and Dalhoff & Peters of Little Rock. The grading and bridges from Leslie to Searcy, were in charge of Burke & Joseph of Cape Girardeau, Missouri, and a construction contract for 40 miles of road out of Helena was awarded to John Scott & Sons. There were to be three bridges over Little Red River, one 155 feet long and two of 255 feet.

Some of the largest machinery ever seen in that part of the state was being used by contractor J. H. Whalen. He had several steam traction engines with immense plows to rip up the earth, rocks, and tree stumps, and he had recently received a giant thirty-ton steam shovel which had cost him $10,000. Freight on this monster was $375 from Toledo, Ohio, to Searcy, and it could do the work of one hundred men in a single day. It certainly proved its worth in the deep, heavy cuts.

The link between Wayne and Neosho was completed June 14, 1907, and construction began between Helena and Brinkley on June 29. Local real estate men were frantically buying as much land as possible from Brinkley to Searcy. The area was sparsely settled because of difficult access, and there were no roads by which produce could be sent to market. A railroad would satisfy the need, and land values were soaring.

Oscar Mize and J. W. Skinner were in charge of bridge construction. There were to be 46 bridges in the 30-mile section from Searcy to Heber Springs, and the two men prophesied that trains would be running from Leslie into Searcy by the first of

January, 1908. Some 1,500 men were working on this section. A large quantity of bridge timbers was required on the M & NA route through the Ozarks. To supply just the structures mentioned above, the Heber Springs Milling Company was given an order for 250,000 board feet of lumber; the Pangburn Lumber Company was to supply an additional 200,000 board feet.

To facilitate passenger service by the one regular train each way every day, a fine gasoline motorcar was put in service in August, 1907, between Eureka Springs and Seligman. It was the largest and most elaborately furnished of any such car ever used in the state. It seated fifty-two passengers and had separate baggage and smoking compartments. The company paid $18,000 upon delivery. It was scheduled to connect with eight passenger trains a day on the Frisco at Seligman, giving rapid and frequent service.

The controversial Carry A. Nation, known throughout America as the "Hatchet Queen," was, indirectly, the motivating factor which caused one employee on the North Arkansas to become violently ill. Carry tamed down her physical destruction of the saloons —dens of iniquity, as they were known—across Kansas in 1908–1909. She embarked upon a speaking tour which took her to Europe and then on to Scotland, where her temperance endeavors landed her in jail.

In 1909, she returned to America and bought a small farm near Alpena, Boone County, Arkansas. She was sixty-three. The next year, she went to Eureka Springs and purchased a two-story frame home which she named "Hatchet Hall." She had a very disturbing effect upon folks who were meeting her for the first time. She was reported to have about as much abhorrence for tobacco as she had for booze.

Ernie Braswell was agent for the M & NA at Eureka Springs during the time Carry was living there. One day he was busy at the ticket office in the depot, his jaw filled with a chew of plug tobacco, when a patron came to the ticket window. Young Ernie turned to the window, shifting his chew comfortably to the other jaw, and came face to face with the stern countenance of the

Hatchet Queen herself. In his startled confusion, Ernie inadvertently swallowed his "chaw." The ticket transaction was completed in the nick of time.

The North Arkansas was determined to become more than a mere feeder road. Her ambition was showing. By early October, 1907, the company had accumulated 350 boxcars, cattle cars, and flatcars, all of the latest design. Of the stable of 14 locomotives, 5 were big Consolidations with Vanderbilt tenders. A complete vestibule train had arrived from the Pullman shops at Chicago.

On the morning of October 6, vice president and general manager George L. Sands left Eureka Springs for the "front," somewhere in the mountain wilderness south of Leslie. He was aboard his private car, No. 305, an ordinary wooden caboose painted a violent crimson. It looked like a blushing crummy from the outside. Inside, however, was a stateroom, beautifully finished in light hardwood paneling, containing a comfortable iron half-bed, toilet, lavatory, and a locker for clothing. A compact kitchen held a small oil stove, a full complement of utensils, an ice box, and a cupboard. In a front compartment were easy chairs and a cot with mattress and bedding, as well as a cushioned bunk in which bedding could be stored. This was a smoker by day and a guest room at night. The rear end was an observation lounge with a long, cushioned seat facing the rear, plus a desk and secretary for writing or for safekeeping of plans, drawings, or books.

While No. 305 did not boast of Pullman-car luxuries, it did provide comforts and conveniences. Sands had designed it for use during the work extending the rails from Leslie through the rugged Ozarks to Helena, for accommodations at the construction camps left much to be desired in the matter of creature comforts. The flaming crummy was to be put in regular service when its tour of special duty was over.

One of the contractors performing clearing work, Frank H. Kennedy, had obtained a crew of thirty-seven prisoners from the state penitentiary at Little Rock and was promised about fifty more. This was a lucrative plum for Kennedy, since their food was just about his only expense. By the middle of January, 1908, the prisoners had completed their particular segment of clearing the right-of-way and were returned to Little Rock. Other crews were busy grading up the embankment so that early in February, 1908, passenger service was begun on a mixed-train basis into Scullin, a short distance south of Leslie.

The little mountain village of Leslie had a half-dozen homes, one store building, and perhaps fifty inhabitants when the shiny rails of the M & NA came in 1902. Then the town was made headquarters for the activities of extending the road toward Helena, and its growth was rapid. The greatest factor in this was the establishment of the H. D. Williams Cooperage Company, which furnished employment for almost everyone in the town. The barrel factory was reported to be the largest of its kind in the world. Once located at Poplar Bluff, Missouri, it was moved to Leslie in the fall of 1907 and began operations in December. When in full operation, the mill employed about one thousand men. There were several portable mills which could be moved about in the mountains of northern Arkansas as the hardwood forest was gradually exhausted. Running at full capacity, the cooperage could produce five thousand barrels a day. The plant at Leslie covered sixty-eight acres, and the company had built fifty houses for its employees. Twenty miles of company railroad were strung out across the mountains, and a steady stream of traffic rolled out of the plant and onto the rails of the M & NA.

Track was pushed southward through the only natural pass in the Boston Range of the Ozarks near Leslie and followed the Little Red River to within a few miles of Searcy. The grade was kept to one-sixth of 1 per cent. One blessing among the many difficulties the road encountered was the fact that there seemed to be plenty of money available during the depression years of 1907–1908.

During April, 1908, the people of Little Rock were again making an all-out effort to secure an extension of the M & NA. They invited railroad officials to town, and at the meeting, the businessmen of Little Rock proposed to furnish all land necessary for terminal facilities in Argenta (North Little Rock), plus right-of-way to a junction with the main line ten miles southeast of Searcy near White River. The railroad fellows were a stubborn lot; they still had their minds set on a Mississippi River terminal.

To stimulate the interest of the traveling folk and to advertise the advantages of riding on the M & NA, it was suggested in May, 1908, that a motorcar run from Searcy northwest to Armstrong Springs, even though it was a ride of only seven miles. Not surprisingly, health seekers soon took advantage of the purported therapeutic values of the many fine springs in the area.

In the vast reaches of the Ozarks, there were no good roads and precious few bad ones. The grading crew preparing the roadbed for the North Arkansas through this rugged country discovered in one of the high ridges a deep notch through which poured the waters of the Little Red River. On a narrow shelf just above lay a deep-rutted wagon trail, rough in good weather and utterly impassable in winter. The grading crew appropriated the shelf, widened it, and made it ready for the gandy dancers. As a compensating gesture, they ran the wagon road up the wooded ridge and brought it down the other side.

On the morning of April 20, 1908, the Burke Construction Company grading crew was working in one of the many cuts in the mountains. Powder monkeys had drilled deep holes in the walls of a narrow passage which had to be widened considerably. Black powder charges were set, fuses lighted. There was a heavy, rumbling roar as the earth bulged and exploded. A huge steam shovel crawled forward to begin gnawing its way through the loosened debris while Greeks with shovels attacked the lower slopes. With no warning whatever, the steam shovel sagged. Cables snapped, the boom crumbled, and the entire machine collapsed. The operator jumped and frantically made his way clear, but one of the unfortunate Greeks, shovel in hand, fell victim to the disintegrating mass of steel. His body was sent to Searcy and held pending funeral preparations, but no one could be found who knew anything about his family or where he came from. He was buried in an unmarked grave.

Still, the men tore their way through the mountains, and warm spring days buoyed their spirits until they reached Heber Springs from the south. At 3:30 P.M. on June 24, 1908, wild shouts from a welcoming crowd and shrill blasts from a locomotive whistle echoed through the surrounding hills. Old Sugar Loaf Mountain had never seen such carrying on.

The train had left Searcy at 11:15 that morning. Conductor Edgar Farrell and engineer Floons, in charge of the train, were to meet railroad officials Scullen and Sauls at Heber Springs for a celebration, but the latter were detained at Eureka Springs and unable to be on hand. This delayed the merrymaking temporarily.

G. W. Musick, the railroad's agent at Searcy, had notified all prospective shippers that he was ready to send freight over the new line as far north as Heber Springs, thirty-six miles away. Other stations along the way to which freight could be consigned were Kensett, four miles; King, six miles; Letona, fourteen miles; and Pangburn, eighteen miles.

A unique development in Arkansas came into being along the M & NA. On July 15, 1908, the Elk Breeders Association of Arkansas was incorporated at Eureka Springs with capital stock of $50,000, fully paid. The association took possession of one thousand acres of land five miles north of town on the White River. The area was enclosed by a strong fence and fifty elk were turned loose. It was a noble effort toward domestication and breeding of these animals.

The U.S. Department of Agriculture sent a representative to Elk Ranch and even issued a special bulletin calling the experiment to the attention of stockmen. General George W. Russ was president of the association; vice president was Colonel G. J. Crump, general attorney for the M & NA; secretary-treasurer was Mrs. Bertie Russ of Elk Ranch. Since the North Arkansas track crossed the ranch, a mail crane was erected and Elk Ranch soon became listed as a flag-stop station on the time card.

Russ believed the elk would improve the forest lands by feeding on the underbrush leaves and buds up to a height of eight feet. The herd increase under domestication was equal to that of cattle, since 90 per cent of the females produced healthy offspring. The adult male weighed from seven hundred to one thousand pounds, while females averaged between six hundred and eight hundred pounds. The meat would bring 40 cents a pound, dressed, on the market at St. Louis. The commercial aspect never did develop because there was a law which forbade sale or shipment of game animals. In New York, prime dressed elk had sold for as much as $1.50 a pound. It was considered as a delicacy in the finer hotels and restaurants.

Russ thought elk could be raised much more easily than beef, pork, or mutton because the elk were natural enemies of wolves and wild dogs, both of which were plentiful in the mountains at that time. His herd of sheep and goats had suffered heavy losses from these predators until he put the elk in with them. There was no further loss and even Russ's own dogs refused to enter the elk park.

Meanwhile, railroad construction trains were operating south from Leslie to Settlement, about thirty-five miles, in Van Buren County and from Kensett to Heber Springs. On these two sections, which were still under the jurisdiction of the Allegheny Improvement Company, the passenger fare was three cents a mile and the freight rate was much higher than on the portions of the road upon which the corporate Missouri & North Arkansas was operating scheduled trains.

This caused much protest from companies shipping to points on these divisions. Their contention was that the Allegheny Improvement Company and the Missouri & North Arkansas Railroad, to all intents and purposes, were one and the same corporation. The improvement company was formed by stockholders of the railroad for the purpose of building the road, a customary procedure in the realm of railroad construction. The operation of trains by the improvement company was a violation of state laws which set the rates that could be charged by a railroad corporation. No formal complaint was filed, but the Arkansas Railroad Commission began looking into the situation, which seems to have been agreeably compromised.

The Doniphan Lumber Company had purchased 85,000 acres of timber land in Cleburne County and had established several mills in the area. Small amounts of lumber and logs were taken out by boats on the Little Red River, but the major portion was stacked at convenient points along the railroad to be loaded for shipment. And there were great quantities of mineral deposits in the mountains, lying undeveloped principally because of the lack of economical transportation. There seemed to be great potentialities for the M & NA if they could be developed.

One deterring factor in the growth of this road was the excessive cost of its construction. It was probably the most expensive railroad in Arkansas on a cost-per-mile basis. The mountains presented tremendous engineering difficulties. The type of soil, which was subject to frequent sliding when cuts were made with steep backslopes, and the presence of subsurface water were troublesome factors. Several of the subcontractors made no profit at all and a few even lost money.

A very heavy cut was encountered seventeen miles west of Heber Springs where the rails spanned the South Fork of the Little Red River. The opening of the road for anything but a minimum of through service was delayed for several weeks in the summer of 1908 because of heavy excavation. Opening this deep notch would require removing 125,000 cubic yards of earth and rock. To facilitate train operations, a 4 per-cent grade shoofly was built; it angled up one side of the ridge and dropped down the opposite slope. By the time heavy traffic could be generated, it was expected the cut would be completed. On the north side of the river, 900 feet of temporary and 148 feet of permanent trestle were constructed. Two 125-foot steel spans were thrown across the river. On the south side, 800 feet of temporary and 562 feet of permanent trestle were required. The temporary trestles were to be filled with earth from the deep cut. One bright aspect of the situation was the fact that in the capital city of Little Rock in 1908, only 44 automobile license plates were sold.

A trip from Little Rock to Neosho, Missouri, by way of the North Arkansas road was an adventure during the spring of 1908. The traveler boarded a varnish run on the Iron Mountain in Little Rock at 7:05 A.M. and changed to the M & NA at Kensett, departing there at 9:30 A.M., to reach Heber Springs at 12:05 P.M. From Heber to Settlement, he rode twenty-five miles over a rough, crooked, seemingly endless road aboard a cumbersome wagon, taking one long day for the trip. At Settlement, he rode the rails to Neosho, arriving on the fifth day after leaving Little Rock.

The folks of Cleburne County had for years refused to vote a tax upon themselves for the purpose of building roads through the mountains. The road from Heber Springs to Settlement was the roughest in the region. It had countless mudholes, which at times seemed almost bottomless, and it was absolutely impassable during the winter months.

Now that the shining rails were conquering the mountains, a new town was being born about halfway between Settlement and Heber Springs: Edgemont. E. W. Stanfield, who had come from Indiana, had formed the Edgemont Improvement Company, had bought twelve hundred acres of land, and was busy laying out two hundred acres in a townsite. Streets had been cleared from the forest, a half-dozen homes built, and they were now waiting for the railroad. To perpetuate the town, the Globe Cooperage & Lumber Company was moving four large mills from Indiana to Edgemont. They would employ about 150 men, and businessmen in Indiana had agreed to come to the little mountain village on the M & NA to establish a bank and other commercial ventures.

On September 5, 1908, the first passenger coach made the trip from Leslie to Heber Springs. Celebrating the occasion were passengers from Leslie, Marshall, and Harrison.

On the southern end of the road, a few days before the rails reached Helena, businessmen of the area and officials of the railroad had agreed to issue free passenger tickets to farmers living along the line. The tickets would ensure rides to Helena for about a week following the opening of the road for service. These folks were future customers of the railroad and their good will was needed. They were holding hundreds of bales of cotton in storage, waiting for a train.

Just when this extra business was needed most, misfortune struck a sneak punch: no cotton shipments to Helena could be accepted after October 14. The Helena compress broke down (it was disabled nearly three weeks) with 23,000 bales of bulk cotton on hand, and another 10,000 bales were already in transit, bound for the port city. Up to that date, the compress had an output of 47,000 bales, compared to only 16,000 bales the year before.

On January 24, 1909, the M & NA completed installing switches to connect its rails to the St. Louis, Iron Mountain & Southern and the Yazoo & Mississippi Valley at Helena. The Y & MV transferred the first foreign car to the North Arkansas, a flatcar of machinery billed for Little Prairie, Arkansas. The M & NA had also completed a telegraph line from Cotton Plant to Helena.

The townspeople of Helena had hopes of persuading the various railroads operating in their town to combine efforts and resources to construct a central depot. Until the M & NA could arrange for its own station, it would use the Y & MV depot.

On January 30, 1909, the rails were made continuous between Helena and Cotton Plant, a distance of fifty-four miles, and the North Arkansas made its first transfer, a freight car, to the Y & MV. Regular train service between Helena and Searcy began March 1, 1909.

The Missouri & North Arkansas was officially complete for 368 miles between Helena, Arkansas, and Joplin, Missouri, when on March 27, 1909, a meeting was held at Little Rock in the offices of attorneys Moore, Smith & Moore to arrange for issuing $4,500,-

000 in bonds to pay the Allegheny Improvement Company for building 178 miles of road between Leslie and Helena. Vice President George P. Sands from St. Louis, W. S. Roberts of Eureka Springs, Powell Clayton, and Judge W. E. Hemingway were at the meeting. They said work was progressing on the union depot at Joplin and that no extensions of the road were contemplated.

The first regular mail schedule went into effect on the completed road April 2, 1909, between Helena and Neosho. The road was divided into the Northern and Southern divisions. The Northern Division extended from Neosho to Kensett, a distance of 266 miles, and the Southern Division lay between Searcy and Helena, just 80 miles. The Northern Division made connection with Little Rock from Kensett over the Iron Mountain. This service handled mail for points west of Springfield, Missouri, and south of Kansas City.

Mail Schedule—Northern Division

Northbound		*Southbound*
7:00 A	Lv. Little Rock (St.LIM & S)	Ar. 11:00 P
9:05 A	Ar. Kensett (St.LIM & S)	Lv. 9:05 P
9:25 A	Lv. Kensett (M & NA)	Ar. 8:15 P
9:45 A	Lv. Searcy	Ar. 8:05 P
2:35 P	Ar. Leslie	————
3:35 P	Lv. Leslie	Ar. 2:45 P
6:15 P	Ar. Harrison	Ar. 12:28 P
9:00 P	Ar. Eureka Springs	Ar. 9:40 A
8:45 A	Ar. Seligman	Ar. 8:45 A
11:40 P	Ar. Neosho	Lv. 7:05 A

Mail Schedule—Southern Division

Southbound		*Northbound*
7:00 A	Lv. Searcy	Ar. 7:53 P
7:12 A	Ar. Kensett	Ar. 7:41 P
9:08 A	Ar. Cotton Plant	Ar. 5:43 P
9:40 A	Ar. Wheatley	Lv. 5:12 P
10:14 A	Lv. Wheatley	Ar. 5:00 P
12:30 P	Ar. Helena	Lv. 2:45 P

To facilitate the handling of passenger and freight traffic at their southern terminal, officials of the M & NA met with those of the other roads involved and on May 5, 1909, formed the Helena Terminal Railway to build a loop road, about four and one-half miles long, around the town. They also agreed to construct a union depot for use by all of the railroads.

In the summer of 1909, a shuffling of office and terminal facilities began. Effective June 1, the division office at Searcy was abolished. Similar offices at Eureka Springs were consolidated and moved to Leslie, and W. H. Dewitt was made general superintendent. DeWitt, chief clerk L. R. Buckley, and dispatchers L. O. Dekovan, R. A. Pigeon, C. T. Eubanks, and J. E. Carr came to Leslie and established their headquarters in a remodeled passenger coach. H. R. Irvine, former division superintendent at Searcy, was made roadmaster of the Southern Division.

The new time card of August 1 showed the first daily through trains each day between Joplin and Helena. The southbound train left Joplin at 6:10 A.M. and arrived in Helena at 11:30 P.M., averaging slightly more than twenty-one miles per hour. In the opposite direction, the Limited left Helena at 6:00 A.M. and arrived in Joplin at 11:20 P.M., averaging the same speed, making the 368-mile journey in seventeen hours and twenty minutes. A thorn in the side for the traveling public was a five-hour layover at Joplin for passengers southbound from Kansas City to points in Arkansas on the M & NA. The Kansas City Southern and the North Arkansas promised to overhaul their schedules to eliminate this inconvenience.

About the time the M & NA had its organization in somewhat of an operating condition, its "friendly" neighbor roads on the north end informed the North Arkansas that other arrangements had been made for an outlet to the Gulf and its service as a bridge road would not be required. A paralyzing blow, this left the North Arkansas in about the same condition as when its rails ended at Harrison: a railroad which began nowhere and went nowhere. The only difference was that it was 230 miles longer.

There wasn't enough on-line business to support a railroad of such proportions, and there was no money in the till, even to pay the interest on the bonds that had been sold. The M & NA (May Never Arrive) was a maverick surrounded by comparative giants in the world of railroading. On the northeast, the St. Louis, Iron Mountain & Southern (St.LIM & S) had a nearly parallel line from Carthage, Missouri, to Newport, Arkansas. The Little Rock & Ft. Smith (later the St. LIM & S) hemmed the North Arkansas in from the southwest. On the west were the Frisco and the Kansas City Southern. The remaining territory of the M & NA's domain was extremely mountainous and void of all except rather minor freight-generating business.

The financial malady grew worse. Receivership claimed the road in 1912, with Jesse McDonald, W. S. Holt, and George Sands appointed as receivers by Judge Jacob Trieber of the U.S. District Court for the Eastern Arkansas Division.

E. M. Wise had been selected to serve as general manager, and he almost made the line self-sufficient. Receiver's certificates for three million dollars were granted, the maintenance department was pruned and reorganized, and the inefficient shops at Leslie and Eureka Springs were combined and moved to Harrison. The holdings were developed into a million-dollar asset, including the general office force. Wise instituted freight runs through the mountains on schedules never even dreamed of before. He said the patronage of customers could be attracted by a time-saving schedule. It was the only method by which the road could compete with other lines for through freight from shippers beyond Kansas City and Memphis. Pullman sleeping-car service was made available on convenient schedules between Helena and Joplin in conjunction with the KCS. Passengers were given the opportunity to see, close up, the extensive beauty of the Ozark Mountain country of northwest Arkansas.

Wise's crash program was beginning to show promise by 1914. The M & NA had instituted passenger service aboard gasoline-powered "doodlebug" rail cars. The doodlebugs gave some relief in the realm of expensive passenger service.

Misfortune visited the North Arkansas to dispel any hopes or dreams of a prosperous future. This fact was most effectively demonstrated on the evening of August 5, 1914. Missouri & North Arkansas motorcar No. 103 was a General Electric rail car. A gasoline engine was used to turn an electric generator, which, in turn, powered electric motors to operate the car. She was seventy feet long and seated seventy passengers; a large horizontal gasoline storage tank was mounted under her floor. The car afforded very comfortable accommodations and could be operated at only a fraction of the cost of a regular steam-powered varnish run.

Car No. 103 left Joplin, Missouri, at 5:30 P.M. as train No. 209, running on the rails of the Kansas City Southern, and was due in Harrison at 11:59 P.M. When she rolled out of Joplin, all seats were filled and a few passengers were standing. Including a three-man crew, there were about 80 persons aboard.

No. 103 rolled through Tipton Ford, about ten miles south of Joplin, right on the advertised. The doodlebug canted to the right as she entered a long, sweeping curve around the foot of a hill. The motorman at the controls had the car traveling about thirty-five miles per hour and she was riding well. Suddenly, his body stiffened and the freezing chill of fear laid hold of his heart. He was staring at the lurching pilot of a steam locomotive swiftly rolling around the curve from behind the shoulder of the hill!

It was impossible for the hogger to see the doodlebug because of the curving track. He saw nothing beyond the swaying, pitching boiler of the KCS 4–6–2 No. 805. He was running with a string of seven or eight deadhead passenger cars and was carrying the green as First No. 56.

"Big-hole 'er!" yelled his fireman as he joined the birds.

The hogger made a frantic, futile swipe at the brass handle of the brake valve, and the motorman on car No. 103 did the same. They were too late.

The high-drivered Pacific and the heavily loaded doodlebug met with a clap of manmade thunder. The forward end of the doodlebug was a shapeless mass of twisted metal fused to the smokebox of No. 805. It contained the crushed body of motorman Herbert Ratliff of Eureka Springs. The engine crew of No. 805 were unhurt, and miraculously, the big Pacific stayed on the rails.

The sound of the collision was still rumbling across the hillside when the gasoline storage tank of the doodlebug exploded with an echoing roar. The forward motion of the KCS train carried the flaming mass more than six hundred feet down the track.

Thirty-eight people met death that August evening, most of them from the crumbling impact. They were the lucky ones. The others were pinned in the wreckage and burned to death. Several were hurled free when the trains met, and others managed to crawl from shattered windows.

William Drury of Webb City, Missouri, was one of the fortunate few who escaped death that day and was able to describe the incident:

> We were running about 35 miles an hour, when suddenly there was a terrific impact which was followed almost immediately by the explosion of the gasoline reservoir. By the time I crawled from the wreck, both the motor car and the train, fed by the burning gasoline, seemed a sheet of flame. Added to this there were the shrieks of the injured and dying. Many persons pinned beneath the wreckage cried to be released or killed rather than face death by fire. Fourteen men were riding in the smoker section and I heard of only one who escaped.

An M & NA foreman of a line crew, J. J. Lauderback, was riding the rear platform of the doodlebug and was thrown clear. Uninjured, he helped free several passengers from the flaming car. Lova Ishelan, a twelve-year-old boy from Dewey, Oklahoma, screaming that his mother was caught inside, was prevented from running back to the car. He had been riding near the rear of the car and was flung through an open window.

Among the dead were Mrs. C. L. Ishelan of Dewey, Oklahoma; Bert Johnson of Oklahoma City; Edward Bradley of Eureka Springs, an M & NA brakeman; and S. A. Nichols, conductor, of Harrison. Many bodies were burned beyond recognition.

The Kansas City Southern sent a train from Joplin with as many nurses and doctors as could be located. It also dispatched a second train to bring the dead and injured to Joplin. Thirty-five bodies were brought to town aboard a flatcar. At 2 P.M. on August 7, a single funeral service was held at Neosho on the courthouse lawn for the unidentified victims. They were buried in a common grave at Odd Fellows Cemetery.

The cause of the accident has never been determined. Several different accounts have been given. It was reported by Donald G. Campbell, of Kansas City, that an order from the KCS dispatcher was addressed to Train No. 209 at Joplin as follows: "First No. 56 meet No. 209 at Tipton Ford and wait at Tipton Ford until 5:50 P.M. and at Saginaw until 6:00 P.M. for extra No. 563 south." This order was supposedly signed by doodlebug conductor Nichols and made complete at 5:08 P.M. Why the entire crew of the doodlebug would overlook a positive meet order is unknown.

When the legal responsibility was fixed, it was shared by both roads. This was a terrible blow from which the M & NA never recovered. Its treasury was completely gutted by payments to families of the victims.

A policy of strict economy was established in 1916 when C. A. Phelan took over the M & NA as general manager. Not a dollar was spent which wasn't absolutely necessary. If trains could be run over the road, there was no sense in spending money for new ties or even second-hand ones. If a locomotive could move a string of cars when the hogger widened the throttle, why should the hog be sent to the shops? What effect this would have had on the economic status of the road was never known—America had to make the world safe for democracy. World War I was going in full swing and on January 1, 1918, Uncle Sam assumed control of all railroads. Standard operating procedures were established, and in

A Time Table in Rhyme
July, 1918

Missouri and North Arkansas is the name of the road
  Always on time and our connections are good,
First train in the morning leaves at eight forty-five,
  With fifteen minutes at Seligman after you arrive
To get a train to St. Louis unless they are late
  But for Ft. Smith and Paris you have a two hours' wait.

The next train arrives at ten fifty-three
  Brings visitors from St. Louis, Dallas and K.C.
Leaves Eureka Springs promptly at eleven o'clock
  Makes connection at Kensett for Memphis and Little Rock
The Iron Mountain South leaves Kensett nine five
  And at eleven o'clock in Little Rock you arrive
Then at one-ten A.M. the Memphis train will be due
  And get you to Memphis about five fifty-two.

Twelve fifty-five is the motor-car time
  Brings visitors from Lebanon and south on that line
Then leaves Eureka Springs promptly at two P.M.
  Takes you to Elk Ranch and Beaver and right back again,
Arrives at Eureka at fifteen past four,
  And leaves at five o'clock for Seligman once more.
The minutes' wait at Seligman for the local train north
  One hour for the train for Dallas and Ft. Worth.
Then the train from St. Louis is just pulling in,
  We get all their passengers and hike out again.
Arrive at Eureka about seven forty-five
  Just before the passengers from the south will arrive.

No. 2 is the last and will leave eight o'clock
  Brought our passengers from Kensett, Memphis and Little Rock
It takes you to Seligman where you make connection north
  But you stay there all night if for Dallas or Ft. Worth.
But passengers for Joplin go right through, you see
  And make good connection for Wichita and K.C.
And various points too numerous to mention,
  But for all these places we make good connection.
If there's any other information, rates, e-t-c.
  Just write, phone or ask the Agent E.R.B.

E. R. ("Ever Ready") Braswell

the process, the men on the M & NA found their paychecks to be about twice what they had been; they were receiving the same standard wages as men on the Iron Mountain or the Kansas City Southern. This aspect of the situation they heartily approved.

Six months after the government took control, the M & NA was returned to a disorganized management on June 28, 1918. The manager said the road was not financially able to continue the standard wage scale set up by Uncle Sam. On July 1, 1918, the government awarded a wage increase for railroad men, making it retroactive to January 1. This was compounding the problem for the M & NA. There was a strike by the men in the shops, and operations were halted for a time. The government stepped in again and leased the road from the management for $175,000 a year, just enough to pay the interest on the receiver's certificates as it came due. This cost $275,000 during the next eighteen months. On March 1, 1920, the road was returned to the owners again.

Except for the time when the road was under government management, it had, since 1908, been running up a deficit which had increased from $7,800 to $683,000 in just twelve years. How the North Arkansas expected to continue operations is a mystery.

In an effort to keep trains running through the mountains, manager Phelan asked for, and received, permission from the Arkansas Railroad Commission and the Interstate Commerce Commission to increase freight and passenger rates. There was an almost immediate decrease in traffic, and revenues were just where they had been.

Phelan notified all employees on February 1, 1921, that wages would be cut back to the level at which they stood before the standard wage was established by the dissension-provoking Decision No. 2 made by the U.S. Railroad Labor Board. Through their representatives, the men suggested that the company retain the wage scale and reduce the number of employees to make up the difference. Phelan refused to consider the proposition and stated that wages were being reduced by $25,000 a month. This brought an angry response from the men, and theretofore unmentioned subjects were brought up. They questioned the propriety of Phelan's cutting wages when his own salary was $1,000 a month.

Why did the employees never receive a portion of the money due them for the time the road was under government control? Where did it go? Why did Phelan sell the company's private official car and credit the proceeds to his personal account? One of the employees was fired for bringing up these questions, to which no answers were ever received. (These incidents were reported in a history of the strike written by O. T. Gooden and published by Columbia University Press in 1926 under the title *The Missouri & North Arkansas Railroad Strike.*)

The employees contended that the manager had violated Decision No. 2 by the Railroad Labor Board, which had set what was considered to be a just and reasonable wage scale. They asked for a new hearing before the board, which was granted. Phelan claimed the board had no jurisdiction over the M & NA because it was in a receivership authorized by a federal court. Moreover, he said, the cost of living was much lower in the area served by the M & NA than in other sections of the country and the men did not need the amount set as the standard wage. To state the case conservatively, Phelan lacked a great deal in the matter of public relations.

The Railroad Labor Board advised the men to accept the lower wage scale under protest and ask the management to request further conferences to resolve the company's ability to pay the higher rate. Meanwhile, representatives of the Federated Shop Crafts were in Chicago for a meeting with Grand Lodge officials, and a telegram was sent to an officer of the local brotherhood at Harrison advising the shopmen to call a strike. This they did, failing to report for work on February 1, 1921.

On February 24, Phelan notified the Railroad Labor Board he was ready to meet with the employees as the board had directed.

The shopmen said they were willing to hold a conference and accept, under protest, the reduced wage scale. Phelan stated that the shopmen had left the service of the road and were no longer considered employees, so he declined to grant a conference.

The other employees were not disposed to holding any conference until the standard wage scale was re-established. On February 25, 1921, they notified the management they would call a strike at three o'clock the following morning. Very quickly the manager notified the Railroad Labor Board that he had recruited a working force willing to accept the lower wage scale. The board apparently made no further effort toward encouraging any additional conferences. A judicious compromise on the part of manager and employees might have resolved the difficulties.

The strike was called, and at 3:00 A.M. on February 26, 1921, there began a conflict destined to attract the attention of the entire United States. It was to be one of the longest railroad strikes in the nation's history.

The people of the rugged mountain country in northern Arkansas were not familiar with the strife and turmoil usually associated with a full-scale strike. Actions were being dictated from remote headquarters by people locally unknown.

When the strike began, the movement of all trains ceased. Within a matter of hours, there appeared in the newspapers of the Harrison area advertisements saying jobs were available to men who wanted to take the place of the strikers on the "open shop" plan. Manager Phelan said he was completely surprised at the action of the men in "leaving the service." He claimed the strikers were violating the order of the Railroad Labor Board recommending further conferences, even though he had refused to meet with the shopmen.

National representatives of unions of conductors, engineers, firemen, trainmen, yardmen, agents, telegraphers, dispatchers, and maintenance-of-way men came to Harrison. They considered the strike a test case which could have a very definite bearing on future wage reductions on other railroads across the country.

Phelan proposed that the strikers accept a 35 per cent reduction in wages and go back to work. A counter offer was made by the men: they would agree if the road would reduce passenger and freight rates by 35 per cent. This was immediately rejected.

At Harrison, a Mrs. Harter, supposedly speaking for Phelan, made a statement that in the future the railroad would operate on the open-shop plan. Phelan declared no such person was in the employ of the company. Said he: "We had to have labor and we hired it where it could be found, regardless of its organization, but the company has not adopted the open shop plan." Phelan said the company had hired 250 men and expected to go into full operation with them, even though this meant 150 fewer workers than the 400 who went out on strike. By March 3, service was about 50 per cent of normal and the freight embargo was to be lifted in about a week. Passenger service would begin at the same time.

On March 2, a locomotive, baggage-express car, passenger car, and four freight cars rolled into Helena late in the afternoon. On board were thirty passengers who milled around the station while one car of the consist, consigned to Armour & Company, was switched to the Yazoo & Mississippi Valley interchange track. Putting the train away for the night, the crew and passengers retired. The next morning at 8 o'clock, the train departed for Harrison. The same thirty passengers were aboard. This substantiated the rumor that they were actually strikebreakers brought in by the company from Kansas City.

So far, the people in the mountain area along the M & NA were in sympathy with the strikers; they were local men known by most as "home folks." Many of the new employees were strangers. The only strike with which the Arkansans were familiar was the short-lived one of 1918, and they had no inkling of what was to come.

A young machinist came from Tennessee in response to an advertisement for new employees, bringing his pregnant wife and three-year-old daughter. The pickets tried to persuade him to go back to Tennessee, but to no avail. He needed the job.

One night he was on duty at the shops when a group of men came to his home. Finding a load of stove wood in the yard, they threw most of it through a window into the house. The man's wife was almost frightened to death, and so was the little girl, but the incident produced the desired result: the machinist returned to Tennessee.

This kind of action was completely alien to both local residents and the workers. Confused and disturbed, they were undecided what to do about it. In such a perplexed frame of mind, they fell easy prey to the persuasive exhortations by the strangers who were directing the strike.

Many of the new employees were now carrying weapons, saying they meant to protect themselves and their families. This served to further strain the relationship between them and the strikers. There was the opinion that the police officers at Harrison were sympathetic toward the cause of the strikers and that they were ineffective in halting the intimidations.

Antagonism between the strikers and the citizens grew almost daily, and a third faction was rapidly developing. On one corner of the triangle were the undiplomatic management of the railroad and the "scabs," who were trying to operate trains in a feeble gesture of defiance. At another point were the strikers, who were known to most of the local people and who gained favor for their cause, at least for a while. Making up the third point were the many hundreds of local citizens, who began to feel they were caught in the middle of an intolerable situation. As tension mounted, those in the latter group became more and more determined to protect their interests, which would be best served by trains operated over the North Arkansas—and they were not primarily concerned about who was operating them. Therefore, they began to hold meetings at various places. It soon developed that their sympathy lay with neither the railroad management nor the strikers, but with the people of the area, who were being deprived of train service which they desperately needed.

Supplies of staple goods were either exhausted or dwindling, and prices were soaring.

On the night of March 16, the darkness which shrouded the steep-sided hills and winding valleys gave way to a faint glow near the little town of Alpena, just fifteen miles west of Harrison. The false dawn slowly brightened as hungry flames licked their way over the creosoted framework of a long railroad trestle. Soon the structure was a solid mass of fire, and its heavy timbers began to sag. The rails buckled and kinked from the intense heat, and the flaming trestle collapsed with a roar, sending sparks and hot brands flying. Only the fact that foliage was in the early budding stage prevented the fire from spreading.

The following morning, it was learned that twenty-two miles south of Harrison, near Pindall, a smaller trestle had also been burned. Harrison was now effectively cut off from rail communication to the north and south.

Manager Phelan charged that the fires were deliberately set by arsonists, while the strike leaders contended they were caused by fire dropping from defective ash pans on locomotives. In any case, all traffic was halted completely. Phelan declared the road could not continue operations in the face of such lawlessness and that no regular trains would be run until protection was offered from some source to guarantee the safety of life and property in the operation of trains.

At Harrison, the sheriff of Boone County sent a telegram to Governor Thomas C. McRae asking that the state contingent of the National Guard be sent to restore order. The Governor said he could not send troops because the M & NA was under the control of a federal court. He also told the sheriff: "It is expected that you will exert all authority to repress lawlessness and protect the property of the company."

Meanwhile, the strikers had been visiting all of the merchants in Harrison and, by threatening a boycott, had endeavored to persuade them not to sell goods to the scabs.

The continued agitation and depredations further alienated local citizens and finally spurred them into an action they felt was necessary to protect their own interests, which meant they wanted the strike ended forthwith and they didn't give a damn who ran the trains, just so they ran.

On the night of March 7, 1921, the Harrison Protective League was formed. The *Harrison Daily Times* of March 8 reported the event as follows:

> "For the purpose of maintaining law and order in Harrison, Arkansas, and for the purpose of safeguarding her business and property interests, we, the undersigned citizens of Harrison and vicinity, fully realizing the gravity of the situation confronting us, hereby organize ourselves into an association to be known as the Harrison Protective League."
>
> The following officers were elected: W. J. Meyers, president; J. W. Wallace, vice president; F. M. Garvin, secretary; R. A. Wilson, treasurer. The Executive Committee was composed of W. L. Snapp, Louis Keck, J. M. Wagley, W. S. Pettit and R. A. Wilson. The sum of $500 was raised at the meeting for the purpose of providing adequate police protection. The qualifications for membership in the League were defined as follows: Every person applying for membership in the league shall not be interested either directly or indirectly in any controversy affecting in any way the property or business interests of Harrison; and any member who so becomes interested in any such controversy at any time shall lose his membership in the organization at once. All representatives of either side were requested to retire from the meeting.

The League's goal was to aid civil authorities in dealing with depredations against the railroad and to preserve order in Harrison. An invitation was sent to citizens at various points along the M & NA to attend a meeting at Harrison on March 22. Special trains were run in both directions to bring people in. The burned trestles had been replaced, but train service had not been resumed.

W. J. Meyers was the logical man to head the organization and face up to those responsible for the acts of sabotage against the railroad, whoever they happened to be. About two weeks after the strike began, Henry Starr, the notorious Oklahoma outlaw, and three confederates attempted to hold up the Peoples National Bank at Harrison. Meyers happened to walk by while the holdup was in progress. Lifting a gun from his pocket as the desperadoes attempted to flee, Meyers coolly and methodically shot Starr. During the confusion, the loot was dropped and Starr's companions fled.

The meeting of March 22 was called to formulate a plan of action. The sentiment of those who attended it left no doubt about their determination to put an end to the unaccustomed acts of violence and intimidation. The many people who had contributed the first $11,000,000 in the North Arkansas had seen their investment completely wiped out. The second bond issue was a financial flop, too. Following the period of government control during World War I, a $3,500,000 issue of receiver's certificates had gone begging. This meant the road was valuable to no one except the 100,000 citizens is served. It belonged to no one else. Those who were feeling the effects of the strike said they wanted the railroad —high wages or low wages, high rates or low rates.

A man from Leslie opined: "Do you know what the people of Leslie would do with that bunch of agitators you have permitted to establish headquarters here in Harrison? They'd be out of town before sunset and they'd stay out." He was referring to the national union representatives: H. S. O'Neil, representing the electricians; W. E. Horn, shopcrafts; W. C. Jenkins, serving for B. B. Jewell, president of Federated Shop Crafts at Moline, Illinois; W. J. Potts, vice president of train dispatchers at Little Rock; L. B. Eddy, telegraphers, San Francisco; George W. Anderson, trainmen, from Sedalia, Missouri; and Martin C. Carey, conductors, Port Huron, Michigan.

Men from points along the line came to the meeting at Harrison's Lyric Theater with blood in their eyes. They felt the season for outlawry should end immediately. The sooner the strikers went about their business, the better it would be for all concerned.

A committee of three citizens went to the Midway Hotel, where the union chiefs were staying, and advised them of the extreme restlessness which prevailed, suggesting that they move their headquarters to another town. The labor leaders refused, saying Harrison was headquarters for the railroad and the unions.

With no advance notice, a special train was run in either direction on April 6 and several hundred people came to Harrison about 1:00 P.M. They proceeded to the Midway Hotel, where the manager, George W. O'Neil, allowed an appointed committee to talk with the union officials. The latter were told that the people believed they were responsible for the various acts of sabotage against the railroad. The committee advised them to leave town immediately and gave them five minutes to hold a conference and make up their minds. The union men left forthwith by automobile for Branson, Missouri, and never returned.

Manager Phelan told a reporter from the *St. Louis Post Dispatch* that when the people did not seem sufficiently sympathetic to the railroad's dilemma, he stopped the trains and announced that none would run until all picketing ceased. He also stated that the M & NA was an open-shop road and would remain so. It would never return to the principle of collective bargaining, he declared, and there would be no contract of any kind with the employees. Wages had been reduced by 22 per cent, and when service was resumed, there would be another reduction. Phelan said he would cease to operate the road rather than accept union workers.

The Harrison Protective League made another determined move on April 12. A statement was prepared, and J. E. Queen, chairman of the local strikers' cooperative committee, Tillman Jines, local representative of the Federated Shop Crafts, and J. T. Venable, secretary of the conductors' local and active as an unofficial strike leader, were called before the League. Former Circuit Judge John T. Worthington, then mayor of Harrison, read the prepared statement and gave a copy to each of the union officials:

Gentlemen:

We have asked you as representatives of the local unions to come before this League for the purpose of stating to you our position. I am speaking directly for and in behalf of the Harrison Protective League and the Leagues of Carroll, Boone, Newton, Searcy, Van Buren, and Cleburne Counties, and I am speaking in behalf of the one hundred thousand people who are served by the Missouri & North Arkansas Railroad.

Every word spoken here has been carefully weighed. There will be no discussion of any description, nor will there be any remarks by any other members of the League, nor will any reply be expected or desired.

We understand from the *Harrison Daily Times* of April 8, that the unions met on that date and decided to continue the so-called strike, and it is for this reason that we have invited you before us.

Now, the United States Railroad Labor Board has dismissed the proceedings which were instituted before it in regard to the strike on the Missouri & North Arkansas Railroad. There is nothing pending before the Federal Court or between the railroad management and its former employees looking for a settlement of the matter.

As there are no negotiations pending, as there are no conferences being conducted between the railroad management and your men, looking to a settlement of this matter, then why should you keep up this everlasting agitation? Why hold the people of the country up and strangle the life out of our industries when it does not benefit you except to get revenge on the railroad management and junk the road if possible?

We are determined that the Missouri & North Arkansas Railroad shall not be junked. That the operation of the railroad shall in no way be interfered with. That the present employees of the railroad shall in no way be interfered with or molested as they have been in the past; and we are determined that every form of intimidation of our citizens, as practiced in the past few weeks must, and shall, cease.

These are not threats, but I want to impress it upon you with all the force and fervor at my command that there is not one single useless or meaningless word in this message.

During the weeks that followed, citizens of the various counties along the road patrolled the right-of-way like a detachment of soldiers on guard duty. Day and night, through all kinds of weather, they guarded the roadbed and trestles. The men who had businesses or farms which required their attention had to abandon the guard camp, but others were hired to take their place. Private citizens of Boone County were paying $500 a week and the Boone County Court allowed $2,000 in public funds to help pay the cost. This sort of action was typical all along the road, except in Missouri and from Searcy to Helena, where no trouble occurred.

In spite of the surveillance, acts of vandalism continued. Blue vitriol (copper sulfate) was poured into water tanks, and the resulting acid attacked locomotive boilers and cylinders, damaging them severely. Machine bearings were given applications of emery dust to render them useless; track switches were tampered with; air-brake hoses were cut and trestles burned.

One day an M & NA train rammed a Rock Island freight where the two roads crossed at Wheatley. The Rock Island wrecker crew was called out to clear the crossing, and in doing so, they turned the M & NA engine on her side and left her there. The M & NA recovered $1,600 in damages from the Rock Island.

All manner of subtle repercussions occurred. When passengers on other lines tried to purchase tickets by way of the North Arkansas, they were informed that it was very dangerous to travel this road and that its trains were running many hours late. In some instances, they were told that no trains were operating on the M & NA. A few passengers were routed over some other road to a point near their destination and had to go the rest of the way in a taxi.

Harassments continued to eat into the meager revenues of the M & NA: bridges mysteriously caught fire; locomotives were crippled or completely disabled by acid in the boilers; spikes were pulled, permitting rails to turn over when trains rolled across; employees were intimidated or beaten. This situation continued until manager Phelan submitted his resignation in June, 1921, and U. S. District Court Judge Jacob Trieber appointed traffic manager J. C. Murray in his place on June 14.

With revenues insufficient to meet expenses, Murray asked the federal court for permission to suspend operations. The request was granted, effective July 31, 1921. Without rail service, the remote mountain communities began to experience real hardships. The wagon roads through the mountains were pitiful excuses for transportation routes, but they were the only means of bringing in necessities. Many businesses went bankrupt, and scores of people moved to towns where employment might be secured. It was impossible to borrow money from sources outside the mountain country; insurance policies were allowed to lapse for lack of money to pay premiums.

The H. D. Williams Cooperage Company at Leslie had an investment of more than one million dollars in plant and materials when North Arkansas trains stopped rolling. It had an eighteen-mile railroad of its own running through the mountains to bring logs to the mill at Leslie; 125 men were without work at its main plant, which was supplied by thirteen smaller mills out in the woods; its payroll was $7,000 a month. In the face of such adversity, this firm allowed its employees to continue living in company houses without paying rent from the latter part of June, 1921, until the trains began running in May, 1922.

Children of the mill employees were hungry victims of circumstance, and they were poorly clothed for the coming winter. The county superintendent said the children in his schools were pitifully undernourished. Entire families lived—rather, existed—on corn bread and molasses for weeks at a time. The Red Cross donated money to prepare two meals a day at school for the children. They feasted on fresh milk, meats, and vegetables.

Most of the strikers were receiving monthly benefits from the various labor unions, enabling them to purchase the necessities of life. It was the helpless and innocent who were the real victims of the controversy. The nationwide depression of 1920–21 was in full swing, and no work was to be had anywhere. Tragedy and suffering were abundant.

The next effort to get trains moving again was a request for representatives of the various unions to meet in St. Louis on October 10, 1921, with Festus J. Wade, a St. Louis businessman representing the owners of the railroad. A proposal was made to the strikers whereby trains could operate once more. Wade asked the men to accept the 25 per cent cut in wages, as approved by the Railroad Labor Board, for one year. At the end of that time, any money remaining from the earnings of the company would be divided on a percentage basis among all employees. This procedure would continue until the standard wage scale was reached, at which time any cash remaining in the treasury would be used to pay the debt owed the U.S. government for its loans. The owners of stocks and bonds would receive nothing until standard wages were achieved and the government debt was paid. The 25 per cent wage reduction would apply to every officer of the road from the receiver on down. If this condition were not met, Wade said, the only alternative would be to scrap the road.

The unions were to select an auditor from their ranks. He would be employed by the railroad and would have full charge of all accounts so the men would know the financial condition of the company at all times. The unions were asked either to accept the offer or to allow the road to operate on the open-shop plan. The entire idea was rejected.

On February 7, 1922, a new development was begun when Judge Trieber, who had jurisdiction over receivership of the M & NA, ordered manager Murray to sell the trouble-bedeviled line within sixty days for not less than three million dollars. At the same time came the announcement that a new company had been formed to take over the road. The new organization substituted "Railway" for "Railroad" in the name, and most of the new owners would be the same men who had directed the former fiasco.

The Interstate Commerce Commission granted the new company a loan of $3,500,000 to pay off the receiver's certificates which had been issued. The additional $500,000 was for improvements to the physical properties. Everybody concerned seemed happy about the reorganization, except the labor unions.

On April 10, 1922, the North Arkansas was sold to Charles M. Gilbert of St. Louis for $3,000,000. To give the new company a boost, an increase was arranged in the division of freight rates from connecting lines. Along with the reduced wage scale, it was estimated that the company would realize a saving of $635,000 a year. With this, it could pay off all debts and maintain operations.

Gilbert was to be president of the new organization, and former receiver Murray was made vice president and general manager. On the staff were H. J. Armstrong, superintendent of transportation, maintenance of way, and structures; C. W. Bugbee, master mechanic; L. A. Watkins, auditor; H. P. Mitchell, assistant general freight and passenger agent; J. R. Tucker, purchasing agent and storekeeper; R. S. Staten, claim agent; Shouse & Rowland, general attorneys.

The first thing Murray did was to call a conference with the union chiefs to determine whether the strikers wished to go back to work at the reduced wages set by the Railroad Labor Board. They refused, so Murray began hiring new men, local and imported.

In addition to the $3,500,000 loan from the government, the new owners invested $560,000 from their own pockets. After paying $3,000,000 for the railroad, they set aside $750,000 for improvements, $250,000 for working capital, and $60,000 for operations.

By this time, the shopmen had been on strike fifteen months and the road had been shut down nine months. The roadbed was in horrible condition, and the locomotives, left sitting with blue vitriol in their boilers and cylinders, were acid-corroded hulks. In sum, the Missouri & North Arkansas was in pitiful shape.

A gentleman from the McNally Machine and Boiler Repair Shops in Pittsburg, Kansas, came to the M & NA shops at Harrison in May. The company made arrangements for him to take four engines—Nos. 3, 5, 12, and 33—to Kansas for general overhaul. Tillman Jines, general chairman of the shopmen's union, wrote to the Arkansas commissioner of labor in an attempt to prevent the railroad from sending the decrepit old hogs out of the state for repairs. He called attention to Section 1, Act No. 220, Acts of the Legislature for 1915, which made it a violation of the law for any railroad company to send cars or engines out of the state to be repaired, PROVIDED that said railroad had proper facilities in the state to do the work.

The matter was referred to Karl Greenhaw, prosecuting attorney at Harrison, who informed Jines that the railroad had no facilities to perform the needed repairs. He also noted that two engines, Nos. 13 and 19, had been sent to Scullin Iron Works in St. Louis for repairs during October and November, 1920, before the strike began. Moreover, during 1919, engines had been sent to Wichita and Pittsburg, Kansas, for repairs. No objections were made at those times, Greenhaw said, and it seemed to him that Jines was more interested in preventing the railroad from serving the people of the area than in seeing the law enforced. It was the opinion of the prosecutor that the 1915 Arkansas statute was in conflict with federal laws governing interstate commerce and that if it were tested in a court case, it would be declared unconstitutional. Nothing more was heard about the matter.

Almost immediately, fresh acts of vandalism began with renewed vigor. Bridges were burned, acid poured into water tanks, switches tampered with. Both the strikers and the new employees were openly carrying guns, supposedly for self-protection. Three of the strikers drove to Springfield, Missouri, where they purchased a large order of cartridges in various sizes, plus 750 12-gauge shotgun shells with nitro powder and No. 2 chilled shot. A few days later, the sheriff at Harrison found in the garden of one of the men two boxes of dynamite caps, a large roll of dynamite fuse, and a quantity of emery dust.

Mounting tension and a sense of impending doom permeated the town of Harrison. It was impossible for citizens to remain neutral in the controversy. Not even their children were spared in the cauldron of ill feeling. The situation continued on this basis through the long winter of 1922–23.

January 15, 1923, fell on Monday. That morning, men began to arrive in Harrison, the number gradually increasing as others arrived. No one was leaving. Several were armed. About noon, a special passenger train rolled into the depot from the south; a group of citizens at Leslie had chartered it for five hundred dollars. Telephones had been busy all day Saturday and Sunday. No one knew just where the rallying call originated, but the people of the hill country had apparently decided to do something about the eternal turmoil that was destroying their homes and businesses.

More than one thousand men responded to the call. They came by train, automobile, wagon, horseback, and on foot, gravitating to the courthouse square in the middle of town. From the vantage point of a pedestal, someone began calling names. Most of these men had known each other for years, and as their names were called, they went directly to the meeting room of the Rotary Club across the street. There was organized what was known as the Committee of Twelve—twelve responsible and respected men. It was their purpose to investigate the strike and the vicious reign of vandalism that had plagued their lives for a year and a half.

The meeting, the committee, and the investigation may not have been legal, but these people had waited many long and anxious months for action and none had come. Now they were through waiting and were determined to get results. An electrifying atmosphere of finality was plainly evident. The situation was tense, and there existed the dangerous possibility that it might get out of hand.

The Committee of Twelve included banker Wilburn Moore, timberman L. M. Clark, and attorney A. B. Arbaugh, all from Jasper; W. T. Mills, S. W. Woods, and J. F. Henley, lawyers from Marshall; W. J. Douglass, editor of the *Berryville North Arkansas*

Star; George Bazore, flour miller, and Tom Morris, grocer and canner, both of Berryville; Dr. Troy Coffman, a Harrison dentist; grocer L. C. Holt, also from Harrison; and Sam Dennis, Valley Springs traveling salesman. Other groups of citizens were appointed to visit the homes of strikers, search for incriminating evidence, and bring the strikers bodily before the committee for questioning.

The circuit court and grand jury were in session at the time, and a message was dispatched to Judge Shinn informing him that the committee was meeting for the purpose of gathering information and evidence concerning the reign of terror against the railroad. The court was in no way connected with the committee, nor did it sanction the actions of the committee.

When such a group goes into action, no matter how moral or well meaning its motives, there is much danger involved. The Committee of Twelve was no exception. It had no legal standing, no right to enter anyone's home. No search warrants were issued, and the committee was given no authority to apprehend or interrogate any citizen. Its members were taking police powers unto themselves.

First on the docket was a raid on the union hall. Records were confiscated, furniture was piled in the street, and everything was destroyed by fire. When some timid soul protested this action, he was told: "They won't have any more use for it."

Homes were searched, and it availed the owners nothing to offer a protest. The number of strikers who were actually guilty of the months of violence and vandalism were very few. They had been trained for this purpose and were most adept at keeping the majority of the strikers in an emotional turmoil.

Soon the roving squads of vigilantes began to appear before the Committee of Twelve with prisoners. These men were questioned about their activities since the strike began. If they were deemed to have given satisfactory answers, they were given a choice: they could join with the citizens in supporting the railroad or they could leave the country. In some instances the men were questioned, then whipped. Some were not ordered to leave town but were told the committee would not be responsible for what might happen to them if they stayed. Usually, they left. The wife of J. T. Venable, one of the strike leaders, was requested to leave under guarantee of safe conduct. She was given just enough time to get her personal effects together.

One of the groups came to the home of Ed C. Gregor, a shopman who, when the strike began, had gone to work at a dam being built on the White River near Branson, Missouri. His wife had remained in their home at Harrison. A couple of days before the committee was formed, Gregor came home to spend a few days before going back to work at the dam. Two of his friends, both strikers, came to his home for a visit; earlier, they had gone to see J. T. Venable. These visits became known to the Committee of Twelve.

When a group of armed vigilantes came to Gregor's home, his wife had gone to town. Ed ordered the gang to leave his property. When they refused, he fired two shots out the back door with a shotgun. Thus the hostilities began. A fusillade of about fifty shots was fired into the house from all sides. Miraculously, Ed and his little daughter were unhurt. His wife came rushing home when she heard the volley of shots. When she screamed that her baby was in the house, the firing stopped, but not until a vigilante had accidentally shot one of his own men. There was an attempt to blame Ed Gregor, but it failed.

Mrs. Gregor finally persuaded Ed to go with the gang to the committee's interrogation room. The answers he gave didn't prove satisfactory, so he was promptly locked in a guarded room, called the "bullpen," for further questioning. During the evening, Sheriff Shaddock sent out an assistant to secure food for the men who were being held in the bullpen.

Pre-dawn darkness shrouded the mountains and wrapped Harrison in peaceful stillness. The door to the bullpen opened, and three masked, armed men stepped into the room (the sheriff had gone to escort a couple of the prisoners to jail).

"Everybody raise your hands high! Ed Gregor, you come with us. You won't need your overcoat, just leave it here."

The door closed as Ed and his abductors disappeared into the darkness. The damp January cold descended again, bringing with it an air of apprehension. The men in the bullpen were not sleeping that night.

Several men were out of bed early the morning of Tuesday, January 16, 1923. They were tense and worried by the action of the day before. Eating a hasty breakfast, they would leave their homes to go uptown for news of what was happening.

Two men were walking along the banks of Crooked Creek near the south edge of town. As they approached the railroad trestle crossing the creek, they stopped abruptly, standing on the rocky pathway which wound its way beneath the trestle. In the murky gray dawn, they saw the body of Ed Gregor swinging and slowly turning in the gentle currents of a cold breeze. Knotted around his neck was a rope tied to one of the bridge timbers.

There was a cursory investigation of Ed Gregor's murder, but no one volunteered to confess to it and persons who were questioned said they didn't know anything about it.

The Committee of Twelve obtained quite a lot more evidence concerning the activities of the strikers while going about its self-appointed task of investigating and abducting suspects. A few were whipped and several were advised to leave town. The committee "held court" for a week, during which time the mayor, the city marshal, and members of the Harrison City Council were forced to resign and leave town. On January 19, 1923, the reign of the Committee of Twelve came to an end. Men had been beaten, flogged, intimidated, run out of town, and one had been murdered, but the strike was broken and all was well.

It was soon learned that unfriendly actions by union men on other lines were cutting into the revenues of the M & NA. Freight shipments were routed over other roads, prospective passengers advised to go another direction. Moreover, the M & NA's equipment and roadbed were in worse condition than ever before. During 1924, the Bureau of Locomotive Inspection, a division of the Interstate Commerce Commission, conducted fifty engine inspections on the road; forty locomotives were found to be defective. Each engine was inspected several times during the year and if found to be defective, was ordered repaired before being put back into service, but repairs were delayed as long as possible. Eight M & NA engines were finally ordered out of service by inspectors.

Business did not revive as the years passed. Roads were finally being built through the mountains, and progress was catching up with the railroad which ran from nowhere to nowhere. In 1927, the M & NA was in receivership again. J. C. Murray resigned, and the court appointed W. Stephenson as receiver. Stephenson soon encountered trouble with the employees, and he, too, resigned. L. A. Watkins succeeded him as receiver, but this still didn't bring prosperity to the M & NA. The road suffered the humiliation of another foreclosure sale in 1935. It was bought by Frank and Joe Kell of Wichita Falls, Texas. Frank and his son, Joe, got the road for the pitiful sum of $350,000. To prevent their inheriting the legal complications associated with the old organization, a new corporation was formed and the name was changed to the Missouri & Arkansas.

The circle now had been completed. When the rails left the Frisco at Seligman and headed for Eureka Springs in 1882, the venture was known as the Missouri & Arkansas Railroad. In 1935, it became the Missouri and Arkansas Railway.

During its difficult days, many tales concerning the M & NA were told. To prevent obvious embarrassment, names will be omitted from the following anecdotes related to me by former employees.

One M & NA conductor remembers winning several bets he made with other employees on the chances of the train's being on the ground within an hour after heading north from the yard at Harrison. He won considerably more than he lost.

The same conductor was making the run south to Helena one day when the hogger was stopped by a red orderboard at a small station. He whistled several times for the board while approaching the station. The board stayed red and the operator didn't come out of the station with an order hoop, so the hogger stopped. The conductor came up from the crummy to see what the trouble was. He found the operator sitting at his desk in the station, dead drunk and wanting someone to talk to. He had no orders for the train and would not issue a clearance for the crew to leave. They could not move the train against the red board. The conductor called the division superintendent and advised him of the situation. The super drove to the station in his car, issued a clearance to the train crew so they could be on their way, then fired the operator.

A section man who lived at Beaver, near Eureka Springs, was planning a vacation in Texas with his young son. They climbed aboard the single coach of the varnish run at Beaver one morning and headed south for Kensett, where they could make connections with the Missouri Pacific for Texas. A short distance out of Beaver, the train stumbled off the rails, the coach and the combination mail-baggage express car tipping tiredly over on their sides at the edge of a watery swamp. The man lifted his son out through a window to a friend, then helped the other passengers out. Several were shaken up but not seriously hurt.

The section man then went forward to help the baggage and mail clerks out of their overturned car. The baggage man had been caught in a deluge when a number of five-gallon cream cans lost their tops and soaked him with fresh cream. The baggage smasher was as slippery as an eel, and the men could hardly hold on to him to help him out.

A freight hog pulled a string of cars out of Harrison one morning, heading north. Not far from Beaver, a rail turned over and several cars swapped ends, breaking open the end of one car. News of the wreck spread through the community, and several people came to see what had happened. The car which had broken open contained sacks of sugar. In the confusion, a local bootlegger managed to make off with several sacks.

When the wreck was cleared away and traffic resumed, M & NA

officials held an investigation. During the questioning, the track foreman was asked what he thought had caused the mishap. "The spikes just won't hold in the bermuda grass," he said. He was fired for insubordination and failure to keep the track in good repair. Good ties and ballast were unnecessary luxuries in those days.

One conductor said the track was in such bad shape that a rail would sag as a freight rolled across a soft spot in the roadbed and box cars would dip and sway till he could read the numbers and initials on the ends of the cars from the cupola on the crummy. To walk the deck from the crummy to the smoky end was impossible if the train were running. He had to crawl while holding to the footboard on top of the cars.

A brakeman, who had passed the examination and was put on the conductor's extra board at Harrison, was called for a trip to Helena. He and his crew began to drink in one of the local taverns and two of the brakemen beat the devil out of him, breaking a couple of his ribs in the process. Getting a doctor to bind him up with adhesive tape, he started on the return trip the next morning. When the train stopped at the first water tank, the brakies climbed down and left it stranded. The conductor and the hogger talked the situation over. Since the hogger had a lady friend in Helena, they just backed the train into town and called for a new crew of brakemen.

There was one advantage in railroading on the old M & NA. When a man asked for work on any other road and said he had worked on the North Arkansas, he was generally assured a job. Any man who could railroad under conditions like those on the North Arkansas was able to railroad most anywhere. There are several former M & NA men still at it in Arkansas.

After the Kells bought the road, manager Watkins was able to make it actually show a profit. The M & A rocked along pretty smoothly until misfortune struck again. Young Joe Kell was killed in an automobile wreck in 1939, and a couple of years later, Frank Kell passed away, leaving the railroad as part of a considerable estate. His heirs did not have the knack or affection for shortline railroading that Frank and Joe exhibited.

Business remained fair during World War II, but increased taxes gave the revenue page of the ledger a generous amount of red ink. The general offices at Harrison burned in 1941, and a few months later, the shops also fell victim to devouring flames. In 1945, a disastrous flood swept away several miles of roadbed on the southern end, and for nearly six months, traffic was routed around the section while it was being rebuilt.

When World War II ended, the nation was caught up in a mad scramble by labor and business in which prices and wages began a bewildering upward spiral. The men of the M & A demanded a wage increase of eighteen and one-half cents an hour in 1946. The manager calmly announced that the road was not financially able to stand the increase and that if the men decided to strike, the road would be abandoned. The men decided to call the manager's bluff: they walked off their jobs September 6, 1946. The company immediately applied to the Interstate Commerce Commission (ICC) for permission to abandon the road. The request was granted, and the M & A was sold to several eastern capitalists, who were represented by M. P. Gross of South Orange, New Jersey. These gentlemen were interested only in dismantling the entire road, for scrap iron was bringing a good price at the time.

This brought forth a stream of protest from various sources and a hodgepodge of schemes to keep the M & A in operation—at least portions of it. The status quo prevailed until February, 1949, when the owners came forth with a proposal of their own.

Attorney Eugene Warren of Little Rock had been acting as liaison man between the road's owners and Governor Sid McMath. Now he announced a plan which would require the cooperation of several "doctors" if the railroad "patient" were to survive. On the condition that all objections to the ICC abandonment order be dropped, the new owners agreed to operate that portion of the road from Harrison to Seligman, Missouri, with no strings attached. The section between Leslie and Heber Springs would be scrapped. The scrapping operation would be halted at Leslie if the citizens from Leslie to Harrison would guarantee the owners against any operating loss on that section if the road were operated from Leslie to Seligman on a one-year trial basis. The owners also would have to be protected against a drop in the price of scrap iron during the trial year in case operation of that segment proved unprofitable and it was then scrapped.

The section from Heber Springs to Searcy would be offered for sale to any group for less than scrap value with one-half the purchase price in cash and the balance in lease rentals over a five-year period.

The line from Kensett to Cotton Plant would be scrapped because it could be bypassed by using the Rock Island track from Searcy to Wheatley by way of Mesa. The owners would operate the road between Cotton Plant and Helena if a group of eastern Arkansas citizens failed in their efforts to purchase it and operate it as a separate railroad.

If this plan were adopted, there would be rail service north from Leslie to Seligman to connect there with the Frisco, but no service between Leslie and Heber Springs. Trains would again run between Heber Springs and Helena by trackage rights over the Rock Island from Searcy via Mesa to Wheatley, making connection with Missouri Pacific and Rock Island to Little Rock, Memphis, and St. Louis.

Warren conferred with M. P. Gross, one of the six men who had bought the road; Senator Ernest Nicholson of Harrison; and A. C. Kennedy of Heber Springs. Senator Nicholson, who had been advocating reopening the road, said the plan was fair and offered relief to all. Kennedy was most enthusiastic about the idea and believed the people in his area would agree to purchase the section between Heber Springs and Searcy. Gross and his associates said they would not scrap the road if they could operate it at a profit. If some arrangement could not be worked out, scrapping would begin April 6. If the line were scrapped, the owners said, they would furnish locomotives for the task and would hire union labor.

On March 4, 1949, the Arkansas Public Service Commission approved a charter for the Arkansas & Ozarks Railway to operate that section of the defunct M & A between Harrison and Seligman. Gross and M. T. Schwartz of New York City were the principal stockholders, but seven Arkansans also had a finger in the pie: Roy Milum of Harrison; Earl B. Hailey, H. G. Leathers, and J. E. Simpson of Berryville; L. A. Watkins and E. R. Vallance of Harrison; and Jim Crain of Wilson. Gross, Vallance, Crain, Milum, and Schwartz were selected to direct the destiny of the new venture. Although the North Arkansas had never really lived as a healthy road should, neither would it give up and die like a respectable corpse. It just kept floundering and struggling.

Official authorization was granted for the abandonment of the Missouri & Arkansas because it could not be legally transferred to the new A & O corporation, whereupon Gross transferred all rolling stock to the A & O. Granting of the charter didn't signify approval of the entire proposal as outlined above, however. Public Service Commission Chairman Charles C. Wine said the plan would require considerable deliberation before a final decision could be made. Meanwhile, negotiations for the purchase of the line from Cotton Plant to Helena had already been completed by a group of eastern Arkansas businessmen, including Jim Crain.

Headquarters for the Arkansas & Ozarks was established at Harrison, and the venture was capitalized for $400,000, including two thousand shares of preferred stock at $100 and two thousand shares of common stock at $10.

The 54-mile section between Cotton Plant and Helena was sold to the Helena & Northwestern, a new company formed to purchase that part of the old M & A. Plantation owner Jim Crain was president; C. W. Ferguson, a financier from Star City, served as secretary; and E. T. Horner of Helena became treasurer. The venture cost $300,000—almost as much as Frank Kell paid for the entire M & A. They gave M. P. Gross $15,000 in earnest money, the entire down payment being $100,000. The remaining $200,000 was to be paid over a five-year period at 4 per cent interest. The Helena & Northwestern was to be operated by steam locomotives, while the Arkansas & Ozarks planned to use diesel-electric motive power.

When the M & A section south of Kensett was being taken up, serviceable creosoted crossties were placed on trucks and hauled to Cotton Plant to be used in rehabilitation work toward Helena. Early in June, 1949, the electric lights in the old M & A depot at Cotton Plant began to shine brightly again after nearly three years of darkness. Signs of life were appearing, and hopes rose daily for the renewal of train operations. Four crews of gandy dancers were at work getting the road in shape. One crew was taking up ties at Georgetown, about fifteen miles north of Cotton Plant on the abandoned section, while a second was busy working on the tracks at Cotton Plant. The other two were putting in ties and straightening track at West Helena and Rondo.

Chris Ferguson was made general manager of the H & NW, and he promptly established its general office in the depot at West Helena. The city of Cotton Plant was making plans for a large-scale celebration befitting the grand occasion of its railroad revival. City officials, residents, and many invited dignitaries were to gather at a huge barbecue on August 25. Governor Sid McMath was to be among the guests.

The morning of the twenty-fifth arrived. Three thousand spectators arrived. Governor McMath arrived. The special train never did arrive.

It was learned at the last minute that the roadbed and bridges would not be safe for train operation, but this didn't interfere with the festivities. The barbecue was ready, the ice cream and watermelon were ready, and the crowd was ready, so everyone retired to Doss Grove. Mr. and Mrs. C. T. Doss announced they were leasing the five-acre site to the city for five years. If it were maintained properly during that time, the title would be transferred to the city. Governor McMath declared Cotton Plant was the only city he had visited which hadn't asked for anything. That, indeed, was unusual.

The terminal facilities at Helena were in good condition, so switching service was begun there and at West Helena on the morning of September 15. Two engines had arrived over the Illinois Central (Yazoo & Mississippi Valley) from the Apalachicola Northern down in Florida. One of them was put into switching service immediately, handling cars between the IC interchange and various industries in the twin cities. The Pekin Wood Products Company and the Chicago Mill & Lumber Company, the two largest industries in the area, had been trucking their products to the IC. Now they would be served by the H & NW.

The little road had some lucky breaks at a most opportune time. Its freight rates were approved by the Interstate Commerce Commission, two locomotives arrived from the AN, and the employees of the Missouri Pacific had gone out on strike. This gave all the switching service in Helena to the H & NW. Some of the most well-known names in Arkansas business circles were listed on its board of directors: J. H. Crain, Colonel T. H. Barton, Chris Ferguson, C. Hamilton Moses.

The strike on the Missouri Pacific actually forced the H & NW into business before it was ready. Freight cars were piling up in the Helena yard, and this gave the new road an opportunity to skim off a little cream. Chris Ferguson announced that the first freight train would leave Helena at 7:00 A.M. on October 11 and would arrive at Cotton Plant at 11:30 A.M. Cotton Plant schools closed in plenty of time for the children to go down to the depot and greet the train, and stores and banks closed their doors to allow the employees to attend the celebration. There was quite a crowd on hand.

After a 45-minute wait, it was announced there had been some delay and a new arrival time of 1:30 P.M. was set. The disappointed kids went back to school and stores opened for business again. A few sightseers, officials, and press representatives came down to the depot, but no train arrived. A couple of new arrival times were announced, but no train showed up. By three o'clock, the schools had closed for the day and some of the children came back to wait. At four o'clock sharp, a shrill whistle was heard. A swelling burst of applause rose from the waiting crowd. In a moment, however, the joyful sound gave way to silence: a near-by veneer plant was closing for the day. At 4:25 P.M., an undaunted old-timer, who had been waiting since morning and was perched comfortably on the depot bench, summed up the situation: "It may have a different name, but its habits are the same—MAY NEVER ARRIVE!"

Gradually, the crowd began to thin out, drifting away by ones and twos. The old-timer still held down his claim on the bench in front of the depot. At 5:00 P.M., a locomotive eased slowly around a curve; her whistle began to scream. As engine No. 200 rolled to a halt, the crowd swelled again—to three hundred persons—and gave the tardy train a rousing welcome.

The cab of No. 200 was pretty well crowded. At the throttle was hogger Ray Thomas, who, incidentally, had piloted the last train into Helena over the M & A three years earlier. Keeping up a head of steam was fireman T. L. "Buddy" Edwards. Keeping them company was general manager Ferguson, his ten-year-old son, Chris, Jr., and a reporter for the *Arkansas Democrat*, Leo D. Martin. Three crummies had been purchased from the Missouri Pacific but, because of the strike, had not been delivered, so a boxcar reeking with a heavy odor had to do the honors of a caboose. Twelve cars rode the drawbar of 2-8-0 No. 200 that day. She had been three and one-half hours late leaving Helena, there was quite a lot of switching to do at the stations along the way, and flood waters nearly covered a considerable portion of the roadbed. In charge of the switching operations were conductor C. C. Atkinson, brakeman Fred McIntire, and flagman-brakeman Fred Bell, another former M & A man.

The H & NW operated as a freight-only road, with no plans for passenger service. On January 14, 1950, a $200,000 mortgage was executed with M. P. Gross and M. T. Schwartz. On April 26,

1951, foreclosure proceedings were filed in federal district court at Helena against the H & NW. The suit, filed by Gross and Schwartz as trustees for the old M & A, which sold the road in the first place, stated that following a $50,000 down payment, the H & NW had made no further payments. Neither had any payment been made on the $200,000 mortgage executed fifteen months earlier. The suit asked for the overdue money and/or a foreclosure order to protect the trustees. Gross and Schwartz said they did not intend to junk the line if the court awarded it to them; they would operate it as a regular freight carrier.

In May, the stockholders of the H & NW announced their determination to hold the road and keep it operating. They selected two men to represent them in legal action to contest the foreclosure suit: C. Hamilton Moses, president of the Arkansas Power & Light Company, and F. W. Schatz, president of the Chicago Mill & Lumber Company of Helena. The stockholders asked the court to appoint J. B. Lambert of Helena and E. T. Horner, Sr., as trustees to operate the H & NW during the litigation. Lambert acted as president and Horner was treasurer.

The heavy expense of rehabilitating the roadbed had given the new company a financial setback, but this condition was supposedly a temporary circumstance. "I am firmly convinced we soon can have this railroad on a paying basis," Moses said. "We do need more support from the general public, but I am convinced the line is vital to the future growth of this community." Colonel T. H. Barton, president of the Lion Oil Company, remarked: "The reason I became a director in this railroad is because I am sure that Helena will grow to be a real city and this railroad is of great necessity to this section and to the state as a whole."

Between May 21, when the above remarks were made, and July 21, a drastic change seems to have taken place: Lambert mailed an abandonment petition to the Interstate Commerce Commission. Cited as reasons for filing the petition were a $30,000 loss in 1950 and a $13,000 loss during the first five months of 1951. Unpaid indebtedness was about $182,000. The familiar nemesis of the old North Arkansas had returned to haunt the offspring: too much money going out, too little coming in.

On October 18, the last freight train ran over the sagging roadbed. The ICC authorized abandonment November 5, 1951. Another piece of the old M & NA bit the dust.

Just when everyone thought the old North Arkansas had been safely buried at last, it heaved one more struggling breath. On February 6, 1952, the ICC authorized the Cotton Plant–Fargo Railway Company to acquire and operate six miles of defunct H & NW road between Cotton Plant in Woodruff County and Fargo in Monroe County. This little outfit was formed by a group of businessmen at Cotton Plant. They would provide freight service only and would run "when necessary," except on Sunday. David D. Bush was president; Joe D. McGregor, vice president; and Ben White, secretary and treasurer. (This abbreviated railroad was operating on the same basis in 1968, connecting with the Cotton Belt at Fargo.)

In the afternoon of February 3, 1950, the first car of freight over the Arkansas & Ozarks, a carload of fir lumber, arrived at the Hammerschmidt Lumber Company in Harrison. The proprietor, John Paul Hammerschmidt, said his firm had received the last shipment of freight over the old M & A when the strike came in 1946.

Formal opening ceremonies for the A & O were held February 9, 1950, at the old passenger depot at Harrison. Many of the spectators had also been among the enthusiastic greeters of the first St. Louis & North Arkansas train back in 1901. The fine display of a locomotive's barking exhaust, billowing coal smoke, and echoing whistle which attended the arrival of the train in 1901 was missing forty-nine years later. The 1950 version was just a 70-ton diesel. The glamor and fanfare were also absent and the crowd was much smaller. The celebration was strictly a hometown affair. There were no out-of-town speakers, and the railroad's owners failed to show up.

At 10:45 that morning, two diesels, Nos. 800 and 900, rolled quietly into sight from the freight yard. The Harrison High School band played *On the Square* as the train rolled by in charge of hogger R. J. Shelton and conductor Hubert Morrison. Charles C. Wine, chairman of the Arkansas Public Service Commission, told the people the future of the road was in their hands. He did not take into account the unpredictable Ozark Mountains.

By the time the A & O celebrated its first birthday, its roadbed had been beefed up. The old office building at Harrison had received a paint job in the company colors of orange with black trim—and new hardwood floors had been installed. M. P. Gross said the road had operated 273 days and had handled 2,088 carload shipments. The volume would have to reach fifteen cars per day to break even. There was a good potential for freight in the area, mostly wood products, and the road was fairly well equipped to handle it. It had forty people on its payroll. J. E. Halter was chief operations officer, C. E. Harris was in charge of all equipment, and Lon Holder headed the bridge and right-of-way crews. Frank Green was business solicitor.

Many local people felt their moral and financial support would keep the railroad operating. This was reflected in record car-handling for the month of July, 1951: 302 carload shipments, including 120 outbound cars. The previous outbound high mark was 90 carloads.

New freight traffic for the road included staves from the Jack Hoskins Stave Mill at Kingston. The staves were hauled by truck to Berryville for shipment over the A & O. Shipments of ties from Berryville and Eureka Springs were made by the Koppers Company of Kansas City. The Kraft Company at Berryville was shipping dried whey to be used in livestock feed. Theo Sutterfield at Marshall averaged from fifteen to twenty cars of ties every month for the Midland Tie Company at Kansas City. Many other firms in Harrison and the surrounding area were doing whatever they could to keep the trains running.

As the years moved along, it became increasingly difficult for the 74-mile A & O to keep its head above water financially. Then, in the spring of 1960, it was literally covered by water. There was a flash flood in the mountains, and Leatherwood Creek went on a rampage near Eureka Springs carrying away trestles and roadbed.

In addition to this baptism, the owners were notified a 2.7-mile section of their track was being condemned by the U.S. Army Corps of Engineers. Table Rock Dam on White River near Branson, Missouri, had been completed, and the lake was filling. The A & O was subject to intermittent flooding. The Corps of Engineers agreed to permit the A & O to continue operating, however, subject to the risk of overflow from the lake. The situation was intolerable to the owners of the road. No shipper was going to route a car of freight over the road when he knew it might be a week or two late arriving at its destination.

Once again the plague returned. In April, 1961, the Interstate Commerce Commission granted the A & O permission to abandon service.

There was a vigorous protest from business people along the road. They had been paying exorbitant prices to have their products moved by truck either to the Missouri Pacific at Bergman, east of Harrison, or down State Highway 65. The 1961 session of the Arkansas Legislature got into the act. It passed—and Governor Orval E. Faubus signed into law—a bill assessing twenty to thirty dollars per ton as a scrap removal tax against any railroad less than one hundred miles long which wished to abandon service. The tax was to be paid before the Public Service Commission would grant permission for abandonment. The law was challenged, of course, and declared unconstitutional by Chancellor Guy E. Williams. It was written in such a way that it applied only to the Arkansas & Ozarks Railway.

The shops and offices at Harrison were closed and the two General Electric diesels were loaded on lowboy trailers and hauled to Bergman, on the White River Division of the Missouri Pacific, where they were billed to a purchaser in Des Moines. Salvage procedures were begun in the winter of 1961–62. In February, 1962, the Frisco filed suit against the A & O to halt removal of the track until a debt of $30,594 for interchange service had been paid. The two companies quickly settled their differences and the A & O was ripped up by the roots.

In April, 1966, a charter was granted to the Ozark Mountain Railroad. The company proposed to operate a three-mile section of the Arkansas & Ozarks track between Beaver and Elk Ranch as a tourist attraction. No freight would be handled. The incorporators were Dreat Younger, Galena, Kansas; R. R. Younger, Springfield, Missouri; and J. M. Parkhill, Berryville, Arkansas.

The new corporation encountered financial problems and has floundered to a standstill. Nothing more has been heard from it.

The old bones of the M & NA may rise again!

DARDANELLE, OLA & SOUTHERN

5

WHEN SETTLERS FIRST CAME TO ARKANSAS, they built homes along the navigable streams, since these provided the most dependable means of transportation. The land along the Arkansas River in the Dardanelle area was found to be unusually fertile and was soon being cultivated. When crop yields proved abundant, additional land was cleared of timber and put under cultivation.

Unfortunately, the river was rather undependable when transportation was needed most, often being too shallow to float loaded barges. When prices were high, the water level was low, leaving warehouses bulging with stored cotton. And moving cotton overland by wagon was impossible during the wet winter or spring months: the roads were impassable.

So it was that the railroad from Dardanelle to Russellville came into being in 1883, thereby relieving the situation for a few years. By the turn of the century, however, cultivation of plantation lands had progressed southward and was well removed from access to the railroad at Dardanelle. The settlers were again confronted by impassable roads, and the only solution to their problem was another railroad.

The St. Louis, Iron Mountain & Southern ran along the north bank of the Arkansas River and was inaccessible. The Choctaw, Oklahoma & Gulf, which connected Little Rock with Indian Territory to the west, lay about fourteen miles south of Dardanelle and offered the most feasible route to outside markets—and the means of survival.

One man was more enthusiastic about the idea of another railroad than most of the community. He was C. C. Godman, and he spent many hours encouraging his neighbors and friends to join him in promoting it for the mutual benefit of all the plantation owners along the route, as well as the folks in Dardanelle. Godman soon enlisted the support of Colonel John B. Crownover, C. B. Cotton, and Fred H. Phillips.

With the groundwork being completed, the state granted a charter on May 1, 1906, to the Dardanelle, Ola & Southern. Residents of the area began to take an active interest when they realized the promoters really intended to build the railroad. As their interest grew, they took a more personal view of the project, and before long, seven miles of right-of-way had been donated. Some who were interested in the road but had no money to buy stock paid their subscriptions in labor, while others furnished materials and construction implements. The response was so favorable that Godman said he expected to have trains in operation by November, 1906.

Money for construction was at hand, and a "great wave of jubilation was felt throughout the land," according to one exuberant newspaper editor. A meeting was called to celebrate the event, and, literally, the fatted calf was killed. A huge barbecue was planned, and some two thousand people were on hand for a day of rejoicing. On Monday morning, March 12, 1906, Mrs. C. C. Godman turned the first shovelful of earth to begin construction of the

Dardanelle, Ola & Southern just five blocks west of Main Street in Dardanelle.

Excavation would be rather limited except for a couple of sharp ridges which would require some heavy cutting. Generally, the rails would follow the flat bottomland along the river and would rise and fall across the rolling hills farther south.

Work progressed very well during the spring months, and by June 15, five miles of roadbed had been completed, culverts built, bridges constructed from timber cut on the right-of-way, and all cattle guards finished. Some of the folks who had subscribed to stock in the DO & S had made the final installment or had discharged their obligation by furnishing labor or materials. The board of directors held its first meeting on June 15, and the secretary presented first-mortgage bonds to those who had fulfilled their subscriptions.

Heavy rains fell in the latter part of June and on into July, but work progressed. Godman had incorporated the Godman Construction Company and had a large crew encamped at Centerville, about seven miles south of Dardanelle, where the heaviest construction was encountered. The Fudge Construction Company was busy cutting its way through Gately Gap, between Centerville and Dardanelle.

Local residents had responded ably in raising $45,000 in stock subscriptions, Godman being the chief stockholder with 800 shares valued at $100 per share. The cost of the venture was estimated at $160,000, a large portion of which was borrowed from the Commonwealth Trust Company at Little Rock.

During the early days of the money-raising campaign and during the initial construction period, the editor of the weekly *Dardanelle Post-Dispatch* printed daily editions to keep everyone informed of the road's progress. Public spirit was good and enthusiasm was running high. There would be no lack of freight for the new road. Abundant timber land surrounded the area, and as the trees were cleared away, the land would be made available for cultivation. Cotton would be plentiful, and there was a world-wide demand for it. By August, real estate values along the DO & S had increased considerably. Dr. McCarthy of Centerville divided forty acres into building lots, which were made available to prospective home builders, and a merchant was planning to construct a brick store building and stock it with $25,000 worth of merchandise.

On October 15, 1906, only one and one-half miles of rails remained to be laid to make connection with the Choctaw Route at Ola. Along the fourteen miles of track from Dardanelle were five bridges and one trestle. Many new business establishments had opened their doors in Dardanelle, and the new depot was only five blocks from downtown.

About this time, there circulated rumors that the Arkansas Central, built from Fort Smith to Paris, Arkansas, in May, 1900, by the St. Louis, Iron Mountain & Southern, was to be extended to Dardanelle. Nothing definite occurred, and a couple of days after Christmas, Godman was visited by a group of men from Paris: Father Boniface of the abbey at Subiaco, J. W. Foster, L. C. Speiler, Henry Stroup, W. B. Rhyne, Conrad Elskin, Dr. A. M. Smith, M. P. Blair, W. Y. McClure, James Cochran, W. C. Roady, Dr. W. H. Bennett, William Greenwood, and M. L. Tucker. They proposed that Godman extend the DO & S to Paris to connect with the Arkansas Central. Many acres of timber land were available and vast bituminous coal deposits lay undeveloped —prime sources of future business for any railroad that would build into the area.

Godman told the group he would build the extension if people would furnish the right-of-way and subscribe to stock in the road to the tune of $5,000 per mile. He proposed to issue thirty-year gold bonds bearing 5 per cent interest as soon as the road was completed. Now $190,000 was more than these men were financially able to raise, and with the debt the DO & S already owed to the Commonwealth Trust Company, Godman didn't feel he was able to assume any additional mortgages. Therefore, no extension was built.

The rails reached Centerville on August 5, 1907, and an old-time picnic was planned for the eighth, proceeds from which were to be used to construct a depot. Five thousand pounds of meat were purchased for barbecuing, and U. S. Senator Jeff Davis was to be the speaker. A brass band was engaged to furnish entertainment. The picnic was well publicized, and more than two thousand people showed up for the feast. Trains ran every hour from Dardanelle to Centerville.

Rails were laid into Ola after considerable delay—in fact, almost a year later than anticipated. Godman had expected to connect with the Choctaw Route by November, 1906, but didn't reach it until the latter part of August, 1907. Business was good from the outset, and by August 24, twelve passenger trains entered Ola every day except Sunday.

A first-class banquet was held at Miller's Hall in Dardanelle on November 26 to celebrate completion of the road and to honor Godman, Phillips, Crownover, and Cotton as its chief promoters. Several prominent persons took this opportunity to make speeches, including Mayor E. W. Farrier and Max Heiman of the Gus Blass Dry Goods Company at Little Rock. The editor of the *Dardanelle Post-Dispatch* observed that the burden of building the railroad rested chiefly on the shoulders of one man whose energy, steadfastness of purpose, and ability had rescued it more than once from what seemed to be a certain death. That man, he said, was Colonel John B. Crownover, who was entitled to the gratitude of every citizen of Dardanelle and the surrounding area.

On October 15, 1907, the DO & S had an experience which was unique in the annals of railroading: it received an order for cross-ties from the United States government, which was building a railroad—its only such attempt up to that time—to extend five miles from Leavenworth, Kansas, to Fort Leavenworth. For about two and one-half miles of this road, the government needed ties, a scarce item on the bald Kansas prairie. The fine hardwood timber along the Dardanelle, Ola & Southern was becoming rather well known.

Business remained good on the DO & S. On July 10, 1908, the first carload of peaches was shipped from Dardanelle, followed by two more cars a few days later. The first three orchards in the area had just begun bearing.

By February, 1909, the DO & S was becoming a full-grown railroad. In the yards just south of the Union Warehouse, a large building was erected to serve as a freight warehouse and machine shop. The shop was equipped with the most modern machinery and tools available, a move which, it was estimated, would save the company almost $150,000 a year. Also installed were a pumping station and storage tank to supply clean water for the locomotives.

On the morning of July 10, 1909, a passenger train, headed for Ola, was passing through the hay meadow of a Mr. Marlowe, who lived near Prosperity. It was rolling along at about fifteen miles per hour when the engine sagged and staggered a bit. The hogger made a swipe at the brake valve and twisted around on the seat box. As he looked back, he was startled to see that the little wooden combine was off the rails, jumping and jerking along on the ties, leaning farther and farther to the right. She reached the point of no return and tiredly lay over on her side, bounced, slid a few feet, then stopped.

Fifteen passengers were aboard the car, and a quick examination showed that only two were injured. A. J. Kuhn had sustained slight bruises on his back and legs, and Miss Lillian Sheegog was bruised and cut rather profusely about the chin and throat, but not seriously.

It was determined that the extreme heat of the previous day had warped one of the rails. How the engine managed to pass over it was a mystery. The wreck was cleared in about a half-hour, and other trains were able to maintain their regular schedules. The damaged combine was hauled into the shop at Dardanelle for repairs.

Business was fairly brisk for the little pike during its youthful years, but hard times came for a visit in 1911. In that year, the

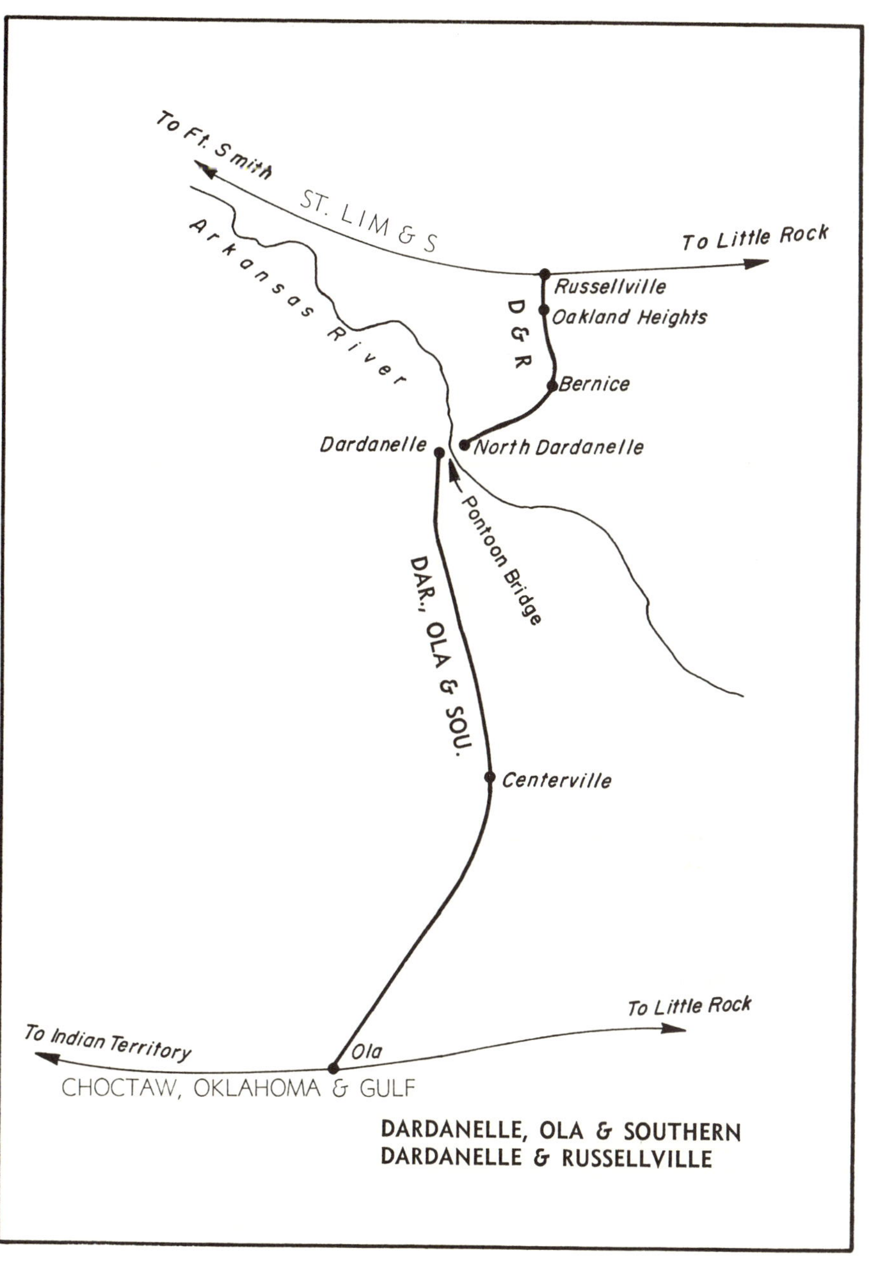
To Ft. Smith
ST. LIM & S
To Little Rock
Arkansas River
Russellville
Oakland Heights
D & R
Bernice
Dardanelle
North Dardanelle
Pontoon Bridge
DAR., OLA & SOU.
Centerville
To Little Rock
To Indian Territory
Ola
CHOCTAW, OKLAHOMA & GULF
DARDANELLE, OLA & SOUTHERN
DARDANELLE & RUSSELLVILLE

road defaulted on its mortgage payments to the Commonwealth Trust Company. Unable to meet the overdue payments, it was sold under foreclosure on February 9, 1911, to Commonwealth Trust Company at Little Rock for the paltry sum of $36,000. At that time, the physical assets of the DO & S included two locomotives, one passenger car, one mail-baggage-express combine, five boxcars, and five flats.

The Dardanelle, Ola & Southern ceased to exist on October 31, 1911, when it was sold to the Rock Island & Dardanelle Railway Company. In December, the road was leased to the Chicago, Rock Island & Pacific for 999 years. New officers had been elected on November 25 in the office of Thomas Buzbee in the Moore & Turner Building at Dardanelle. W. C. Fordyce was chosen as president, F. S. Yantis as vice president and general manager, and H. C. Rockhold as secretary-treasurer, with W. V. Delahunt as Rockhold's assistant. After the Rock Island took possession, new officials were appointed. James E. Gorman became president and George Crosley secretary-treasurer. Rockhold remained as ticket agent and assistant treasurer.

In 1915, the fine two-story depot and office building at Dardanelle burned. It was replaced by a smaller and more conventional depot having a traditional bay window next to the main line to accommodate the telegraph operator.

The years moved slowly along, and progress began to overtake the little road. Hard-surface highways were built across the state, and soon freight was moving along these public roads aboard large trucks, which became ever larger and more numerous. The Rock Island men saw the handwriting on the wall, and on September 8, 1920, the road was leased to a neighboring shortline railroad which had built into Dardanelle from the west—the Ft. Smith, Subiaco & Eastern. The new company was known as the Ft. Smith, Subiaco & Rock Island.

The next seventeen years saw a steady decline in the movement of freight along the rails, and the family automobile cut huge gaps in the passenger business. A gasoline-powered doodlebug was substituted for the regular twice-a-day passenger train from Fort Smith to Ola. Later, the car made only one trip a day.

Then came the paralyzing days of the Great Depression, and when the struggle was over, the little streak of rust through the weeds never recovered. Early in March, 1938, a crew of twenty-three men under the direction of G. S. Temple came to Dardanelle. They were a wrecking crew from the Hyman-Michalls Company in Chicago. Rusty spikes were pulled from soft, aging ties, fishplates were unbolted, and rails were loaded on flatcars. The Dardanelle to Ola railroad was abandoned.

The people in Dardanelle and all along the road had worked hard to save their little pike. Senator F. D. Majors, Joe Goodier, S. F. Meek, and Roy E. Pate even went to Washington to ask the Interstate Commerce Commission to reverse its abandonment order, but their plea was rejected.

The weatherbeaten, dilapidated Dardanelle depot still stands, and if you have imagination, you can see a dim figure at the oper-tor's table scan the faint, weed-grown roadbed for the approach of a short train behind brass-bound ten-wheeler No. 2—she's nearly thirty years late.

CROSSETT LUMBER COMPANY—CROSSETT RAILWAY—CROSSETT, MONTICELLO & NORTHERN—ASHLEY, DREW & NORTHERN

As WAS THE CASE with many Arkansas shortlines, the railroad at Crossett was born when men with saws and axes began to make a determined assault upon the forests of south Arkansas. In 1901, the Crossett Lumber Company sent a large crew to cut its way west from the village of Hamburg. There wasn't even as much as a wagon road—no indication of civilization at all. But when the men established their headquarters, they cleared the forest and laid out a small town, which they named Crossett in honor of their employer. By 1907, it had 2,500 residents, every one of whom was dependent on the company for livelihood.

The town was owned, lock, stock, and barrel, by the Crossett Lumber Company, for the company believed that a contented worker was a dependable one. The business section consisted of a hotel, commissary, bank, post office, butcher shop, printing office, laundry, and an office building for a doctor and dentist. Every building was owned by the company, and each business was a subsidiary of the company. Nearly all the taxes for the school were paid by the company, as was half the money to support the town's churches. Workers rented the houses, most of which had either three or four rooms, at the rate of $1.50 per month per room. Electric lights were available at 25 cents per month per bulb.

Crossett was honored by the presence of the only Methodist deaconess in the state of Arkansas. She was Miss Mae McKenzie, assigned to that duty by the Women's Home Missionary Society.

The main lumber plant consisted of two mills with a capacity of more than 100,000 board feet a day, two planing mills, a hardwood mill, eleven dry kilns, and many auxiliary buildings, such as machine shops. In 1906, the Crossett Lumber Company shipped 70,000,000 board feet of lumber and owned 150,000 acres of timber, most of it yellow pine. Three camps were maintained, each consisting of 100 portable houses, which were placed on flatcars and moved to new locations as the timber was logged out.

It was soon evident that bull teams could not transport downed logs very far, so the Crossett Railway was incorporated. It was granted a charter May 22, 1905, to build ten miles of railroad from Crossett in a northerly direction to a point near the north line of Section 32, Township 16 South, Range 8 West. It was estimated that $2,500 per mile would be sufficient to build and equip the line. From this it can be seen that the construction and equipment left much to be desired; perhaps that is why the corporation was granted a chartered life of only four years. C. W. Gates and E. S. Crossett each owned 62½ of the railway's 250 shares.

The little road extended nearly to Stephens. It leased four miles of track from the Crossett Lumber Company there, thus making a total of fourteen miles of railroad. Its charter was extended, and on April 11, 1912, it made arrangements to buy right-of-way from the Crossett Lumber Company in order to establish a terminal at Crossett. The Crossett Railway ceased to exist on May 1, 1912, when it was purchased by the Crossett, Monticello & Northern.

The Crossett, Monticello & Northern was granted a charter to build from Cremer Junction, about five miles south of Crossett, into Crossett, then in a northerly direction to Fountain Hill and on to Monticello, where connection was to be made with the St. Louis, Iron Mountain & Southern. At Crossett, it could tie into the Rock Island and the Mississippi River, Hamburg & Western, a subsidiary of the Iron Mountain.

By May 2, rails had been laid to near Fountain Hill, about twenty miles, and a new two-story depot and office building was under construction at Crossett. Lack of ready cash had prevented the rails being extended to Monticello. It was estimated that $200,000 would be needed to build the additional twenty miles. The company expressed its desire to issue first-mortgage bonds on the entire roadbed, rolling stock, office, and fixtures and to liquidate the mortgage from the first gross earnings after the road reached Monticello. The editor of the *Monticellonian* was enthusiastic about the railroad and the proposal:

> What can be done by our city to solve this dilemma? It seems if the Chamber of Commerce has any reasonable excuse for its existence this is the opportune moment to get busy. Banquets may appease the appetite and wind jamming may please the ear, but they do not carry freight and build cities. To say that the Chamber, composed of 80 members of mostly wealthy and prosperous business men, could not arrange for the floating of these bonds would be tacit acknowledgement that it, in reality, had no decent excuse for an existence. The bonds would be secure and bear six per cent interest, so why prolong acting? The Chamber should arrange for the prompt sale of these bonds, either here or elsewhere.

On June 28, 1912, a meeting was held at the courthouse in Monticello and a committee of businessmen was appointed to secure right-of-way through the southern part of Drew County and through the city itself to a connection with the Iron Mountain. The committee was to take care of getting land for a depot and terminal facilities. The actual route of the road would depend upon the generosity of the property owners, since it would be built along a route where right-of-way was donated by the owners. The campaign proved unsuccessful, and on August 8, 1912, a charter was granted to the Ashley, Drew & Northern Railway. On August 23, the Crossett, Monticello & Northern was sold to the AD & N. The new company acquired its name from the two counties through which the rails were laid: Ashley and Drew.

The AD & N ("All Day & Night") belonged to R. O. Roy of Crossett, who owned 4,100 shares of stock valued at $410,000. Serving with him as directors were Sherman Cook of Alexandria, Louisiana; J. T. Sifford and T. J. Gaughan of Camden, Arkansas; and B. A. Cannon of Crossett, all of whom owned only one share each. They set the capitalization of their venture at a whopping $600,000 to acquire and build a railroad from Cremer Junction to Monticello.

In mid-September, 1912, Roy announced he had purchased twenty flatcars, five boxcars, three coaches for passenger service, and one coach to be used on the local freight as mixed-train service. He also bought enough rails from the Tennessee Coal, Iron & Railway Company at Birmingham, Alabama, to lay thirty miles of track. Rails to build five miles of road had been sent to Monticello, along with the necessary spikes and angle bars. A steam shovel had also been acquired, and an advertisement for seventy-five thousand white oak ties had been placed in the newspaper.

The new company agreed to build into Monticello *if* the town would donate right-of-way within the city limits, this being the most expensive land it would need. The townspeople appointed a delegation to get in touch with property owners and negotiate for the purchase of land. The group soon discovered that many property owners were asking five times what their land was really worth. This was, of course, very frustrating to the railroad's promoters, and the outspoken editor of the *Monticellonian* suggested they pay the folks who were asking a reasonable price and have the court condemn the other parcels of land and set a fair price so they could go ahead with building the railroad. It must have been appropriate persuasion because there was no letup by the construction crew. "No, that wasn't thunder you heard!" he wrote. "Workmen are using dynamite to blow stumps from the right of way for the Ashley, Drew & Northern. After waiting and wanting for forty years for a North-South railroad, work has started at last!"

Monticello's business prospects were looking up. A sawmill operator said two large mills could prosper in the area if the railroad were built. Several businessmen had shown an interest in the town.

In mid-October, 1912, Roy announced the AD & N would be extended beyond Monticello and on to Little Rock by way of Rison and Sheridan. Then a new tentacle was to project from Monticello to either Stuttgart or Helena on the Mississippi River. There was a great flurry of construction, and between fifty and seventy-five teams of mules and oxen were at work about a half-mile south of Monticello. Quite a bit of embankment work was completed before bad weather brought everything to a halt for the winter.

In the latter part of April, 1913, the AD & N construction superintendent, a Captain Lucas, inspected the work that had been completed and found only three to four hundred dollars' worth of damage caused by heavy rains. Fortunately, the road crossed no large streams, so it was fairly immune to overflows. Grading was almost completed by June 5, and rails had been laid to within five miles of Monticello. President Roy moved his family to Monticello. Late in July, the rails entered Monticello and made connection with Jay Gould's Iron Mountain. The All Day & Night was in business. Almost immediately a forty-passenger gasoline motorcar began operating between Monticello and the agricultural school, now known as Monticello A & M College, making a round trip every hour.

The grand plans which Roy had made for his "little giant" were not reflected on the pages of the ledger books. There were no extensions. In fact, there was not much of anything, especially business. To say the least, the two years from 1912 to 1914 were

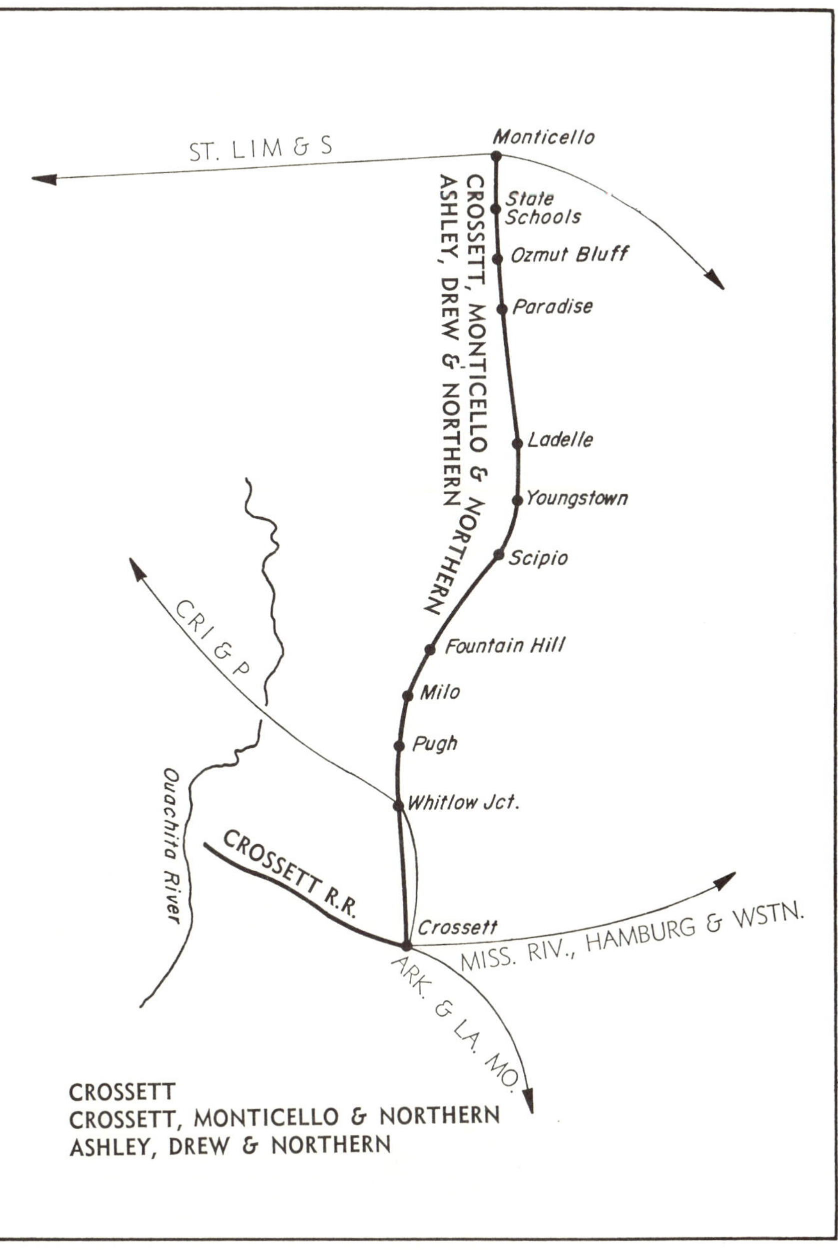

CROSSETT
CROSSETT, MONTICELLO & NORTHERN
ASHLEY, DREW & NORTHERN

not profitable ones. Finally, on December 1, 1914, the AD & N was leased to the Arkansas, Louisiana & Gulf, which ran from Monroe, Louisiana, to Crossett—the road now known as the Arkansas & Louisiana Missouri.

The AL & G was based in Monroe, Louisiana, but was incorporated to build northward through Bastrop, Hamburg, and Monticello to Pine Bluff. This brought a bonus of $130,000 from the town of Monroe for the Southwestern Development Company. It stumbled and stalled around from 1907 until July, 1908, when the rails reached Crossett. Then it wanted the construction time limit extended until January, 1911, and the terminus changed from Pine Bluff to Monticello or "some point equally distant." This caused much concern among the folks at Hamburg and Monticello. They were afraid the AL & G would absorb two logging roads: the Crossett Railway, extending north from Crossett, and the Wilmar & Saline Valley, running south out of Wilmar. By closing a six-mile gap between the two roads, the AL & G would have a road extending to Wilmar, which was "equally distant" from Monroe, as was Monticello. This would leave Hamburg on a spur, and Monticello would be left out entirely.

General manager J. M. Parker of Colorado Springs said the officials had no intention of buying up logging roads. Colorado capitalists were building the AL & G for the revenues which would be derived from its operation. He informed the people that the company had bought fifteen thousand acres of land and planned to establish five towns between Hamburg and De Valls Bluff. The objective had always been to build into West Memphis through the rich rice and hay country east of Pine Bluff.

It has been said that the best-laid plans of mice and men often go astray. So it was that Brother Parker and the AL & G fell upon hard times and no rails ever were laid east of Monticello—nor in any other direction. Parker struggled along until February 28, 1920, when he gave up, and the Crossett to Monticello portion was once again known as Ashley, Drew & Northern. C. W. Gates was elected president, A. Trieschmann served as general manager, and W. B. Anderson was auditor. Revenues during the next nine months were disappointing, however. The credit side of the ledger indicated an income of $102,499, but the outgo was $205,129, leaving a net loss of $102,680.

The next ten years were very difficult and discouraging. It was 1930 before the AD & N was able to make a profit. Then a little shot of prosperity came when the Crossett Chemical Company was establishd in 1934. Until that time, the railroad had depended primarily on the movement of logs, lumber, and various other wood products for its existence. Much miscellaneous business was received from on-line points, principally shipments of agricultural products from the Monticello area. The Crossett Lumber Company began a diversified program of expanding its operations to include various manufactured products—from wood, of course. It shipped out 972 carloads of charcoal and other products, including acetic acid, methanol, and pitch, in 1935.

The real booster of business for the railroad, however, was the huge paper mill at Crossett. Construction began early in 1936, and it was completed about a year later. The materials used in constructing the mill totaled 1,311 carloads: 532 cars of sand and gravel, 214 cars of machinery, 136 cars of structural iron and steel, and 277 cars of brick and cement, plus miscellaneous materials. During the portion of 1937 in which the mill was in operation, 1,070 cars were dispatched. The first full year of operation produced a total of 1,500 carloads (36,000 tons), bringing much needed revenue of $41,000. The Crossett Lumber Company and the chemical firm brought $110,000 into the AD & N cash register in 1938. In that year, revenues were $272,000, while expenses amounted to $180,000, leaving a tidy profit of $91,000.

In 1945, the first "foreign" manufacturer established a beachhead in Crossett: Chase Paper Bag Company. Seven years later, the Crossett Lumber Company prepared many acres of land for industrial sites along the railroad on the west edge of town. Several companies have taken advantage of this, among them Crossett Concrete Products Company, manufacturers of ready-mix concrete and concrete blocks; Simplex Paper Corporation, waterproof building paper and wrapping paper; Bemis Brothers Bag Company, special types of paper bags; and Textile Paper Products Company, paper cores. Each of these firms contributes to the total tonnage of freight which rolls over the AD & N rails.

The All Day & Night may be lacking in some respects when compared with the Illinois Central, but it is serving its purpose well and is making a profit. Like those of other shortline railroads in most sections of the country (except in the mountainous areas), the AD & N's rails rise and fall while following the earth's natural contours. No deep cuts, no high fills plague it with maintenance problems. The AD & N even fabricated its own reinforced concrete pipe to install for drainage structures instead of using wooden trestles. Untreated white-oak ties were used until the early 1940's, when it was discovered that a residue from the manufacture of charcoal was ideal for the preservation of wood, so the American Lumber Treatment Company is now treating railroad ties. The untreated ties resulted in crews frequently having to rerail cars or a locomotive. One unruly tank car was on the ground *seven times* in one 41-mile trip.

According to a retired conductor, there were a few non-aggravating incidents on the AD & N. A bulk gasoline distributor's plant lay on the line, and the spur track at its storage tank was not quite level. Train crews soon discovered that a tank car would not drain completely at that particular spot, so, after leaving the plant when picking up an "empty," a crew would spot the car on a level place and loosen the cap from the drain at the bottom of the car. Their reward was usually two No. 3 washtubs full of gasoline. Since there were no filling stations at Crossett, anyone who owned an automobile was a prime customer. Most individuals got their gasoline shipped in barrels in merchandise cars.

The AD & N was dieselized in 1948, and its present motive power consists of five diesel electrics. Two are 70-ton General Electric units—purchased new in October, 1948—equipped for multiple-unit operation. The other three are 124-ton, 1,200-

horsepower EMD units from General Motors. These were bought in June, 1952; December, 1955; and June, 1963. The AD & N also owns 210 cars, 120 of which are in interchange service; the others are used for local hauling of pulpwood and chips and inter-plant switching service. Since December, 1956, the road has maintained its own locomotives and other equipment in a fully equipped machine shop. The main line is predominantly laid with 90-pound rail on rock ballast. The Crossett yard has 65- to 85-pound rail.

With an operating ratio of 58.59 per cent in 1967, the All Day & Night racked up a handsome net profit of $322,853 and paid a dividend of $10.00 in 1965. Its future looks bright.

DARDANELLE & RUSSELLVILLE

7

One of the few success stories in the realm of shortline railroading in Arkansas is to be read in pages from the life story of the Dardanelle & Russellville Railroad, a five-mile freight-only independent pike in west-central Arkansas. Its rails do not enter the home terminal of Dardanelle, the road has never been in the hands of a receiver, and it still retains the same corporate name with one exception: the title was changed in January, 1900, from *Railway* to *Railroad.* It connects with the Missouri Pacific at Russellville, and trains have been running since the first engine whistled off in August, 1883.

The first house on the site of what was to become the town of Dardanelle was built about 1845. Soon a few newcomers moved in and erected homes near by. This nucleus was conveniently situated on the banks of the Arkansas River. The river was the only artery of transportation and commerce through the central portion of Arkansas from the capital city of Little Rock to Fort

Smith, the U.S. Army garrison established on the border between Arkansas and Indian Territory to the west. Situated about midway between these seats of civilization, the settlement of Dardanelle was the most obvious point along the river to develop as a port for the surrounding region. Wharfs were built at which steamboats plying the treacherous and unpredictable Arkansas docked to discharge cargoes of raw materials, hardware, household goods, and passengers. More homes were built as settlers moved in, and Dardanelle became a center of commerce.

As the number of settlers increased, the agricultural possibilities of the area began to draw attention. The delta region south and west of town was soon being cleared of timber. This rich alluvial deposit was found capable of producing great quantities of cotton, at that time the prime money crop. A fine stone wharf was built, and Dardanelle was well established as a riverboat town. By 1870, the rails of the Little Rock & Ft. Smith were penetrating the Arkansas River Valley on their way west. In 1873, they reached Russellville, across the river from Dardanelle and five miles north.

The Little Rock & Ft. Smith began to divert some of the freight traffic from the river. After all, its trains could operate when many a riverboat was stranded because there wasn't enough water in the Arkansas. Several of the small towns in the valley had perished when the rails bypassed them, and Dardanelle folks were afraid the same fate might befall them.

A ferry boat of sorts had been operating to transfer wagons loaded with cotton so that they could make the journey to Russellville and ship their cargo to market via the railroad. This permitted the precious bales to reach St. Louis or New Orleans when demand for cotton was greatest. Shippers could not depend upon the erratic schedules of the riverboats. They also discovered that the road from the river to Russellville would not support the enormous weight of the loaded cotton wagons. A better means of transportation was mandatory if the town were to survive.

The idea of bringing the railroad to the riverbank opposite Dardanelle was voiced by D. L. Bourland, James K. Perry, Thomas

Cox, G. L. Kimbal, Ed W. Cunningham, Z. J. Price, and C. M. Freed. There was sufficient response to their plan that the Dardanelle & Russellville Railway was granted a charter by the state on February 13, 1883, for the purpose of "transporting persons and property, and constructing a telegraph or telephone line along the road to transmit messages for private or public use." It was determined that capital stock of fifty thousand dollars would be sufficient to build and equip the five-mile pike.

After receiving its charter, the D & R lost no time in breaking ground. A young civil engineer, J. Burgess, who had been working for the Frisco, was engaged to survey the route. When this stage of progress had been reached and it was almost certain the road would be built, Captain Ed Shinn of Dardanelle boarded a riverboat and headed for Cincinnati. There he ordered construction of a transfer boat by which freight could be moved back and forth across the river from the town wharf to the railroad freight house. Moreover, the boat would be capable of transferring freight cars if the railroad decided to use this plan. There's nothing like being prepared.

The most prominent public figure guiding the destiny of the D & R was D. L. Bourland. He was not a railroad magnate, he was not a sharp speculator, neither was he a foreigner to the people in the area. He was a very lively, thoroughgoing, upright Christian gentleman whose home was up the river a few miles at Ozark. And he was the nephew of U.S. Senator Solon Bourland, whom Arkansas first elected in 1848. The young fellow had the reputation of being a very active salesman for a St. Louis firm, was faithful to the company's interests and ethical in all of his transactions, and by prudence and economy he had accumulated a little more than twenty-five thousand dollars in cash. Looking for a sensible venture in which to invest his money, he was keenly interested in the D & R.

When the corporate structure of the D & R was formed, Bourland was elected superintendent and general manager, with James

K. Perry as secretary. All legal technicalities were handled by attorney T. M. Gibson. E. L. Bourland, a brother of the superintendent, was awarded the contract to grade the right-of-way, furnish and place all crossties, and lay all rail. In addition, he had the contract to furnish one locomotive, one coach for passengers, and one baggage car, with the stipulation that the entire road be in operation by August 1, 1883. Freight cars would be leased from the Little Rock & Ft. Smith.

Simultaneously with the beginning of roadbed construction, a wooden cotton storage shed was built on the riverbank opposite Dardanelle, and Captain J. L. Shinn was retained to transfer all freight and passengers across the Arkansas. The depot was to be in Dardanelle, and all freight and passengers were to be delivered there.

On April 24, 1883, a subcontract was awarded to a Mr. Moore to grade the route. He put several crews to work grading up the roadbed at various sections instead of beginning at one terminal and working his way toward the other end. One mile of grading had been completed south from Russellville by mid-May, and a half-mile was finished in the other sections. Railroad officials promised an excursion run on July 4, terminating at the ferry landing at North Dardanelle. They had to renege, but even this failed to dampen the spirits of the folks at Dardanelle.

Making preparations for the day when its rails would be ready, the D & R purchased an 0-4-0 Porter and a single passenger coach and baggage combine in May. They were delivered and ready for service in the latter part of July.

The first tramps to travel the Dardanelle & Russellville were a party of three—J. H. Bell, Robert Toomer, and the editor of the *Dardanelle Post*. They walked the five miles of roadbed August 1 and found that about half of it had received ties and the rails were spiked in place. A full day of celebrating was scheduled for August 15. The little Porter mill, named *Petit Jean* in honor of the near-by mountain resort of the same name, and the wooden combine were shined to a high gloss and were ready to roll. Excursion trips were to be run to Russellville, and the ten-mile round trip could be made for only thirty cents.

August 15, 1883, was a typical lowland Arkansas day. The bright, brassy sun rose into a cloudless blue sky, its rays laden with penetrating heat. The people, not being spoiled by the comforts of air-conditioning, were out early in eager anticipation of the festivities. The crowd numbered almost five thousand in spite of the fact that the westbound Little Rock & Ft. Smith train was an hour and a half late and Captain Shinn's steam ferryboat chose that particular day to become contrary and prevent three hundred people from attending a fine barbecue feast. Twenty-six hundred pounds of beef, pork, and mutton were served with appropriate amounts of bread and vegetables. The brass bands from Dardanelle and Russellville seemed to play at their very best, and there were few minutes during the day when music could not be heard. The grounds were generously decorated with the usual conglomeration of swings, slides, flying jinnies, and bunting-draped stands dispensing lemonade, watermelon, and ice cream.

There was also the usual abundance of long-winded speeches, all of which were duly applauded. D. L. Bourland was one of the honored speakers, and in his discourse he made what proved to be a rather prophetic statement: "Whether this railroad makes money or loses money, it is here for good and it is a monument to the public spirit and enterprise of the men who built it."

(To clear up what has been a general misconception for many years, the Dardanelle & Russellville has *never* been a narrow-gauge pike. All of its business was interchanged at Russellville with the LR & FS, a standard-gauge road.)

Only one discordant note was sounded in connection with the inauguration of service on the D & R. It is to be found in an editorial which appeared in the *Arkansas Democrat* at Little Rock:

> The "lemonade fiend" cried his wares by the hour with no semblance of weariness and without a trace of pity for the nerves of

> his unfortunate and unwilling audience. I have always wondered why lightning from Heaven did not strike this fiend, or why the earth did not open and swallow him bodily. For the lemonade fiend who yells at the top of his voice and never ceases to yell, I have nothing but the bitterest and most withering maledictions.

To keep himself in the good graces of the people, the writer concluded by saying that the day marked a new era in the life of Dardanelle and that if her live men would push things, build more manufacturing establishments, and reach out for more railroads, a most marvelous growth would be the result.

By early September, the dinkey was making three round trips a day, affording very favorable connections with the Little Rock & Ft. Smith for Little Rock or Fort Smith. When freight from Russellville was shipped overland by wagon, the incoming rates were fifteen to eighteen cents per hundredweight higher than the rates to Russellville; after the D & R went into operation, rates were only *three cents* higher. Thus the people began to receive tangible benefits immediately from their Lilliputian railroad. The traveling public noticed advantages, too. It now was a matter of only twenty minutes from the time conductor E. L. Bourland cried his "all aboard" until passengers were stepping down at the depot in Russellville. The Little Rock & Ft. Smith train covered the seventy-five miles to Little Rock in just five hours.

Aggravations began to crop up. The Arkansas River's level began to drop, the water's edge receding from the bank on the town side. When passengers were transferred across the river, they had to wade a muddy slough from the deck of the ferry to the riverbank. Also, the old ferryboat was plagued by frequent breakdowns, leaving its passengers stranded. Sometimes they were as much as three hours getting from Russellville to Dardanelle. Now all of this provoked the editor of the *Dardanelle Post* to refer to the D & R as the Dardanelle & Russellville "mud, sand, river and rail road."

As the old adage has proclaimed, it is darkest just before the dawn. When it seemed that the old steam ferry would collapse before she could cross the river one more time, the new ferry Captain Shinn had ordered finally arrived. A proud and beautiful craft, she was immediately christened the *Martha* when she steamed in on October 3, 1883.

The *Martha* was 120 feet long, with a beam of 30.5 feet and a hull four feet deep. The United States government had rated her capacity at 147.81 tons. Her hull was constructed of the best oak timbers available, all bolted 3 inches by 6 inches, and she was powered by two poppet-valve engines having cylinders with 12-inch diameter and 48-inch stroke. Her twin paddle wheels were 15 feet in diameter and had buckets 7 feet, 1 inch long by 2 feet wide. Steam was furnished by two steel boilers 22 feet long and 38 inches in diameter, each having two 14-inch return flues. On deck was a large fire pump equipped with 100 feet of hose. The *Martha* was built at Marysville on the Ohio River under the personal supervision of engineer Rickard and Captain Shinn and had cost the grand sum of ten thousand dollars.

In the depot at Dardanelle, Joe Cox was passenger agent and W. B. Lemoyne had charge of all freight shipments. The railroad also had a horse-drawn omnibus which picked up passengers around town and transported them to the train for a fare of twenty-five cents. The ticket to Russellville cost the traveler another fifty cents.

The *Martha* was eventually replaced by a very handsome double-decked stern-wheeler named *Elva,* which served the railroad faithfully for several years. Finally, the idea of ferry transportation began to lose favor, and there was heard talk about building a bridge. After some investigation, it was ascertained that the cost was prohibitive. However, railroad officials came up with an idea which evolved into a noteworthy enterprise: a pontoon bridge. When the river stage was at normal elevation, the bridge would float on the surface; when the water dropped to the aggravating level, the bridge would rest on the exposed riverbed and would at least give the traveling public access to both banks of the Arkansas.

A contract for the bridge was negotiated with the South McAlister Fuel Company in 1890, and construction began in October of the same year. To span the Arkansas from bank to bank would require a structure approximately 2,300 feet in length. Upon 72 pontoons (wooden boats) were to rest 13 sections of wooden deck, with handrails, having an 18-foot clear roadway. The various sections were built and stored on the riverbank at Dardanelle. The steam ferry *Elva* struggled through another winter, but her days of service were numbered. With the coming of spring, the ferry maneuvered a pile driver out across the river, and upstream from where the bridge was to be, five large log cribs were anchored into the riverbed. The thirteen sections of the bridge were towed into position, fastened end to end, and anchored to the cribs with heavy wire cables. When this structure was secured to the opposite banks of the Arkansas, it was the longest pontoon bridge in the world and possibly the only one ever owned by a railroad.

Captain Richard Keilch was placed in charge of the floating bridge, since passage across it was subject to a toll. A man on horseback could cross for fifteen cents, but for a wagon, the toll was thirty-five cents. A man on foot could cross for a dime. In those days, many traveled on shanks' mare, with no possessions except the threadbare clothes they wore. These unfortunate persons were allowed to pass without charge. When automobiles began to appear, the one-seaters were charged fifty cents, while the fancy two-seaters paid seventy-five cents for the privilege of crossing.

Much sentimentality was associated with the bridge. It was a favored spot with young people in their courting days. Its length provided ample space for privacy, and just above the water's surface was the coolest place in the neighborhood. In the lazy days of summer when there were no school sessions to make life miserable, many a barefoot, jean-clad boy fished for bullheads from the ends of the pontoon boats, or learned to swim in the river shallows when sandbars formed near the pontoons. Patriotic men traversed the dipping and swaying deck on their way to three wars in defense of their country, and many of them crossed it in caskets on their final trip home.

Cotton from the fields of a half-dozen counties crossed the bridge on the way to the distant markets of the world. Many times it was torn asunder when the Arkansas raged in an unexpected flood during the night. Long sections of it would be rebuilt and traffic resumed. If there were ample warning, the sections were disconnected and towed to the riverbank, where they were anchored securely to ride out the flood.

For thirty-eight long years, Captain Keilch endured the hardships of caring for his bridge. He repeatedly gathered its broken sections, supplemented them with new ones, and resumed operations. Progress finally defeated him. On November 18, 1927, the Arkansas Highway Department signed a contract with the Lakeside Bridge & Steel Company for construction of a permanent steel and concrete bridge, which was opened to traffic in January, 1929. The pontoons and deck timbers from the old bridge were salvaged and sold.

Extensive deposits of coal underlay the area north from the rail terminal at Dardanelle toward Russellville, and their development furnished a generous slice of revenue to the D & R. They were mined by the Southern Anthracite Coal Company, later named Bernice Coal Company in honor of Mrs. Victor Lelaurin. During World War I, the mines operated at full capacity, thereby generating much passenger traffic. A small settlement sprang up, and the railroad established a station at Bernice where miners could wait comfortably for the train. A round trip was made each morning and evening.

In the early days of the D & R, there was a small settlement, known as Norristown, on the riverbank a short distance upriver from Dardanelle. Here resided Mrs. Sam Norris, known to everyone as Grandma Norris. One day she was preparing to step off the four miles into Russellville and came by the spot where conductor Pete Rice was preparing for the run to town. He invited Grandma aboard for a free ride. She gave the little engine and its combine an amusing glance. "Thanks, Pete, but I'm in a hurry. I'll just walk on."

One of the early D & R engineers was rolling toward Russellville for a noon meeting with a southbound Little Rock & Ft. Smith varnish run. Gazing drowsily ahead from the cab window, he saw a sheet of newspaper fluttering about between the rails. As the train drew closer, he noticed that the newspaper's behavior was rather peculiar. Giving it his full attention, he discovered that it wasn't a newspaper, but a baby, toddling and crawling along. With brakes only on the engine, the hogger knew he could never stop in time, so he frantically scrambled out through the cab window, made his way down the footboard along the boiler, and climbed down onto the pilot. Hanging precariously from his insecure perch, he leaned out and down, snatching the little toddler from between the rails. None of the several accounts of the incident reports the names of the baby and engineer.

The earliest D & R engine about which there is any information is No. 7, a Porter 0-4-4 T built as No. 1689 about 1883. The greatest popularity must go to 4-4-0 No. 8 (Cooke No. 1861), built in 1888 for the Ft. Worth & Denver City. She was unofficially put on retirement status by the D & R when she was run onto a spur in 1933. Here she sat for five years, gathering rust and dust while the weeds climbed higher and higher about her drivers. One hot summer day in August, 1938, a man named Henry King approached D & R officials. He was a motion-picture director for Twentieth Century-Fox Studio in Hollywood. Would the Dardanelle & Russellville be interested in leasing old No. 8 and two wooden coaches to be used in a movie, *Jessie James*? It certainly would!

The picture was to be filmed in the rugged, beautiful Ozark Mountains near Noel and Pineville, Missouri, under the general direction of Sidney Bowen, financial unit manager, and George Dudley, art director. The role of Jesse James was played superbly by Tyrone Power. Henry Fonda was cast as Jesse's brother, Frank, while Arleen Whelan portrayed Jesse's wife, Zee. The movie, filmed in Technicolor, was released January 19, 1939.

No. 8 had run for quite a few years on the St. Louis, Iron Mountain & Southern. When only ten years old, she pulled the first trainload of soldiers from Arkansas on their way to the Spanish-American War. When the movie scout asked whether the Missouri Pacific shop force could put her in good running condition, he was told that it most certainly could, so she rolled into the shops at North Little Rock, where she was dismantled and rebuilt for about two thousand dollars. Her boiler was repaired, a new smokebox was installed, and a new crown sheet was put in. Flues and side sheets of the firebox were renewed. Finally, the old girl got new boiler lagging and jacket. A dummy diamond stack was anchored around her tall bootleg stack. A large phony oil-burning headlight was installed atop the smokebox, leaving her with the small electric lamp and reflector as well as a steam dynamo. She was given a coat of bright olive-green paint and gold trim, which reflected the blazing Arkansas sun when she rolled out of the shop on August 31, 1938. Across the upper edge of the tender had been lettered "St. Louis Midland R. R."

No. 8 was proudly wheeled to Van Buren by Missouri Pacific hogger A. C. "Charlie" Keese, fireman S. E. Orr, and master mechanic Hanna. After the movie had been completed, the old eight-spot and two wooden passenger coaches were purchased by the studio. They later appeared in *Centennial Summer*, *Sentimental Journey*, and *Walls of Jericho*.

Taking her place was Mogul No. 9, just one year younger than the pike on which she was running, being outshopped in 1884 by Baldwin as No. 7469 for the New Orleans & North Eastern as its No. 235. A plate on her boiler states she was rebuilt by the NO & NE in 1904 at its shop in Meridian, Mississippi. In July, 1917, she came to the D & R by way of Birmingham Rail & Locomotive Company for $7,100. No. 9 was retired in 1955 when the first diesel appeared on the roster. Then in 1957, the 73-year-old Mogul was recalled to service. Uncle Sam was going to overhaul the Arkansas River and make it suitable for navigation again.

A multi-million-dollar concrete dam was to be constructed a

short distance upstream from Dardanelle, and large quantities of materials would be required. The old Mogul was overhauled, her boiler was painted a brilliant green, a red number plate adorned her smokebox, and her running gear received a silver trim. A slotted sheet-steel pilot and a new steel cab spruced up her appearance. She was ready to roll again.

When the heaviest traffic was over and additional diesels had come in, the kind hand of fate beckoned for the nine-spot: she was sold to the Mid-Continent Railway Museum at North Freedom, Wisconsin. She served the 1964 season of rail fan tourists as she steamed merrily along, her tall stack barking sharp and clear.

Mogul No. 10 had the reputation of being the most powerful engine on the road. She had a low, slope-backed tender which gave the hogger a clear view of the track when she made the return trip from Russellville running backward. She was built in 1907 for the Isthmian Canal Commission and served two years during the early construction days of the Big Ditch. She came to the D & R in 1921 at a cost of $13,500 and was given the number 10 and the nickname *Panama Mogul.*

Old No. 10 served the D & R steadily for thirty-four years. She was left standing on a spur track in 1955—replaced by a diesel—where she attracted the interest of the Civitan Club at Shreveport, Louisiana, in 1956. A fund was begun to purchase the old Mogul and rescue her from the ignominy of the scrap heap. The club bought her in 1956, and she was taken to Shreveport and enshrined in Ford Park, a tangible reminder of America's hey day of railroading.

There was a No. 11, but no information about her seems to be available.

The bugaboo of railroading—the family automobile—appeared, and it was only a matter of time until no passenger service was available on the D & R. It was listed in the official guide as "freight only." Still, the coal mines disgorged sufficient "black diamonds" to keep the five-miler solvent. Then these gave way, but revenue-producing Arkansas Valley Industries established a bulk-feed mill just across the highway from the rail terminal at North Dardanelle. Several carloads of grain are trundled in each day from the Missouri Pacific interchange at Russellville.

Came May 11, 1955, when a new engine appeared. No. 12 was sporting two Cummins diesel engines which turned an electric generator. For fifty thousand dollars, the D & R showed it had faith in the future prosperity of the area it served. No. 12 was a General Electric job, No. 32337, weighing forty-five tons and exerting a tractive force of twenty-seven thousand pounds. The cost of operating the diesel for several days was less than the expense of raising a head of steam in Mogul No. 9 just sufficient to move her. Steam was doomed on the D & R.

Internal combustion provides power for moving freight to and from Keenan Grain Company, as well as the Osburn Grain Elevator, and frozen poultry from the plant of Arkansas Valley Industries. A liquid petroleum company, a rendering plant, and a sand and gravel company contributed to the D & R's $10,559 net income for 1967. The Dardanelle & Russellville is alive and kicking.

PLATE 1. The Augusta Tramway & Transfer ex-elevated railway triple-domed 0–4–2 "T" Forney No. 2 sits proudly at Augusta in 1903, sporting a home-made footboard as wide as a tabletop and leading the only varnish car of the AT &T road. (*Courtesy R. H. Carlson*)

PLATE 2. The Augusta Railroad 2–6–0 No. 300 at the park in Paragould, Arkansas. (*Courtesy William J. Husa, Jr.*)

Plate 3. The Hot Springs Railroad (the Diamond Jo Line) 2–4–0 No. 2 sits beside the depot at Hot Springs in 1877. The hogger has just finished oiling. No. 2 was built by H. K. Porter & Company, Pittsburgh, Pennsylvania, in 1875, as No. 227 and was named the *Diamond Jo*. It was sold to the Missouri Southern in 1889.
(*Author's collection*)

PLATE 4. On a fine spring day in 1893, the Hot Springs Railroad Baldwin Mogul 2–6–0 No. 3 paused at the beautiful mansard-roofed depot at Hot Springs. The proud crew, including the conductor, Walter Beauchamp (far left), and the eagle eye, McMillan (at the cab window) paused for a photograph. Beyond No. 3's pilot are two of the numerous wagons, hacks, and buckboards that frequented the depot at train time. (*Author's collection*)

PLATE 5. A contemporary issue of *Leslie's Illustrated Weekly* depicted this scene at the Malvern depot. The lithograph shows persons suffering from various infirmities who are being transferred from the cars of the St. Louis, Iron Mountain & Southern to those of the narrow-gauge Hot Springs Railroad. (*Author's collection*)

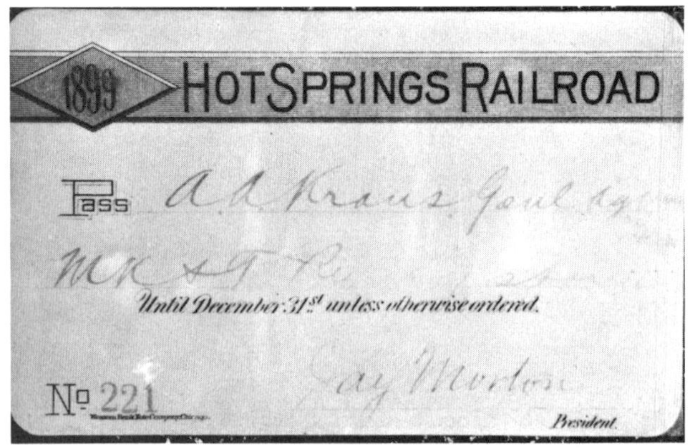

1899 HOT SPRINGS RAILROAD

Pass

Until December 31st unless otherwise ordered.

No 221

President.

PLATE 6. An 1899 Hot Springs Railroad pass. Many annual passes were issued by the 25-mile line to officials and employees of other roads. (*Author's collection*)

PLATE 7. The Missouri & North Arkansas 4–4–0 No. 16, a regal beauty with a capped stack and extended wagon top boiler. After No. 16 was scrapped in 1936, the boiler was used to furnish steam for the Silica Sand Company at Everton, Arkansas. (*Courtesy H. L. Broadbelt*)

PLATE 8. Missouri & North Arkansas Consolidation 2–8–0 No. 12 at Baldwin Locomotive Works in 1907. (*Courtesy H. L. Broadbelt*)

PLATE 9. Missouri & North Arkansas 2-8-2 Mikado No. 36 with her distinctive Vanderbilt tender, as she looked new at the Baldwin Locomotive Works in April, 1914. (*Courtesy H. L. Broadbelt*)

PLATE 10. Missouri & North Arkansas 2-8-2 Mikado No. 21 at the Baldwin works in November, 1912. About 1914 she was renumbered 32. (*Courtesy H. L. Broadbelt*)

PLATE 11. Missouri & North Arkansas 4–6–0 No. 20. In 1949 she became the Arkansas & Ozarks No. 20. (*Courtesy H. L. Broadbelt*)

PLATE 12. Missouri & Arkansas freight train No. 212, pulled by 2–8–2 No. 52, awaiting highball from the Harrison Yards, December 28, 1940. (*Courtesy E. G. Baker, National Railway Historical Society*)

PLATE 13. Missouri & Arkansas southbound freight, pulled by 2–8–2 No. 54 and 2–8–2 No. 55, near Harrison, February 8, 1942. (*Courtesy E. G. Baker, National Railway Historical Society*)

LATE 14. Missouri & Arkansas northbound passenger train No. 202, pulled by 4–6–0 No. 18, near Harrison, Arkansas, December 27, 1940. (*Courtesy E. G. Baker, National Railway Historical Society*)

Plate 15. Missouri & Arkansas 4-4-0 No. 17. (*Courtesy Charles E. Winters*)

Plate 16. Missouri & Arkansas motorcar No. 705, the *John E. Martineau,* running as train No. 1, its rock-battered pilot betraying a continued lack of maintenance, rolls into Eureka Springs a few days before the fatal strike in September, 1946. (*Author's collection*)

PLATE 17. This 1940 Buick traveled many miles as the official vehicle for the Missouri & Arkansas. (*Courtesy Witbeck Studio, Hammond, Louisiana*)

PLATE 18. The Yazoo & Mississippi Valley 4-4-0 No. 1901 with extra varnish run at Beulah, Mississippi, in 1898. This little engine met many Missouri & Arkansas trains at Helena, Arkansas. (*Author's collection*)

PLATE 19. Dardanelle, Ola & Southern 4–6–0 No. 2 at Dardanelle about 1907. She was built by Rome Locomotive Works as No. 260 in 1887 for Western New York & Pennsylvania as their No. 72. They renumbered her 116, and when the WNY & P was taken over by the Pennsylvania Railroad, she was renumbered 6252. Later she was sold to the St. Louis, Indianapolis & Eastern as their No. 579. In 1907 she came to the DO & S. (*Author's collection. Original photograph by C. W. Witbeck*)

PLATE 20. Crossett Lumber Company 2–8–2 Mikado No. 12 at the mill in Crossett, Arkansas. Note the unusual pilot coupler (two-level link-and-pin), as well as the slotted knuckle of an automatic coupler. The dented cylinder casing and damaged pilot footboards indicate some extremely close clearances. (*Author's collection*)

PLATE 21. Crossett Lumber Company 2–8–2 Mikado No. 12 emerging from the dense forest, pulling a typical log train to the mill in Crossett. (Author's collection.)

PLATE 22. The well-kept Crossett Lumber Company 2–8–0 Consolidation No. 15 with a full head of steam and white flags flying for a run as an extra. (*Courtesy Witbeck Studio, Hammond, Louisiana*)

PLATE 23. A turn-of-the-century yard scene at the Crossett Lumber Company, showing an interesting array of motive power and steam log loaders. The engine in the foreground is a Shay No. 4. (*Author's collection*)

.ATE 24. Crossett Lumber Company log loader No. 3 in operation. The steam g loader was a great improvement over the anchored chain and ox team or obstin-atc long-eared Missouri mules. (*Author's collection*)

.ATE 25. Crossett Lumber Company timberjacks, about 1905. The man on the ar platform of the flat-roofed crummy appears to be rolling a Bull Durham quirly—or perhaps he is simply camera-shy. (*Author's collection*)

PLATE 26. Crossett Lumber Company 2–8–0 Consolidation No. 10, shown new at the works. This little low-drivered locomotive wheeled many trainloads of logs from the forests of southern Arkansas to the Crossett mills. (*Courtesy H. L. Broadbelt*)

PLATE 28. Ashley, Drew & Northern 2–8–0 No. 125, photographed in Crossett, Arkansas, April, 1949. (*Collection of William J. Husa, Jr.*)

PLATE 29. Ashley, Drew & Northern 2–8–0 Consolidation No. 135. No. 52234 from Baldwin in August, 1914, she was ex-Louisiana Railway & Navigation Company No. 98 and ex-Louisiana & Arkansas No. 98. (*Courtesy Charles E. Winters*)

15

31

60

PLATE 33. Dardanelle & Russellville 0–4–4 "T" No. 7, waiting at North Dardanelle with a trainload of cotton. (*Author's collection*)

ATE 30 (top, opposite). Arkansas & Louisiana Missouri 4–6–0 No. 15; ex-Texas Mexican No. 15. (*Collection of Harold K. Vollrath*)

ATE 31 (middle, opposite). Arkansas & Louisiana Mis-ıri 4–6–0 No. 31; ex-Cisco & North Eastern No. 31. (*Collection of Harold K. Vollrath*)

ATE 32. (bottom, opposite). Arkansas & Louisiana Mis-ıri 2–6–0 No. 60; ex-Union Sawmill No. 60, photographed in Monroe, Louisiana, in 1934. (*Collection of Harold K. Vollrath*)

PLATE 34. Dardanelle & Russellville 4–4–0 American Standard No. 8 at the engine house at North Dardanelle, Arkansas, about 1928. She was built by Cooke Locomotive Works in 1888 for the Ft. Worth & Denver City and was retired to the weed-grown spur in 1933. She was rescued in 1938 and leased to Twentieth Century-Fox Studio for a movie about Jesse James (see Plate 35). (*Author's collection*)

Plate 35. When the Dardanelle & Russellville No. 8 was leased to Twentieth Century-Fox Studio for use in the movie *The Return of Jesse James,* she was sent to the Missouri Pacific shops at North Little Rock for overhaul and camouflage. A few days later she posed outside the shops for the picture above. She had acquired a new name (*St. Louis Midland*), a new coat of paint, and a fake square "oilburner" headlight (with an electric bulb inside, powered by a "square" dynamo just behind the sand dome). A fake sheet-metal diamond hood had been anchored around her straight stack. (*Author's collection*)

Plate 36. The Dardanelle & Russellville No. 8 in Hollywood. With her movie makeup on she is hardly recognizable. (*Author's collection*)

Plate 37. Dardanelle & Russellville 2–6–0 Mogul No. 9 after being rebuilt at the Missouri Pacific shops in North Little Rock. She had a new pilot and headlight, and the cab was from the D & R No. 11.
(*Author's collection*)

Plate 38. Dardanelle & Russellville No. 9, a classic example of the Mogul locomotive, rests beside the D & R water tank in the summer of 1963.
(*Photograph by author*)

LATE 39. Cab interior of the Dardanelle & Russellville No. 9. Her cab as relatively simple compared to the cabs of her sister steam hogs of the Missouri Pacific. Most conspicuous was the Armstrong reverse, or Johnson bar. rying to "hook 'er up" a couple of notches when the engine was in motion ould produce a reaction similar to the kick of the crank on a Model "T" Ford. (*Photograph by author*)

PLATE 40. Tallowpot's view from the cab of the Dardanelle & Russellville No. 9. (*Photograph by author*)

PLATE 41. Dardanelle & Russellville 2-6-0 Mogul No. 10 beside the coal chute. This little Mogul was built in 1907 for the Isthmian Canal Commission and served in the construction of the Panama Canal. She was sold to the D & R in 1921 for $13,500. (*Author's collection*)

PLATE 42. Dardanelle & Russellville No. 10, the "Panama Mogul." In 1956 the Civitan Club of Shreveport, Louisiana, acquired her and placed her on permanent display in Shreveport's Ford Park, where she is shown in this photograph. (*Author's collection*)

Plate 43. Dardanelle & Russellville 2–6–0 Mogul No. 11 with wood combine No. 4 at Dardanelle, June 18, 1946. She was built by Schenectady Locomotive Works as No. 25088 in September, 1901, and was ex-Katy Nos. 444, 402, 931, and 1205. Subsequently she was sold to Rockdale, Sandow & Southern and then to D & R. She was scrapped at North Dardanelle in 1955. (*Author's collection*)

Plate 44. Dardanelle & Russellville stern-wheel steam ferry *Elva,* which transferred passengers and freight from the terminus of the rails on the north bank of the Arkansas River to Dardanelle on the opposite bank. (*Courtesy Dardanelle & Russellville Railroad*)

PLATE 45. Dardanelle & Russellville steam ferry *Elva* and her freight barge at Dardanelle about 1885. The captain was Richard Keilch. Later a pontoon bridge was built across the Arkansas River at this location (see Plate 46), after which the contractor bought the *Elva* and took her to Kansas City. (*Courtesy Dardanelle & Russellville Railroad*)

PLATE 46. Dardanelle & Russellville pontoon bridge across the Arkansas River from the railroad terminus to Dardanelle. It was the longest pontoon bridge in the world—a little more than 2,300 feet long. The bossy (0-4-0 "T") crossed the bridge in 1906. (*Author's collection*)

PLATE 47. Dardanelle & Russellville wood combine No. 12. This combine was a jewel of the car builder's art. It was paneled in solid walnut, oiled, and hand-polished. It had three sections—two for passengers and one for mail, express, and baggage. (*Author's collection*)

PLATE 48. William Hope "Coin" Harvey, builder of the Monte Ne Railway. (*Courtesy Don Goforth, editor,* Rogers Daily News)

PLATE 49. A 1905 Monte Ne Railway pass. (*Author's collection*)

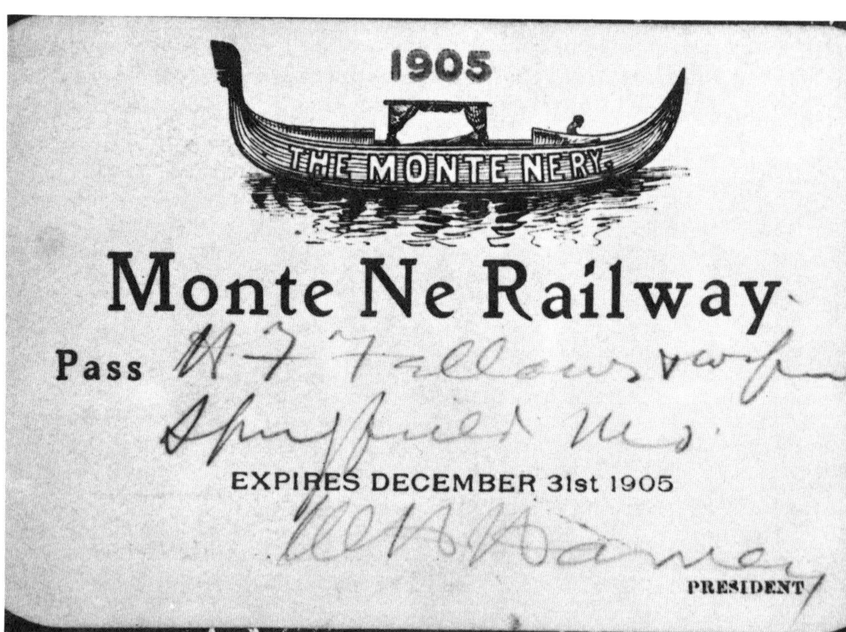

PLATE 50. With concrete and stone "Coin" Harvey created this series of terraced seats and stairways at Big Springs in Monte Ne, Arkansas. Here fine plays were to be presented out of doors for the diversion of the distinguished guests of Oklahoma Row, the Hotel Monte Ne, and the numerous cottages. (*Author's collection*)

PLATE 51. The Hotel Monte Ne. Hotel guests were taken to the depot of the Monte Ne Railway in gasoline-powered canopied launches like the one shown in the photograph. (*Courtesy Don Goforth, editor,* Rogers Daily News)

Plate 52. Kansas City & Memphis 4-6-0 No. 7, acquired new from Baldwin in 1913. The apple emblem prominently displayed on the Vanderbilt tender proclaimed the "Fruit Belt Line" across northwestern Arkansas. This No. 7 later became the Midland Valley No. 7 and later still the Missouri & North Arkansas No. 21. (*Courtesy H. L. Broadbelt*)

Plate 53. Kansas City Southern 4-4-0 No. 101, built by Baldwin in 1897 and shown here in 1900 at Ft. Smith, Arkansas. (*Author's collection*)

PLATE 54. Kansas City, Pittsburg & Gulf 4-4-0 No. 1. This beautiful piece of machinery, photographed at the Baldwin plant in all its gleaming splendor, was to conduct many a trainload of excursionists over the Kansas City, Pittsburg & Gulf for exchange with the Arkansas, Oklahoma & Western at Siloam Springs, Arkansas. (*Courtesy H. L. Broadbelt*)

Plate 55. Memphis, Paris & Gulf 4–6–0 No. 1 about 1906 (later Memphis, Dallas & Gulf No. 201). Note the unballasted track and gaps in ties. (*Courtesy Joe Wilson*)

PLATE 56. Memphis, Paris & Gulf pile driver and crew setting piling for the railroad bridge at Dillard Creek, one-half mile north of Mineral Springs, Arkansas, about 1906. Joe Wilson, the assistant engineer, is standing behind the 22-inch Gurley level. (*Courtesy Joe Wilson*)

PLATE 57. Memphis, Paris & Gulf inspection train and passengers after completion of road to Ashdown, Arkansas, in 1908. W. W. Wilson, a special agent, is ninth from the right. (*Courtesy Joe Wilson, son of W. W. Wilson*)

LATE 58. Memphis, Paris & Gulf 2–8–0 Consolidation No. 8, shown at the South-rn Iron & Equipment Company, from whom the MP & G bought her in 1909. This hort-legged locomotive was built by Baldwin as No. 11993 in June, 1891, with 19-y 26-inch cylinders. Ex-Pennsylvania Railroad No. 6297, ex-Western New York & Pennsylvania No. 171. (*Photograph by C. W. Witbeck*)

LATE 59. Antoine Valley 4–6–0 No. 1. This lovely Baldwin ten-wheeler carried ne prestige of number 1 on the little Antoine Valley. She pulled many a trainload f logs between Graysonia, on the Gurdon & Ft. Smith, and Arkadelphia, on the St. Louis, Iron Mountain & Southern, in the early years of the twentieth century. (*Courtesy Earl Saunders, Jr.*)

PLATE 60. Antoine Valley No. 1 pausing near the Arkadelphia Lumber Company mill to have her rare beauty preserved by some unknown photographer in the early 1900's. Her deep firebox dropped just ahead of the rear drivers and barely cleared the crossties. The Antoine Valley Railroad was purchased by the Memphis, Dallas & Gulf in 1910. (*Courtesy Earl Saunders, Jr.*)

PLATE 61. Antoine Valley 4-4-0 American Standard No. 5. This aristocratic engine proudly displayed a shotgun stack, steam jam brakes, and a clerestory cab roof. Those arch-bar trucks on her tender look

Plate 62. Caddo & Choctaw 2–6–2 Prairie No. 2, photographed at Baldwin Locomotive Works. Note the backup lamp on the top of the cab. (*Courtesy H. L. Broadbelt*)

Plate 63. Caddo & Choctaw 2–6–2 Prairie No. 8. (*Courtesy H. L. Broadbelt*)

PLATE 64. Caddo & Choctaw 2–6–2 Prairie No. 9 at Baldwin plant in Philadelphia, ready to roll toward the Arkansas forests. (*Courtesy H. L. Broadbelt*)

PLATE 65. Caddo & Choctaw 2–8–2 Mikado No. 10. This little locomotive rode the logging rails of the Caddo Lumber Company west from Roseboro, Arkansas, until the Caddo & Choctaw was purchased

PLATE 66. Graysonia, Nashville & Ashdown 2–6–0 No. 26, photographed at Nashville, Arkansas, June 30, 1940. (*Courtesy John B. Fink Collection, Division of Manuscripts, University of Oklahoma*)

PLATE 67. Graysonia, Nashville & Ashdown 2–6–0 No. 26, photographed at Ashdown, Arkansas, January 22, 1943. She later went to the Nebraska-Kansas Museum road, and then to Wilson Carlgren, of Concordia, Kansas. (*Courtesy Charles E. Winters*)

Plate 68. Graysonia, Nashville & Ashdown 4-6-0 No. 45, photographed at Nashville, Arkansas, July 3, 1951. She was built by Brooks as No. 3805 in April, 1901, and was originally St. Louis, Iron Mountain & Southern No. 1725, Missouri Pacific No. 2331. Note the dents in her cylinder casing. She was scrapped at Federal, Illinois, in 1955. (*Courtesy Charles E. Winters*)

Plate 69. Graysonia, Nashville & Ashdown 4-6-0 No. 2630 pulling the first trainload (125 cars) of cement from the Okay, Arkansas, plant, on October 2, 1929. (*Courtesy Ideal Cement Company*)

PLATE 70. Remodeled Graysonia, Nashville & Ashdown depot at Nashville, Arkansas, June 30, 1940. The old roof had been removed and the building remodeled for use as a station and general office. (*Courtesy John B. Fink Collection, Division of Manuscripts, University of Oklahoma*)

PLATE 71. Murfreesboro & Nashville 4-6-0 No. 6, ex-Missouri Pacific 2600 series. (*Courtesy Charles E. Winters*)

PLATE 72. Murfreesboro & Nashville 2–6–0 No. 7, photographed at Murfree
boro, Arkansas, October 21, 1952; built by Baldwin as No. 52233 in May, 192
(*Courtesy Charles E. Winters*)

PLATE 73. San Augustine County Lumber Company 2–6–2 Prairie No. 108 (later Reader No. 108). This handsome little "Prairie Schooner" left the Baldwin shops on February 11, 1920, with the shop number 52820 and went to the San Augustine County Lumber Company, where she stayed until purchased by the Reader in 1956. She has borne road number 108 all her life. In this photograph, made at the Baldwin plant, the spelling on the tender is incorrect. (*Courtesy H. L. Broadbelt*)

PLATE 74. Reader 2–6–2 Prairie No. 11 in the engine house at Reader, Arkansas. She was completed as Baldwin No. 58194 on February 2, 1925, for the Caddo Lumber Company, owners of the Caddo & Choctaw. She came to the Reader in the 1940's. Here Chief Mechanical Officer Kim Bryne and his crew are overhauling her innards. (*Photograph by author*)

Plate 75. Reader 2–6–2 No. 11, photographed in August, 1963, at Reader. With her "pops" spewing and a white feather showing at her cylinder cock, she waits for a rail-fan group to climb aboard the parlor car *Rambler* and the crimson ex-Cotton Belt crummy. (*Photograph by author*)

Plate 76. Reader 2–6–0 No. 403, photographed at Reader in 1937; ex-Cotton Belt. She was scrapped at Reader. (*Courtesy Charles E. Winters*)

PLATE 77. Reader 2–8–0 No. 1702, photographed at Reader on April 1, 1966; ex-Warren & Saline River (Bradley Lumber Company, Warren, Arkansas); originally U.S. Army No. 1702. Built at Baldwin Locomotive Works as No. 64641 in September, 1942, she came to Reader in June, 1964. (*Courtesy Charles E. Winters*)

PLATE 78. Reader 4–6–0 No. 12, photographed in Reader in 1951; ex-Texas Mexican No. 12. (*Courtesy Charles E. Winters*)

PLATE 79. Reader 4-6-0 No. 17, photographed at Reader in 1937; ex-Arkansas Lumber Company, Warren, Arkansas. She was sold to Meriwether Gravel Company. (*Courtesy Charles E. Winters*)

PLATE 80. Reader 2-6-2 Prairie No. 108, photographed after a summer shower in August, 1963. She was built by Baldwin as No. 52820 on February 11, 1920, for the San Augustine Lumber Company, owners of the Angelina & Neches River Railroad. The Reader bought her in 1945. She has carried No. 108 since she left Baldwin. Here she is setting the crummy out near the depot before switching the Missouri Pacific interchange track. (*Photograph by author*)

PLATE 81. Reader 2–6–2 Prairie No. 108. Brakie Sykes rides the rear footboard while bringing the little Prairie from the engine house to the interchange track. (*Photograph by author*)

PLATE 82. Reader 2–6–2 No. 108 and 2–6–2 No. 11, photographed at t engine house in 1966. The two locomotives comprised two-thirds of the Reade motive power. (*Photograph by author*)

Plate 83. Reader combine No. 501. When Mr. Tom decided to put his Reader road into passenger service, the hunt was on for suitable equipment. The Milwaukee had for sale a surplus combine, designed for mixed train service, which was purchased by the Reader in 1962. She was 59 feet 8½ inches long and weighed 56,000 pounds. (*Photograph by author*)

Plate 84. Reader *Rambler* No. 500. In 1962, to supplement the combine in passenger service, Mr. Tom purchased the parlor-lounge car shown here. She was built by Pullman in 1927 for the New Haven and named *Taunton*. In 1937 she was rebuilt and assigned to the Wabash and renamed *Rambler*. In 1953 she went to the KCS, and was numbered 500. (*Photograph by author*)

PLATE 85. Reader steam derrick. This steam-powered A-frame derrick d[illegible] many heavy jobs on the Reader before it was replaced by a "big hook." (*Photograph by author*)

Plate 86. The author prepares to enter the Reader's crimson crummy at Reader, Arkansas, July, 1966. (*Author's collection*)

PLATE 87. The Reader "big hook" is not called upon very often. Here she is on stand-by alert at the engine house. (*Photograph by author*)

PLATE 88. Little Rock, Maumelle & Western diamond stack No. 50, photographed about 1904. With his hat at a jaunty angle, hogger Reece Jones is holding up the pilot on the right. His diamond-stacked little hog is pulling an American log loader at the Neimeyer lumber camp.
(*Courtesy Harold Jones*)

PLATE 89. Little Rock, Maumelle & Western 4-6-0 No. 101. This short-legged little ten-wheeler came from Baldwin to the Neimeyer road in 1907. She hauled log trains from Saline and Perry counties to the Neimeyer Lumber Company mill in southwestern Little Rock.
(*Courtesy H. L. Broadbelt*)

Plate 90. Malvern & Freeo Valley 2–6–0 Mogul No. 16. The Malvern & Freeo Valley, the Wisconsin-Arkansas Lumber Company's railroad, indirectly caused the Neimeyer Lumber Company to build the Little Rock, Maumelle & Western. The Wisconsin-Arkansas built the M & FV, cutting off Neimeyer from access to timber he planned to buy. (*Author's collection*)

Plate 91. Ozan-Graysonia Lumber Company No. 3, photographed in the late 1920's. Previously, her furiously barking stack talk was heard on the Neimeyer road, the Little Rock, Maumelle & Western. (*Courtesy Dr. Fred Henker*)

PLATE 92. Arkansas Central 4–6–0 No. 1, photographed in 1917. (*Courtesy Harold K. Vollrath*)

PLATE 93. Ft. Smith, Subiaco & Rock Island 2–6–0 No. 439, photographed at Paris, Arkansas, about 1938. (*Author's collection*)

PLATE 94. Ft. Smith, Subiaco & Rock Island 2–6–0 No. 489, photographed at Paris, Arkansas, September 30, 1938. (*Author's collection*)

Plate 95. Ft. Smith, Subiaco & Rock Island 4–6–0 No. 614, photographed at Ft. Smith on August 30, 1932; ex-Frisco No. 614, she was traded by Frisco for Subiaco No. 101, a 2–10–0, and became Frisco 2d No. 1621. (*Author's collection*)

Plate 96. Ft. Smith, Subiaco & Rock Island 0–4–4–0 motorcar No. A-1, photographed when it was new. (*Courtesy R. H. Carlson*)

Plate 97. Fayetteville & Little Rock 4–6–0 No. 168. This ten-wheeler hit a split switch at Pettigrew, Arkansas, in the summer of 1900 and rammed her nose into the ground, while several stock cars swapped ends. (*Courtesy Marion Bayles*)

Plate 98. Fayetteville and Little Rock 2–6–0 Mogul No. 345, shown on the Cassville & Exeter in Missouri. She was formerly Frisco No. 345 from the St. Paul, Arkansas, branch. (*Author's collection*)

PLATE 99. View of St. Paul, Arkansas, from the east, about 1915. Th unballasted Fayetteville & Little Rock track is symbolic of the newness c the town. (*Author's collection*)

PLATE 100. Teams of mules pulling the wagons of tie haulers about 1919 i St. Paul, Arkansas, on the Fayetteville & Little Rock line. (*Courtesy Marion Bayles*)

PLATE 101. Fayetteville & Little Rock, St. Paul branch, section crew in front of the St. Paul depot about 1925. Left to right: Aug Riley, Harve Thomas, Willard Patrick (foreman), Gus Lackey, and station agent T. V. Griffith. (*Courtesy Marion Bayles*)

PLATE 102. Scene at St. Paul depot, about 1925. (*Courtesy Marion Bayles*) The words of an old railroad poem, author unknown, adequately describe this scene:

Down around th' deepo when th' keers come in,
What a hustle an' a bustle an' a clatter an' a din!

PLATE 103. St. Louis, El Reno & Western 4–6–0 No. 3, photographed in El Reno, Oklahoma, about 1905. (*Courtesy John B. Fink Collection, Division of Manuscripts, University of Oklahoma*)

PLATE 104. Ft. Smith & Western 4–4–0 1st No. 2, photographed at Ft. Smith with shop crew. (*Courtesy Charles E. Winters*)

PLATE 105. Ft. Smith & Western 4–4–0 2d No. 2, photographed at Ft. Smith, August 25, 1938. (*Courtesy Charles E. Winters*)

Plate 106. Ft. Smith & Western 4-4-0 No.3, photographed in 1932. This regal old lady was rebuilt by the Union Pacific in 1895 and came to the FS & W in 1902. (*Courtesy Charles E. Winters*)

Plate 107. Ft. Smith & Western 4-4-0 2d No. 4, photographed in 1938 on passenger train at Oklahoma City. (*Courtesy Charles E. Winters*)

Plate 108. Ft. Smith & Western 4-4-0 2d No. 4, photographed in use as the shop boiler in Ft. Smith, March 27, 1938. (*Courtesy Charles E. Winters*)

PLATE 109. Ft. Smith & Western 4-4-0 1st No. 5, photographed in front of engine house in Ft. Smith, August 20, 1924. (*Courtesy Charles E. Winters*)

PLATE 110. Ft. Smith & Western 4-4-0 2d No. 5, ex-2d No. 10, photographed in Ft. Smith, April 18, 1939. (*Courtesy Charles E. Winters*)

PLATE 111. Ft. Smith & Western 4-4-0 1st No. 6, photographed at Ft. Smith depot. (*Courtesy Charles E. Winters*)

PLATE 112. Ft. Smith & Western 4-4-0 2d No. 6, photographed in Ft. Smith about 1925. (*Courtesy Charles E. Winters*)

PLATE 113. Ft. Smith & Western 4-6-0 1st No. 8, photographed with crew in McCurtain, Oklahoma. (*Courtesy Charles E. Winters*)

PLATE 114. Ft. Smith & Western 4-4-0 2d No. 9, photographed in Ft. Smith about 1925. (*Courtesy Charles E. Winters*)

PLATE 115. Ft. Smith & Western 4-6-0 1st No. 10, photographed in Guthrie, Oklahoma. (*Courtesy John B. Fink Collection Division of Manuscripts, University of Oklahoma*)

PLATE 116. Ft. Smith & Western 4-4-0 2d No. 10, photographed at Ft. Smith. Note the dangling stack cover. (*Courtesy Charles E. Winters*)

PLATE 117. Ft. Smith & Western 4-6-0 No. 14, photographed in Ft. Smith, February 14, 1934. (*Courtesy Charles E. Winters*)

Plate 118. Ft. Smith & Western 0–6–0 1st No. 20, photographed at McCurtain, Oklahoma, about 1912. (*Courtesy Charles E. Winters*)

Plate 119. Ft. Smith & Western 0–4–4 "T" 1st No. 21, photographed with crew at Piedmont, Oklahoma, on the St. Louis, El Reno & Western in January, 1914. (*Courtesy Charles E. Winters*)

Plate 120. Ft. Smith & Western 2–8–2 No. 23, photographed at Ft. Smith, May 10, 1936. (*Courtesy Charles E. Winters*)

Plate 121. Ft. Smith & Western 2–8–2 No. 24, photographed at Ft. Smith, June 13, 1936. (*Courtesy Charles E. Winters*)

Plate 122. Ft. Smith & Western 2–8–2 No. 25, photographed at Ft. Smith, June 15, 1936. (*Courtesy Charles E. Winters*)

Plate 123. Ft. Smith & Western 2–8–2 No. 26, photographed at Ft. Smith, June 12, 1936. Note the temporary tender. (*Courtesy Charles E. Winters*)

Plate 124. Ft. Smith & Western 2–8–2 No. 27, photographed at Ft. Smith, March 15, 1936 (*Courtesy Charles E. Winters*)

Plate 125. Ft. Smith & Western 2–8–2 No. 28, shown new at Baldwin in 1920. (*Courtesy H. L. Broadbelt*)

Plate 126. Ft. Smith & Western 2–8–2 No. 28, photographed at Ft. Smith in 1936, sixteen years after she was built. The air reservoir tanks on top of the boiler were a peculiarity of the FS & W. (*Courtesy Charles E. Winters*)

PLATE 127. Ft. Smith & Western 4-8-0 No. 32, photographed in 1938. This ungainly gal, built by Brooks in 1900, came from the Buffalo, Rochester & Pittsburgh in 1918. (*Courtesy Charles E. Winters*)

PLATE 128. Ft. Smith & Western Nos. 28, 25, and 27 posing for a photograph which appeared in 1937 in the "Coal Edition" of the *Ft. Smith Times Record.* (*Author's collection*)

PLATE 129. Prescott & Northwestern 2-6-2 No. 7, photographed by Joe Collins at Prescott, Arkansas. She was built by Baldwin as No. 51771 in May, 1919; ex-Caddo & Choctaw No. 7; ex-Ozan Lumber Company No. 7. She was sold in 1962 to a tourist road, Black Hills Central, running between Keystone and Oblivion, South Dakota. (*Courtesy Charles E. Winters*)

LATE 130. Prescott & Northwestern 2–6–0 No. 14, photographed at Lewis-
ille (Old Town), Arkansas, March 16, 1950, at Meriwether Gravel Company.
he was built by Baldwin as No. 33159 in January, 1909. Note the stack cover.
(*Courtesy Charles E. Winters*)

LATE 131. Prescott & Northwestern 2–8–2 Mikado No. 16, the *R. F. Smith*.
his triple-domed, low-drivered Mikado came from Baldwin in 1914. She
heeled many trains of luscious Elberta peaches to the P & NW connection
with the St. Louis, Iron Mountain & Southern at Prescott, Arkansas.
(*Courtesy H. L. Broadbelt*)

PLATE 132. Prescott & Northwestern 2–8–2 No. 17, photographed at Pre cott, November 12, 1951. She was built by Baldwin as No. 43057 in Marc 1916. She later went to the Arkansas Railroad but was not relettered c renumbered. (*Courtesy Charles E. Winters*)

PLATE 133. Prescott & Northwestern Model "T" rail car No. 19. This P & NV 0–4–0 ran mostly as an extra, occasionally at night, as indicated by the outsi headlight. Note the different style of wheels front and back and the finge pinching accordion running-board luggage rack. (*Courtesy Earl Saunders, Jr*

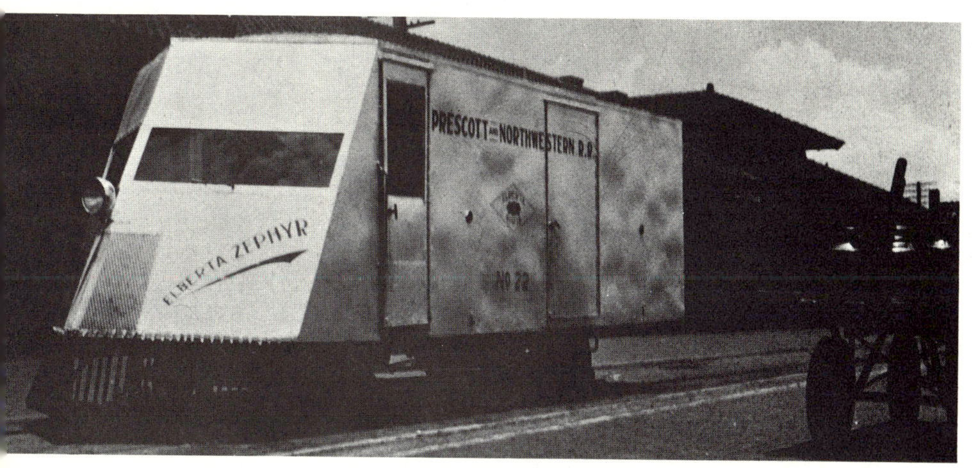

PLATE 134. Prescott & Northwestern aluminum sheet-bed truck, the *Elberta Zephyr*, photographed at the Missouri Pacific depot in Prescott, Arkansas. When the Burlington ran the first streamlined train in the United States between Denver and Chicago nonstop on May 26, 1934, the impact was felt all the way to southwestern Arkansas. The P & NW soon inaugurated the *Elberta Zephyr*. Her speed was slightly less than the 92 miles per hour reached by other Zephyrs, and her run of 31 miles was somewhat shorter than the 1,015-mile record run, but her presence was a matter of pride to residents of Arkansas. (*Courtesy Earl Saunders, Jr.*)

PLATE 135. Gould Southwestern 2-6-0 Mogul No. 6, built at Baldwin as No. 41647 in 1914. (*Courtesy H. L. Broadbelt*)

PLATE 136. Southern Indiana 4–6–0 No. 39, shown new at Baldwin in 1903; later No. 8 on the Arkansas Railroad. (*Courtesy H. L. Broadbelt*)

PLATE 137. Arkansas Railroad 4–6–0 No. 8. (*Author's collection*)

PLATE 138. Arkansas Railroad 2–6–0 No. 150, ex–Warren & Saline River No. 150, photographed at Gould, Arkansas, June, 1957. (*Courtesy Harold K. Vollrath*)

PLATE 139. Arkansas Railroad 2-6-0 No. 300. (*Author's collection*)

PLATE 140. Texas State 2-6-0 No. 7, later Arkansas Railroad No. 412, shown new at Baldwin in 1915. (*Courtesy H. L. Broadbelt*)

PLATE 141. Arkansas Railroad 2-6-0 No. 412, photographed at Star City, Arkansas, May 26, 1957; ex-Texas State No. 7. (*Author's collection*)

PLATE 142. Warren, Johnsville & Saline River 2–8–0 Consolidation No. 101, shown new at Baldwin. (*Courtesy H. L. Broadbelt*)

PLATE 143. Warren & Saline River 2–8–2 Mikado No. 10, photographed at Warren, Arkansas, in 1938. (*Courtesy R. H. Carlson*)

PLATE 144. Warren & Saline River 4–6–0 No. 153, photographed at Warren in 1938. (*Courtesy R. H. Carlson*)

Plate 146 (above). Warren & Saline River crummy No. 8, photographed at Warren, June, 1961. (*Author's collection*)

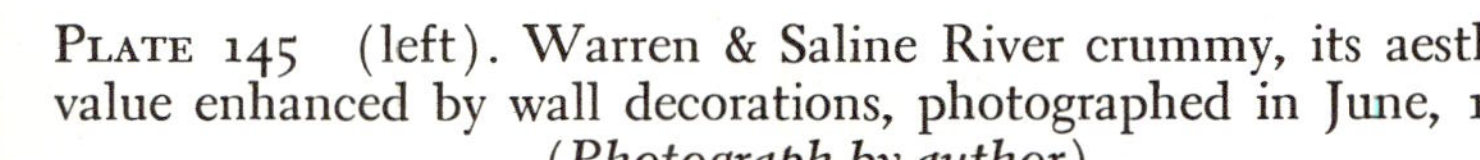

Plate 145 (left). Warren & Saline River crummy, its aesthetic value enhanced by wall decorations, photographed in June, 1961. (*Photograph by author*)

PLATE 147. Warren & Ouachita Valley 4–6–0 No. 123, photographed at Warren, Arkansas park, September 4, 1957. (*Courtesy William J. Husa, Jr.*)

PLATE 148. Warren & Ouachita Valley 4–6–0 No. 1, photographed at North Freedom, Wisconsin, July 2, 1966. (*Courtesy William J. Husa, Jr.*)

PLATE 149. Jonesboro, Lake City & Eastern 2–6–0 No. 32, shown new at Baldwin. (*Courtesy H. L. Broadbelt*)

PLATE 150. Blytheville, Leachville & Arkansas Southern 0–4–2 "T" No. 2, photographed at Blytheville, Arkansas, in 1903. (*Courtesy R. H. Carlson*)

PLATE 151. Blytheville, Leachville & Arkansas Southern 0–4–2 "T" No. 3, photographed at Blytheville in 1903. (*Courtesy R. H. Carlson*)

PLATE 152. Blytheville, Leachville & Arkansas Southern 4–4–0 No. 5, photographed at Blytheville in 1903. (*Courtesy R. H. Carlson*)

PLATE 153. Bradley Lumber Company 2–8–0 No. 101, photographed in September, 1912. (*Author's collection*)

PLATE 154. De Queen & Eastern 2–6–2 Prairie No. 200, shown new at Baldwin in 1905. Note the unusual lettering on the tender and the cab. (*Courtesy H. L. Broadbelt*)

PLATE 155. De Queen & Eastern 2–6–2 Prairie No. 208, made by Baldwin as No. 47437 in 1918. (*Author's collection*)

PLATE 156. De Queen & Eastern 4–6–0 No. 351, left side, photographed in July, 1934. (*Courtesy Harold K. Vollrath*)

PLATE 157. De Queen & Eastern 4–6–0 No. 351, right side, photographed in June, 1943. (*Courtesy Charles E. Winters*)

PLATE 158. Dierks Forests, Inc. 2–6–2 No. 207, photographed in De Queen, Arkansas, September, 1953. (*Courtesy Charles E. Winters*)

PLATE 159. Dierks Forests, Inc. 2–8–2 Mikado No. 226 in front of the engine house and machine shop at Mountain Pine, Arkansas. (*Photograph by author*)

PLATE 160. Dierks Forests, Inc. 2–8–2 No. 227, photographed on the Texas, Oklahoma & Eastern at Pickens, Oklahoma, December, 1959. (*Courtesy Charles E. Winters*)

PLATE 161. Dierks Forests, Inc. 4–6–0 No. 360, photographed in February, 1966, on display atop Rich Mountain at Wilhelmina State Park, near Mena, Arkansas (see Plate 164). (*Photograph by author*)

PLATE 162. Link-and-pin couplers on log cars of Dierks Forests, Inc., at Mountain Pine, Arkansas, in 1960—seldom seen in railroading today. The link and one pin are in the author's possession. (*Photograph by author*)

Plate 163. Dierks Lumber & Coal 2–8–2 Mikado No. 226, shown new at Baldwin. She was built as a woodburner with a fine "cabbage" stack. Later she was converted to an oilburner and became Dierks Forests, Inc. No. 226. Today, retired, she rests in the city park at Benton, Arkansas.
(*Courtesy H. L. Broadbelt*)

Plate 164. Dierks Forests, Inc. Mikado No. 226, with a new coat of paint, sitting on a Missouri Pacific station track on her way to the city park at Benton.
(*Photograph by author*)

PLATE 165. Dierks Forests, Inc. loader and train of logs at mill in Mountai
Pine, Arkansas. (*Photograph by author*)

PLATE 166. Dierks Forests, Inc. D-2 spelled "doom for steam" on the rails at Mountain Pine. (*Photograph by author*)

PLATE 167. Texas, Oklahoma & Eastern 4–6–0 No. 360, photographed January 15, 1943. She later became Dierks Forests, Inc. No. 360 (see Plate 161) (*Courtesy Charles E. Winters*)

PLATE 168. Doniphan, Kensett & Searcy 2–6–0 Mogul No. 6, photographed at Doniphan, Arkansas. This sad old Mogul was probably an ex–3600–class Missouri Pacific. (*Author's collection*)

PLATE 169. Doniphan, Kensett & Searcy 4-6-0 No. 7.
(*Courtesy R. H. Carlson*)

PLATE 170 (opposite, top). Ozark & Cherokee Central 4-6-0 No. 2679. In 1900, J. H. McIlroy, of Fayetteville, Dr. McCormick, of Prairie Grove, and a few other influential men began talking about building a railroad from Fayetteville to the Illinois River Valley in Indian Territory. It would cross the Kansas City Southern (brand-new successor to the Kansas City, Pittsburg & Gulf) at Westville, I.T., then head for Tahlequah.

W. A. Bright, a railroad contractor at Little Rock, was engaged to build the road, but he failed in his effort, and the promotors hired W. A. Kennefic. With Paul H. Easby as chief engineer, the Kennefic Construction Company completed the Ozark & Cherokee Central to Tahlequah, and the road was almost immediately extended to Muskogee and Okmulgee, connecting two parallel lines running north and south through Indian Territory and Arkansas, both of which were built by the Frisco.

The O & CC had plenty of traffic, and towns rapidly developed along the route. In 1903 the Frisco bought the line and greatly improved the roadbed and equipment. (*Author's collection.*)

PLATE 171 (opposite, bottom). Fordyce & Princeton 2-8-0 No. 101, ex-Tennessee, Alabama & Georgia No. 101, photographed at Fordyce, Arkansas, in 1952. (*Courtesy Harold K. Vollrath*)

The Fordyce & Princeton was chartered on February 25, 1890, with a total of 18.82 miles of 40-pound rail to serve the Fordyce Lumber Company. In the list of directors are two names familiar to the timber industry of Arkansas: C. W. Gates and E. C. Crossett, who controlled the Crossett Lumber Company and the Ashley, Drew & Northern Railroad. The Fordyce & Princeton had an authorized capital stock of $140,000 (changed to $35,000 in June, 1948).

The line extended 11 miles northwest from Fordyce, on the Cotton Belt and the Rock Island, to Bryant's Spur, and 6 miles from Cynthiana to Trigg. The rails were originally laid as narrow gauge but were changed to standard gauge in October, 1907. The line from Cynthiana to Trigg was put into operation on January 11, 1911.

In 1956 there were 42 stockholders, and the operating ratio was 84.67 per cent, producing a net income of $2,420. By 1963 the stockholders had dwindled to 1, and the ratio was 136.39 per cent, with a deficit of $6,703. The road mileage had shrunk to 1.70 miles.

Fordyce & Princeton 2-8-0 No. 101 was donated to Little Rock in April, 1960. She was brought to town over the Rock Island and was kept at the Rock Island's Biddle yard until placed on display at War Memorial Park. Her plaque reads in part: "This steam locomotive was built by the Baldwin Locomotive Works in Eddystone, Pa., in 1922 and was sold to the Tennessee, Alabama & Gulf R.R. Co., that year. It was operated by this company until 1931 and then was sold to the Fordyce and Princeton R.R. Co. who used it for logging and switching for the Fordyce Lumber Co. of Fordyce, Ark., until 1948. It was retired from active use at that time. On April 19, 1960, F. & P. donated it to the city of Little Rock. The L. R. Optimist Club made arrangements for it to be moved to this site for the enjoyment of those who care to see an 'iron horse' of yesterday."

FORDYCE AND PRINCETON R.R. CO.

PLATE 172. Fordyce & Princeton on permanent display at War Memorial Park in Little Rock. (*Photograph by author*)

PLATE 173. Bauxite & Northern 0–6–0 No. 3203, shown new. Owned by Aluminum Company of America, it connects the plant at Bauxite, Arkansas, with the Missouri Pacific. (*Author's collection*)

PLATE 174. Bauxite & Northern shown new at Dupo, Illinois, on her way to Bauxite in 1938. (*Courtesy Harold K. Vollrath*)

ARKANSAS & OKLAHOMA—MONTE NE RAILROAD—ROGERS SOUTHWESTERN—ARKANSAS, OKLAHOMA & WESTERN—KANSAS CITY & MEMPHIS—ARKANSAS NORTHWEST

8

On May 10, 1881, a beautiful 4-4-0 diamond-stack wood-burning locomotive built at the shops of Baldwin Locomotive Works in 1870 rolled into a little Arkansas settlement, leading two open-vestibule wooden passenger coaches. Thus the town of Rogers was born, named in honor of one of the gentlemen aboard the last coach of the two-car special: Captain C. W. Rogers, vice president and general manager of the St. Louis & San Francisco, known throughout the nation as the Frisco. From that day, the people of Rogers and the surrounding area realized the importance of having a railroad.

As far back as 1860, the levying court of Benton County had voted an appropriation of five hundred dollars to assist in the preliminary survey for a railroad to run from Van Buren, in Crawford County, to a point on the Pacific Railroad (now the Missouri Pacific) somewhere in Missouri. C. W. Rice, Sr., was selected as the Benton County representative, and it was specified that the road was to cross Crawford, Washington, and Benton counties. The Civil War began a short time later, and construction was never begun. But a peculiar incident is recorded with regard to the effort—the five hundred dollars was returned to the county.

In the early 1880's, a few private citizens built a railroad of sorts from Rogers to Bentonville. It didn't amount to much as far as equipment was concerned, but it did serve as a connecting link and was a convenience for the people of both towns. Finally, in May, 1898, a group of eight men, including John M. Bayliss, E. J. Glascow, W. A. Miller, T. Mallen, W. K. Bayliss, William R. Felker, J. A. Rice, and D. H. Woods, secured a state charter for the Arkansas & Oklahoma Railway. They were authorized a capital stock of $200,000, whereupon the promoters asked Rogers residents for a donation of $20,000. The road was to extend from Rogers to Gravette, where connection would be made with the Kansas City, Pittsburg & Gulf (later the Kansas City Southern). The event was celebrated with a free lunch, music by a brass band, great bonfires, and even greater speeches.

The A & O secured the old right-of-way of the private road to Bentonville, relaid the rails, purchased new equipment, and pushed the end of track to Gravette in the fall of 1898. The next year saw the penetration of Indian Territory as far as Grove. The A & O didn't last long, however: it was bought by the Frisco in November, 1900. Its forty-eight and one-half miles of track was principally owned by W. K. Bayliss and W. R. Felker, the only names mentioned when the sale was made final.

The Monte Ne Railroad was the brainchild of William Hope "Coin" Harvey, a controversial figure on the national scene as well as in northwestern Arkansas. The man and his railroad cannot be separated; you cannot tell of one without the other.

Harvey was somewhat eccentric concerning finance, especially as it concerned the monetary standard of the American business world. He felt that surely civilization must perish from the earth because "usury" could lead only to financial ruin. The standard or legal definition of *usury* is "interest in excess of a legal rate charged to a borrower for the use of money." Harvey preferred to use the word in its absolute sense: "a premium charged for the lending of money or goods." Interest, or a usurious charge for the lending of money, would wipe out all capital, not only of individuals, but of nations as well.

Harvey began his monetary-reform efforts in the early 1890's, and they came into full bloom in 1896 when he managed the presidential campaign for "The Great Commoner," William Jennings Bryan. The main plank of the Democrats' platform was free silver coinage. They wanted to make legal coins of silver, with the value of the silver stipulated as 1/16 that of gold. During the campaign, Harvey wrote a book entitled *Coin's Financial School*, millions of copies of which were sold, earning him the nickname of "Coin." It stayed with him the rest of his life. The campaign was in vain, however, for William McKinley was elected president. Harvey became disenchanted with the country and its policies, so he retreated to the sanctuary of the Ozark Mountains near Rogers.

Southeast of Rogers was a tiny settlement known as Silver Springs. It nestled in a hollow of the hills near a meandering spring-fed stream. Here Harvey bought 325 acres of land and a fine home from the Reverend J. G. Bailey, who was postmaster at the time. Just a short time before Harvey's arrival, Rev. Bailey had petitioned the Post Office Department to change the name of the office to Vinola in honor of the well-known vineyard of a neighbor, Carl A. Starck. The letter was written in longhand, and the *o* and *l* were spaced so close together that a clerk misread the name as "Vinda," which is the way it was recorded. *Vinda* meant nothing to Harvey, and he found a name more to his liking in "Monte Ne," which he said was Spanish for "mountains of water."

On December 13, 1900, Harvey organized the Monte Ne Investment Company, with offices at Rogers. In 1901, it was moved to Monte Ne. He had ambitions to revive at Monte Ne the rural entertainment so popular in many districts of the southern mountain country, a part of which was a fiddler's contest. He also had plans to make Monte Ne a social center second to none in that part of the state. The major deterrent was the lack of convenient access to Monte Ne.

First he proposed a good gravel road to connect Monte Ne with Rogers. This effort proved in vain, but it did accelerate the beginning of the Monte Ne Railroad. Petition was made to the Arkansas Railroad Commission, and a charter was granted on April 26, 1902. It was brought about through the efforts of W. H. Harvey, Carl A. Starck, P. G. Davidson, A. L. Williams, B. R. Davidson, J. H. McIlroy, J. W. Kimmons, F. F. Freeman, J. E. Felker, Robert H. Harvey, and Thomas W. Harvey—eleven men to build a five-mile railroad. There was some evidence that the project was financed by a brother of Coin Harvey, a banker at Huntington, West Virginia, who gave the company a capital stock of $25,000, although 240 shares of the total of 250 were registered in Coin's name.

The road proposed to make connection with the Frisco at Lowell, five miles south of Rogers. The rails followed the grass-roots grade of the undulating countryside eastward via Limedale and Cross Hollows (where two distinct ravines crossed) and terminated at a spacious log depot, the center portion of which was two stories high. One end was an open-sided waiting room. The station was located near a huge spring which formed a large and beautiful lagoon, from which Harvey constructed a series of canals to the various hotels and cottages he had built—or planned to build—for the many expected tourists or visitors of the social strata.

Harvey had a novel and unusual arrangement here. The little one- or two-car trains arrived at the impressive log station with a reverberating blast from the engine's whistle and a tolling of its bell. Passengers alighted from the coaches and were met with a royal welcome. Upon naming their desired destination, they were escorted to the near-by lagoon, where deep blue-green waters from Big Spring reflected stately trees of the forest. At the lagoon visitors were ceremoniously ushered aboard a long, low Venetian gondola in which they were leisurely transported to the hotel or cottage of their choice. The gondoliers were dressed in colorful costumes, and the final minutes of the journey were made as pleasant and inviting as possible.

Upon the rounded knolls and wooded hillsides were spacious hotels, lodges, and cottages. In 1904, the Monte Ne Club House, Hotel and Cottage Company, Inc., was formed to build a hotel 220 feet long and four stories high. The "cottages," between 300 and 350 feet long, were known as Arkansas, Texas, Louisiana, and Missouri rows. The Missouri Row and the Oklahoma Row (the latter was added to honor the newly-rich oil barons) were the only two ever built. Harvey encountered considerable trouble with organized labor and stopped all construction.

Monte Ne was envisioned as one of the finest resort hotels and social centers of the state, and Coin Harvey worked unceasingly for three years to bring his dream to reality. Special trains were run by accommodation on the Frisco from Springfield, Joplin, and Fort Smith, bringing large crowds to the mountain resort on Sundays. Ironically, many of Coin's Arkansas neighbors did not take kindly to his making a general holiday of Sunday; they resented his desecration of their Sabbath.

Coin was born thirty years too soon as a developer of the resort trade. Two teams of the Western Baseball Association were brought to Monte Ne aboard a special train for an exhibition game. Again the good people frowned upon such goings-on on Sunday. The attraction was not repeated. Then Harvey and the Frisco agreed to disagree on several problems, whereupon the Frisco refused to handle the special excursions.

The Monte Ne Railroad had an auspicious beginning. The first train to arrive at Monte Ne was greeted with a speech by none other than William Jennings Bryan on June 19, 1902. Also present was U.S. Senator Ben "Pitchfork" Tillman of South Carolina. There were great plans for extending the influence of the embryo village. For political aspirants, it was a place where they could meet the socially elite as well as the "stocks and bonds" group. And all came via the Monte Ne Railroad.

Adversity and disappointment seemed to plague Coin Harvey. He received more than a million dollars from the sale of *Coin's Financial School,* but this had disappeared by the time he came to Arkansas. On December 14, 1901, the log home he bought from Rev. Bailey burned to the ground. The Harveys lost their piano, silverware, clothing, books—everything that had been shipped from their Chicago home a few weeks earlier. In October, 1903, Halliday Harvey, Coin's oldest son, was killed while braking on a Frisco freight in Oklahoma Territory. A law student in Chicago, he had accompanied his father to Arkansas. A couple of days before his death, Halliday had received word of his appointment to the Railway Mail Service. He was making his last trip braking when he was killed.

Coin was talked out of running for Congress in 1904 because of lack of support. In 1932, he was nominated for president of the United States and was badly defeated. He began a huge concrete monument, designed to withstand the ravage of time for thousands of years. In it were to be placed articles depicting life in his time: books on industry and scientific achievement, pictures of inventions and discoveries, encyclopedias and histories, and articles in common use, from a safety pin to an automobile. These items were to be discovered by a new generation of people after civilization had perished because of the usurious charges for loans of money or goods. The monument fell victim to the Great Depression of 1929 and was never completed.

Coin Harvey died at his home in Monte Ne on February 11, 1936, at the age of eighty-five, an embittered, frustrated man of dreams. His body was entombed, along with that of his son Halliday, in a huge concrete monolith (above ground) at Monte Ne. The site of the town, Harvey's tomb, and all of his ambitious dreams now lie buried under eighteen feet of water, backed up through the valleys of the Ozarks after the government completed Beaver Dam across White River.

For a few brief years, the Monte Ne Railroad served the full-scale dreams of Coin Harvey. Pleasure-seeking tourists were the principal source of revenue, but there was a fair trickle of income from the Rogers White Lime Works, a reduction plant located at Cross Hollows, just west of Monte Ne. Here was produced industrial and commercial quantities of lime from the once-abundant deposits of limestone in the area. F. F. Freeman, one of the railroad's original stockholders, state senator, and son-in-law of Rogers financier William R. Felker, was also the owner of the Rogers White Lime Company.

In June, 1907, Senator Jeff Davis swept the state with his demands that Arkansas railroads be taxed in proportion to their substance, even as the poor man pays on his lowly chattels. This led the Board of Railroad Commissioners to assess the Monte Ne at three thousand dollars per mile, whereupon Coin Harvey asked Davis, who was a friend of his, to have the assessment lowered. The road was unable to make both ends meet, even though its literal ends were only five miles apart. The income from Coin's literary efforts and from those who came to "salubriate at the salubrious resort" did not meet the expense of operation. Although Davis did not reverse his stand on equal assessments for railroads, he did prevail upon the commissioners to lower the Monte Ne assessment for friend Harvey.

The little road finally went broke, and Harvey's banker brother paid off the accumulated debts and gave the property to Tom Harvey and Tony Le Blanc, a secretary to Coin. The pair took turns at being engineer and conductor or brakeman. They had a lot of fun and wrangled annual passes from railroads all over the country. The railroad went from nowhere to nowhere, its schedule was erratic at best, and it finally gave up and died.

Soon after the first of the year in 1904, there was heard quite a bit of talk about a railroad extending west from Rogers toward Siloam Springs, just short of Indian Territory. Either Siloam Springs or Gentry would provide a connection with the north-south main line of the Kansas City Southern (which had been the Kansas City, Pittsburg & Gulf until 1900). This would put the little town of Rogers on two large rail systems—the KCS and the Frisco—and competition would guarantee local shippers the lowest possible rates. Moreover, the connecting railroad would be able to secure a favorable rate division.

Thus it was no surprise when the Arkansas Railroad Commission approved the granting of a charter to the Rogers Southwestern on February 2, 1904, climaxing the diligent efforts of William R. Felker, the same man who was instrumental in building the Arkansas & Oklahoma from Rogers to Gravette in 1898. The A & O gave the town its first connection to the Kansas City, Pittsburgh & Gulf, but it was quickly bought up by the Frisco. Who knows? Perhaps the promoters of the RSW thought they would be able to sell another road. At any rate, the Rogers Southwestern was financed to the tune of $300,000, or about $10,000 per mile to build and equip. Associated with Felker were R. L. Nance, J. E. Applegate, W. R. Cady, A. R. Potters, S. M. Morris, George D. Locke, W. F. Rozelle, J. W. Walker, J. E. Felker, and McQueen Rozelle. These gentlemen had sufficient faith in the venture to subscribe to $60,000 in stock, and within a year they had paid $15,000 in cash.

During the summer of 1904, the city of Rogers passed Ordinance No. 22, which granted a fifty-year franchise to the Rogers Southwestern, giving it right-of-way up First Street from the south edge of town to Cherry Street, thence through the alley between First and Second streets to Elm. Several months were spent in survey sorties during the summer of 1905. The line was staked out southeast from Rogers to Hazelwood, a short distance northwest of Lowell, then headed almost due west to Springtown. Here it was only two and one-half miles from Gentry and a connection with the Kansas City Southern.

Construction began in November, 1905. Ten graders were put to work under the supervision of J. H. G. Brown of Gravette, with Ned Whitcomb surveying the final grades. Grading began in McGaughey Addition on the west side of the Frisco tracks at Rogers.

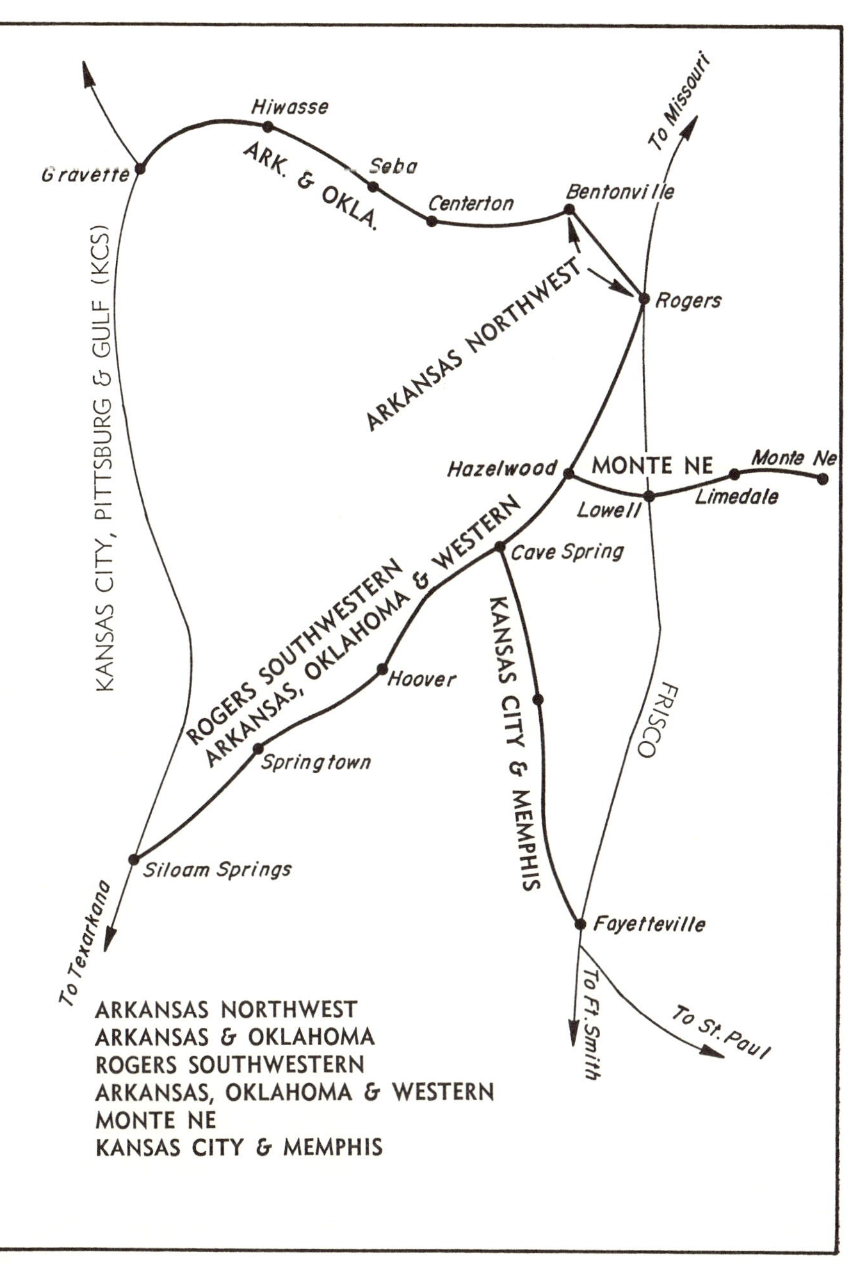

Hiwasse
Gravette
Seba
ARK. & OKLA.
Centerton
Bentonville
To Missouri
KANSAS CITY, PITTSBURG & GULF (KCS)
ARKANSAS NORTHWEST
Rogers
Hazelwood
MONTE NE
Monte Ne
Lowell
Limedale
Cave Spring
ROGERS SOUTHWESTERN
ARKANSAS, OKLAHOMA & WESTERN
KANSAS CITY & MEMPHIS
FRISCO
Hoover
Springtown
Siloam Springs
Fayetteville
To Texarkana
To Ft. Smith
To St. Paul
ARKANSAS NORTHWEST
ARKANSAS & OKLAHOMA
ROGERS SOUTHWESTERN
ARKANSAS, OKLAHOMA & WESTERN
MONTE NE
KANSAS CITY & MEMPHIS

The first carload of rails arrived at Rogers and track crews began placing them on April 18, 1906. Work progressed rather slowly; money was becoming more scarce as each mile of rail was laid. Fall was approaching, and days were getting shorter. On September 1, 1906, the railhead reached Springtown, about twenty miles west of Rogers. On September 4, a picnic dinner, band concert, baseball game, and extensive speeches were combined to celebrate the arrival of the first passenger train at Springtown. And William R. Felker announced that the Rogers Southwestern was heading for Siloam Springs. Its rails never reached that point.

On January 26, 1907, a meeting of Rogers Southwestern stockholders was held at Rogers. It was decided that the railroad would be sold, but this time the Frisco was not the purchaser. The sale was consummated for the magnificent sum of one dollar and other good and valuable considerations to the newly formed Arkansas, Oklahoma & Western on February 13, 1907.

The AO & W was formed by ten men living in the counties through which it was to run: William R. Felker, J. E. Felker, F. F. Freeman, Alf L. Williams, S. M. Morris, A. Newton, J. S. McLeod, J. W. Walker, H. Van Smith, and C. E. Speer. Some of these names seem to be found in the list of incorporators of each new company.

The purpose of the AO & W was to purchase all physical properties and franchises of the Rogers Southwestern. Then the owners proposed to complete the line into Siloam Springs to give Rogers a connection with the KCS, then continue into Indian Territory to a point at or near Pryor Creek. From Rogers the rails were to be laid eastward to the resort town of Eureka Springs. This would represent a rail system in northwest Arkansas totaling sixty-two miles, a very nice network.

On New Year's Day, 1908, the section from Springtown to Siloam Springs was opened to traffic. To complete the proposed route into Eureka Springs—and thus make connection with the Missouri & North Arkansas—a speculative eye was cast upon the defunct Monte Ne, undulating eastward from Lowell. About

December 1, 1909, Senator Freeman, one of the principal stockholders of the AO & W, purchased the Monte Ne.

In order to join the Monte Ne and the Arkansas, Oklahoma & Western, it would be necessary to build a connecting link from Hazelwood to Lowell. This would require an underpass to bring the road beneath the Frisco rails at Lowell (the Frisco would not permit a direct crossing). The underpass proved to be a long and expensive job. The Frisco attempted to block its construction by repeated court actions, but an agreement was finally reached and the underpass was completed. Some evidence of the old cut still may be found south of Rogers along Highway 71.

The AO & W was envisioned to run from Harrison, Arkansas, to Wagoner, Oklahoma, a distance of about 150 miles. A branch from Monte Ne to Huntsville was begun, but money ran out and construction was halted. Lack of money continued to plague the builders, and the rails never extended beyond Siloam Springs to the west.

One more attempt was made to lace northwestern Arkansas with an interconnecting network of railroads. On December 17, 1910, the Kansas City & Memphis filed its application with the secretary of state for a charter. Again we find some familiar names: William R. Felker, J. E. Felker, F. F. Freeman, J. W. Walker, J. S. McLeod, A. L. Williams, and a few newcomers.

There was no diminishment in the ambitions shown by the promoters. They proposed to build a line south from Cave Springs, a few miles west of Rogers, to the university town of Fayetteville, where the rails were to bend eastward across Madison, Newton, Johnson, Pope, Conway, Van Buren, Cleburn, White, Woodruff, Jackson, Cross, and Crittenden counties. This would justify the corporate title designation of Memphis. A branch was to leave the main line at Hindsville and proceed north to Eureka Springs. From a point in either Van Buren County or Faulkner County, a southern branch was to penetrate Little Rock. West of Siloam Springs, train service was to enter the three-year-old state of Oklahoma as far as Wagoner. A survey party soon was working its way laboriously eastward from Monte Ne, crossing White River and winding through the valleys of the Ozarks.

In the early days of 1911, the Kansas City & Memphis bought the Arkansas, Oklahoma & Western properties. Then it began securing right-of-way from Cave Springs to Fayetteville by way of Elm Springs and Tontitown, an Italian settlement west of Springdale. Stations along the 31-mile route were established at Steele, Litteral, and Mount Comfort, and the first regular KC & M train entered Fayetteville on August 22, 1912. About the only celebration along the route was held at Tontitown, and the Italians really made a day of it.

A new steel bridge was erected to span the White River east of Monte Ne. For several years it was the subject of much speculation by people who could see a fine bridge in the valley of the White but no sign of a railroad approaching it from either side. The rails never reached the bridge.

The company equipment register in 1914 showed the presence of five locomotives, two cabooses, forty-two freight cars, and three passenger cars. Financial troubles began to appear then, too. Efforts were made to sell the little rail empire of 50- and 60-pound steel to one of the large companies with main lines in the area, the thought being that the Frisco or the Kansas City Southern could use the branching network as a feeder system, but the proposal fell on deaf ears. On July 18, 1914, the stockholders threw the road into the hands of a receiver and Roscoe C. Hobbs of Rogers, who had been associated with the company in various capacities, was named as general manager.

When the federal government assumed control of all railroads in the United States during World War I, the Kansas City & Memphis was marked for abandonment. With little or no fanfare, the rails came up for salvage, the buildings came down, and the KC & M marched off into history.

Completing the network of independent railroads in northwestern Arkansas was the Arkansas Northwest, whose existence was rather brief. J. D. Southerland came to Bentonville in 1912 or 1913 and bought the Park Springs Hotel, a fine resort, and it is reported that he built the Arkansas Northwest to aid the tourist business at his hotel.

Construction began in the spring of 1914. The company had a local franchise in Rogers to lay rails down the center of Second Street from Cherry Street north to the Frisco track, about 1.10 miles. From here the rails followed the swales and rolling hills northwest to Bentonville. Stops were made along the way at Apple Spur, Arlan Spur, and the Massey Hotel, and the route terminated at the Park Springs Hotel in Bentonville. The mortgagees employed the Ozark Trust Company of Springfield, Missouri, to take charge of constructing the road. It acted as trustee while a company headed by John T. Woodruff, also of Springfield, did the actual work.

The fledgling pike soon ran into legal difficulties, all because the cities of Rogers and Bentonville both owned water companies. The Rogers Light & Power Company halted construction of the road and had the interurban officials haled into court. It was contended that the water company would suffer damages because its main water lines would probably be ruptured. The court decreed that inasmuch as the complainant had not complied with city ordinances in laying the water mains at the required depth, it had no business being in the middle of the street in the first place, and in the second place, the court could grant no legal relief. The rails were laid.

Service was to be provided by a knife-nosed McKeen car with distinctive round porthole-type windows. Ninety-two feet long and seating 130 passengers, it was painted bright red and trimmed in black with gold lettering. On a hot, humid July 1, 1914, more than 100 citizens from Bentonville, accompanied by the town band, came to Rogers on the motorcar's first trip. An informal reception was held for the visitors, and a short time later, folks from Rogers returned the call to the Park Springs Hotel at Bentonville, where they were honored with a formal dinner and a picnic.

The round-trip fare was finally set at 40 cents, with a 21-cent one-way ticket. Many banks closed their doors in 1914, and the big red car proved to be a very popular means of making a quick trip to the county seat at Rogers. Seven round trips were made each day. The car left Bentonville at 6:15 A.M. and returned on its final trip at 11:30 P.M., being in charge of Bob Fowler or a man named Ketter as conductor. Motormen who handled the controls were Ed Largette, Ben Guoh, Art Mayhall, and Jake Kohley. Henry Cavness was its brakeman during the entire life of the Arkansas Northwest. The motorcar seemed to be a little less than reliable, and a good many scheduled trips were missed for various and sundry reasons.

From Rogers, "Big Red" rolled on Frisco track to Bentonville, where she switched to Arkansas Northwest rails down the city streets to a small shed near the Park Springs Hotel. Here she spent her nights. The trackage rights were on a lease basis from the Frisco.

On June 11, 1916, Big Red made her last trip; the Frisco had ordered her removed from its rails because leasing fees had not been paid. Company officials announced publicly that the dues would be paid and that service would resume "in the near future." But "in the near future" it was discovered that Big Red had been sold and was already gone, never to return.

This left the city of Rogers with somewhat of a problem. Who had authority to tear up the rails and remove the ties from the middle of Second Street? someone asked. The city council condemned the track, but this didn't solve the situation. The street department removed the ties after a creditor had salvaged the rails.

It is ironic that the last northwestern Arkansas railroad was destined to operate over the route of the first. The Arkansas & Oklahoma was chartered in 1898 to take over the defunct and decrepit line between Rogers and Bentonville. Just eighteen years later, the Arkansas Northwest made the final run between Bentonville and Rogers as a privately owned line. Located in Washington and Madison counties southwest of Fayetteville were the

Fayetteville & Little Rock (known as the St. Paul Branch of the Frisco) and the Combs, Cass & Eastern, but they were so closely related to the parent Frisco that they cannot be included in the group forming the rail empire of northwest Arkansas.

The network had been built largely through the efforts of one man: William R. Felker. Born near Washburn, Missouri, on September 22, 1855, he landed a job as a clerk in a store at Washburn when he was eighteen years old. In a very short time, he was made a full partner in the business. Felker came to Rogers in 1883, when the town was two years old, and established its first bank. His business acumen made him an outstanding financier in northwest Arkansas. In 1914, the Felker bank at Rogers failed, and the rail system he had fostered and nurtured began to crumble and disintegrate. Its passing was a relatively unmourned affair, but there are a few fond remembrances of it.

The Arkansas, Oklahoma & Western was affectionately known as the "All Off and Walk." One day an excursion train was returning to Siloam Springs from Monte Ne. The little teakettle engine and one coach were leisurely dipping and swaying through the dells. The train clanked and clattered to a halt at Healing Springs, where the crew and passengers were informed that the strawberry harvest was in full swing and that many of the pickers were still in the fields. The growers would consider it a mighty nice favor if the train could wait a little while so that the berries could be shipped out fresh.

The train waited an hour.

The crates of crimson berries were loaded aboard the express car.

The railroad had gained several friends and a few extra dollars.

On many occasions during the fall months, train crews would take a burlap tow sack along on every run. When business required a stop at some small station, they would climb down and quickly make their way to a convenient tree and gather a good supply of black walnuts. These were always shared with any member of the crew who was detained by business, such as a fireman who might have had to take on a tank of water.

Almost unbelievable quantities of cordwood went to market behind the straining little engines. Stacks of it lined the track through the hill country.

Many carloads of apples—dried, otherwise processed, or in their delicious raw state—went to markets all over the country by way of northwest Arkansas trains every year. The interior of Benton County was opened to trade as never before, for its few wagon roads were in poor condition. Thus the shortline railroads served their purpose well before they died.

MEMPHIS, PARIS & GULF—MEMPHIS, DALLAS & GULF—ANTOINE VALLEY—CADDO & CHOCTAW—HOT SPRINGS, GLENWOOD & WESTERN—ULTIMA THULE, ARKADELPHIA & MISSISSIPPI RIVER—GRAYSONIA, NASHVILLE & ASHDOWN—MURFREESBORO-NASHVILLE SOUTHWESTERN—MURFREESBORO-MURFREESBORO & NASHVILLE RAILROAD NASHVILLE RAILWAY

WHEN THE TWENTIETH CENTURY was very young, a rash of small railroads began to penetrate the timber land of southern, southwestern, and western Arkansas. Here were millions of acres of trees, mostly pine, and the demand for lumber was heavy: homes were needed, especially for newcomers to Arkansas, as were buildings to house the increasing number of business establishments.

In 1905, a group of ambitious citizens in southwest Arkansas had sufficient faith in the future of the area to incorporate a railroad whose terminal points were to be Memphis, Tennessee, and Paris, Texas. It had the corporate title of Memphis, Paris & Gulf. But for some reason, nothing was accomplished with this venture. Then on June 16, 1906, a new charter was granted, and the MP & G was revived. The same title was retained, but the promoters deflated their initial ambitions. Now the objective was to build a standard-gauge road from Nashville to Ashdown, twenty-five miles to the southwest, where connection could be made with the Kansas City Southern. This would provide a nationwide outlet for an area having great potential in fruit-bearing orchards.

The greatest incentive for building the road was the Nashville Lumber Company. The Memphis, Paris & Gulf and the lumber firm were both incorporated at the same time and by the same people: Brown-Henderson Improvement & Timber Company, formed by W. W. Brown and C. C. Henderson. Brown was from Camden, Arkansas, while Henderson hailed from Arkadelphia.

When the railroad was resurrected, it was financed by a capital stock issue of $375,000, owned predominantly by Brown; Henderson; R. E. Major, W. E. Barkman, and J. H. Hineman, all of Arkadelphia; and L. L. Cooper and T. M. Dodson of Malvern.

Their plan was to have the railroad serve in several capacities. For example, along the route to connect with the KCS at Ashdown, the MP & G would tap an area embracing many thousands of acres of heavily timbered land. This was being bought by Brown-Henderson Improvement & Timber Company as quickly as its timber scouts could cruise the countryside and make satisfactory deals with the owners.

Through the forest, spur tracks would lead from the main line to temporary camps set up by timber cutters. As the trees were felled and trimmed, the logs could be loaded aboard coupling pole-connected rail trucks and delivered to the Nashville mill. When the road was completed, a steady supply of fine Arkansas pine lumber would be dispatched to the markets of America.

As an additional service, the rails would bring settlers into the quickly developing territory, the fruits of their labor would leave by way of the same rails, and the commodities they required would of necessity be shipped in by rail. It would be a profitable cycle. To select the most feasible route, a crew of civil engineers was brought in. Then on June 20, 1906, equipment began to arrive at Nashville: wagons with heavy, iron-tired wheels; many teams of mules and several saddle horses; canvas bedrolls, blankets, transits, level rods, axes, and saws; a wagon outfitted with implements and provisions for preparing three meals a day for men with ravenous appetites. The survey crew had arrived.

On the morning of June 25, a field camp was set up near Midway Church, about three miles out of Nashville. The chief engineer in charge of the survey party drove the first stake between the iron rails of the Arkansas & Louisiana Railroad at the northwest edge of town. The A & L was a lightweight extension of the St. Louis, Iron Mountain & Southern, branching off the high iron at Hope. The engineer set up his transit, turned an angle of south and approximately sixty degrees west, and the crew began driving stakes at 10:00 A.M. Connection was to be made with the A & L near the north side of its depot. The men quickly made their way across the grassy pasture lands.

Early in July, the final route was established and bids were taken for the grading work. J. F. Anders was awarded the contract for grading the first two-mile section out of Nashville. Various other sections were given to other contractors. Along the six-mile segment from Nashville to Mineral Springs, there would be no cuts more than three feet deep. The same held true from a point two miles beyond Mineral Springs. Some heavier cutting was required for a couple of miles beyond the Mineral Springs depot site, which was located on property owned by Hattie Mulkey. Several contracts were signed after negotiations for right-of-way and land for the depot had been completed.

The year 1906 saw the beginning of immigration in the Nashville area. The community's industries had been founded and developed by home-grown talent and were proving to be very efficient. Nashville now had fifteen hundred people, twenty-six business houses, seven churches, two wholesale houses, two banks, one of the state's largest brick cotton warehouses, and a very efficient school system. A new brick courthouse had been erected at a cost of $16,000, while the school, grounds, and dormitory were valued at $20,000. Assessed property valuation in Howard County was $1,747,489, with less than $14,000 on the debit side of the ledger. During the previous season, the shipment of cotton totaled nearly twenty thousand bales. The folks at Nashville enjoyed the convenience of natural gas in their homes, were soon to have electric lights, and the town was working on a system for piping water from artesian wells to all homes and businesses.

Through the sultry heat of summer, there was great activity around the campsites of the construction crews. Teams of long-eared, methodical mules strained against Fresno slips to grade up the roadbed across rolling swells of grassland or snake downed trees from the right-of-way through the forest. The robust shouts and blasphemous curses of the mule skinners added to the general din and riotous confusion. The roaring blast of powder boomed hour after hour as stumps were torn from the earth. By the time darkness smothered the fading glow of day, the dancing flames of the cook's fire had retreated to leave a radiant bed of coals. The camp's swamper made a great clatter as he washed the piles of heavy pots, pans, kettles, and tin plates. Weary men lounged near the canvas tents, appearing as ghostly shapes in the gathering darkness. Pipe bowls nestled in the palms of rough, horny hands and cigarettes glowed intermittently, then died. Soft bars of guitar music were gently strummed, and the mournful, vibrant tones of a mouth organ drifted through the warm evening air. Here and there a figure rose, stretched, and moved to one of the tents. The mutter of voices grew quiet, and a peaceful night settled on a camp of weary men.

Day by day, the roadbed was graded through the forest toward a promised connection with the KCS and the Frisco at Ashdown. Preparations were proceeding nicely for construction of the large sawmill at Nashville. To feed its hungry saws, Brown-Henderson had purchased from Dierks Lumber Company 5,300 acres of timber land lying east of Saline River and south of the road between Locksburg and Centerpoint, about seven miles west of Nashville, for the princely sum of $37,000. Thousands of acres more were acquired for as little as a dollar an acre.

While the grading crews were busy, C. C. Henderson, president of the MP & G, visited Ashdown. Here, early in September, 1906, he promised citizens to run his road into their town and establish his car and engine shops there if they would subscribe to a nice cash bonus and donate land for a depot and the right-of-way through town. The townspeople gave him twelve thousand dollars and acquired the right-of-way, not only through town, but all the way to White Cliffs, a distance of about six miles. The clincher was his hint that the MP & G would terminate at White Cliffs and use the rails of the KCS branch to Wilton, then continue down the main line to Ashdown.

Charles Dodson, manager of the Dodson Construction Company, which had the general contract for grading the right-of-way, went to Monroe, Louisiana, in the latter part of July to ship a carload of mules to Nashville to be used in grading. Two cars of long-eared motive power were en route already. Meanwhile, Henderson had made arrangements with the Nashville Telephone Company for the use of three rooms in its building "uptown" as the railroad's main offices while the depot was being erected.

By October, 1906, nine miles of roadbed had been graded and now awaited ties and rails. The first shipment of rails was expected the third week of October. Ten carloads were all the dealers could supply, for rails were scarce. The first locomotive had been ordered and was expected to arrive at about the same time as the rails.

The engineering corps said the route would require fifteen bridges, two of which would be of considerable size; one would cross the Saline River, and the other would span Little River. A contract for building them was awarded to the Covington & Parks Bridge Company.

On the morning of October 19, the first carload of rails for the MP & G arrived on the Arkansas & Louisiana. A crew of gandy dancers quickly used them to construct a temporary branch line from the A & L track about three hundred yards to MP & G right-of-way. There was no time to lose because if the MP & G engine arrived and could not be transported to its home road, the A & L would charge storage on it. So a few ties were dropped and rails were spiked into place.

About the first of November, additional rails were received and the anxiously awaited locomotive came rolling in. A little sixty-ton job, she was immediately put to work distributing rails and ties. Construction would proceed much faster now.

The MP & G wanted to install a crossing at grade with the A & L track, but the A & L men said it would be much too close to their depot and would be very dangerous. Bitter words were exchanged until roadmaster Woods of the Arkansas & Louisiana arrived on the scene. He said that any Memphis, Paris & Gulf man who came onto the A & L property would be arrested for trespassing. MP & G officials immediately had Judge Steele issue a restraining order forbidding the A & L to interfere with the crossing installation in any manner.

Meanwhile, Brown-Henderson had purchased another five thousand acres of timber land in Hempstead and Little River counties contiguous to the railroad, assuring more business once the trains and sawmill were in operation. The price of land was on the increase, however; the tract cost slightly more than six dollars an acre.

To begin 1907 in the proper manner, the MP & G received its second engine on January 11. She was a small lightweight hog and was assigned the task of bringing loaded log trains from the temporary logging camps to the main line, where they could be picked up by engine No. 1 and taken to the Nashville mill. A third engine had been ordered.

Speed was held down on the new road because the track had been laid with only ten ties to each rail in the area around Nashville. Here timber was scarce, and transportation would remain a problem until the rails could reach the timber country to the south. To remedy this situation, gandy dancers were rapidly pushing through the forest and over the grassland swells.

The route through Ashdown followed the center of Whittaker

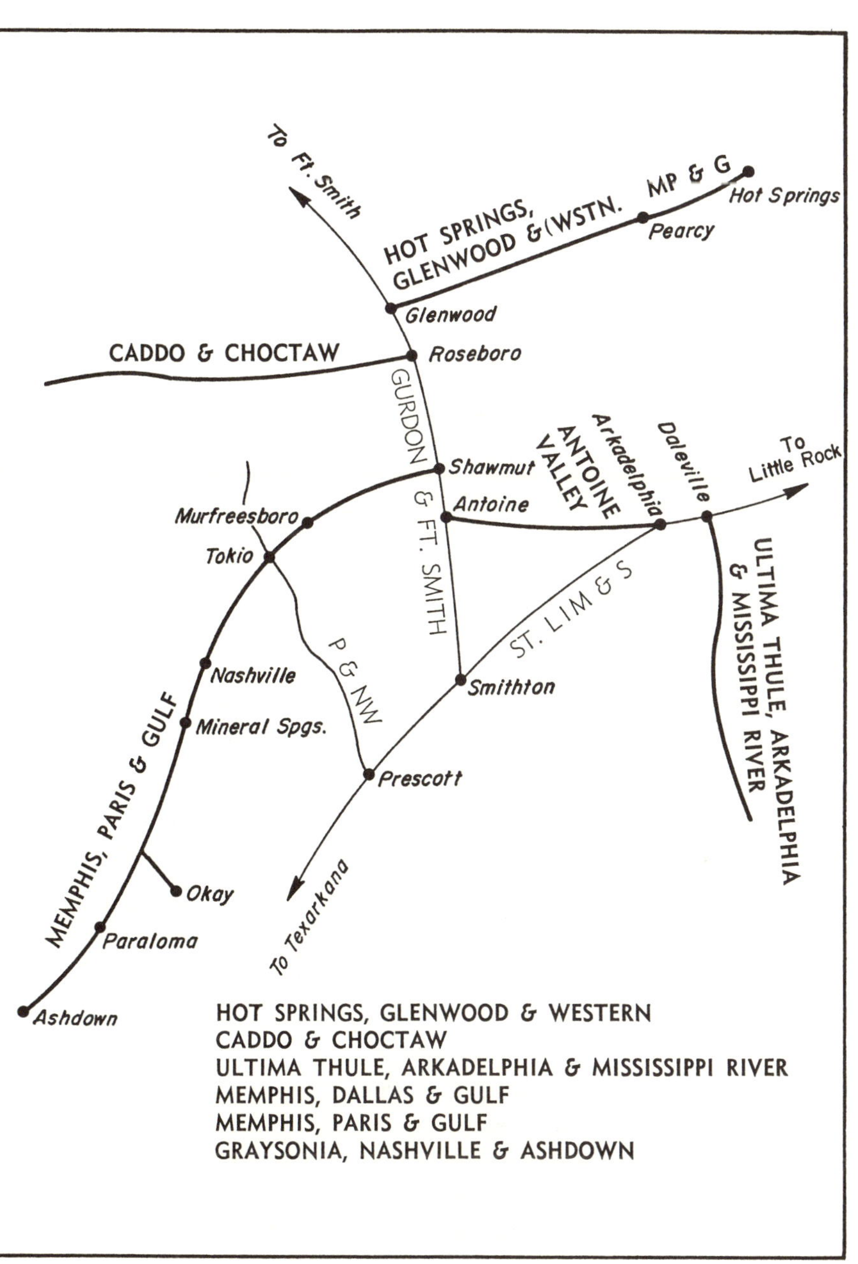

To Ft. Smith
HOT SPRINGS,
GLENWOOD & (WSTN.
MP & G
Hot Springs
Pearcy
Glenwood
CADDO & CHOCTAW
Roseboro
GURDON & FT. SMITH
Shawmut
Antoine
ANTOINE
VALLEY
Arkadelphia
Daleville
To
Little Rock
Murfreesboro
Tokio
ULTIMA THULE, ARKADELPHIA
& MISSISSIPPI RIVER
ST. L I M & S
P & NW
Smithton
Nashville
Mineral Spgs.
Prescott
MEMPHIS, PARIS & GULF
Okay
Paraloma
To Texarkana
Ashdown
HOT SPRINGS, GLENWOOD & WESTERN
CADDO & CHOCTAW
ULTIMA THULE, ARKADELPHIA & MISSISSIPPI RIVER
MEMPHIS, DALLAS & GULF
MEMPHIS, PARIS & GULF
GRAYSONIA, NASHVILLE & ASHDOWN

Avenue, passing directly through the business district between the Frisco and Kansas City Southern depots. Ballast, consisting of gravel hauled from Mine Creek near Nashville, was eight to twenty-four inches deep.

Late in February, 1907, the Arkansas Legislature passed a bill giving the MP & G permission to construct a bridge across Little River at White Cliffs. The stream was navigable, so spanning it was subject to approval by the state. The railroad was authorized to construct a bridge without a swing span. Thus navigation up the Little River would now terminate at White Cliffs.

All legal problems had now been resolved, and a crossing diamond was installed in the Arkansas & Louisiana track near its depot at Nashville on April 19. The third MP & G engine had arrived, and the Brown-Henderson mill blew its whistle for the first time. Full operation was rapidly approaching. The first car of logs to travel over the MP & G rolled into the mill on April 27, 1907, coming from an area served by a spur track along Dillard Creek.

Enthusiasm pervaded the area served by the MP & G. For several years, Dr. T. J. Garner, of the old capital city of Washington, Arkansas, had maintained a hotel a short distance east of where the MP & G had recently installed its crossing with the A & L at Nashville. Early in April, he asked contractor F. M. Buxton to estimate the cost of a new brick structure on the site of the old building.

On May 3, 1907, an impressive group of men arrived in Nashville. Spokesman for the delegation was Edward F. Cost, vice president of the Kansas City Southern. He was accompanied by twenty bankers and capitalists, some from Kansas City and others from Missouri, Kansas, and Michigan, who were interested in the huge limestone deposits discovered at White Cliffs in 1890, which, they had determined, contained "an inexhaustible supply." Although a previous attempt at development had fizzled out and nothing had been done in more than four years, these men proposed to invest $1,500,000 to rehabilitate the cement plant and put it into production. Half the money would be supplied by investors from Holland, the other half by American capitalists; the new firm's principal office would be established at Texarkana. It promised to be a profitable venture, since cement was selling for $1.70 a barrel when the plant was in operation earlier and the price had now risen to $3.50.

With the coming of winter in 1907, the Memphis, Paris & Gulf had joined the towns of Nashville and Ashdown, and on December 23, this schedule went into effect.

Daily No. 1	* No. 3		Daily No. 2	* No. 4
4:30 A	2:10 P	Lv. Nashville Ar.	12:10 P	6:00 P
———	3:30 P	Ar. Paraloma Lv.	———	4:40 P
6:30 A	———	Ar. Ashdown Lv.	9:40 A	———

* Daily except Sunday

The full complement of passenger equipment had arrived on the Arkansas & Louisiana evening train December 21 and was immediately pressed into service. There was a varnished wood coach for white passengers and a highly polished combine for mail, express, baggage, and Negro passengers.

A momentous occasion for the 25-mile pike was April 13, 1908, when U. S. mail service was inaugurated. This important cargo was transported in sealed pouches only, so no clerk was required for sorting and handling.

When regular service had been established, the rolling stock and all business letterheads were decorated with a diamond-shaped monogram with a many-faceted jewel in its center. This was to call attention to the newly discovered diamond fields near Murfreesboro, Arkansas, the only diamond-producing area on the North American continent. John Huddleston had found the first stones there on August 1, 1906. Inside the diamond insignia and surrounding the sparkling gem there was lettered "Diamond Route," by which the road was known. There was speculation that the MP & G rails would be extended northeast from Nashville to the diamond fields.

During the fall and winter months of 1907, the final touches were being put on the ballasting work. The gandy dancers' camp was set up just a few miles from Ashdown; it would be the last campsite until the job was finished. Since the days were growing shorter, there was a longer interval between quitting time and bedtime.

Quite a few members of the work gang were Negroes, and their presence was resented by the native white people. For one thing, the whites felt the Negroes should not be holding jobs which local residents believed were rightfully their own and which they needed very much.

One of the contractors was approached by a delegation of white citizens one evening after supper. It was their studied opinion, they said, that it would be most beneficial for all concerned if he would discharge his Negro laborers and replace them with men from near-by communities.

The group happened to be standing near the mule corral, where the corral boss, a Negro, was on guard, sitting on a bale of hay. A ring of lanterns, hanging from tree branches, surrounded the corral, enabling the guard to spot an intruder from any side of the enclosure. Across his lap lay a rifle.

The Negro guard heard the demand made by the visitors. He raised his rifle to his shoulder. Methodically and rapidly, he sent a bullet crashing through each of the lighted lanterns. Discretion being the better part of valor, the whites decided they had business elsewhere. The Negro crews continued working on the railroad.

The winter of 1907 saw the beginning of growing pains for the Memphis, Paris & Gulf. The name "Paris" in the corporate title grew more and more alluring. About noon on Saturday, December 5, H. L. Remmel, president of the Mercantile Trust Company of Little Rock, and W. W. Brown, president of the Ouachita Valley Bank at Camden, returned to Nashville from St. Louis. In the midst of the 1907–1908 depression, they had been successful in their efforts to sell $500,000 worth of MP & G bonds. This, indeed, spoke very well of their ability to convince strangers of the value of a 25-mile newly built railroad in Arkansas.

The money was to be used for extending the MP & G from Ashdown to Paris, Texas, by way of Clarksville. Another extension was to be built from Nashville to a connection with the Bemis Road—the local name for the Prescott & Northwestern—about eight miles northwest of town. The next step was to proceed through Hot Springs, then follow an uncertain route to Hopefield or West Memphis on the Mississippi River.

The townspeople of Paris promised a donation of $100,000 when the rails reached their town. If the rails reached Paris, there existed the possibility of making connection with several other roads: the Paris & Mt. Pleasant, the Frisco, the Gulf, Colorado & Santa Fe, the Southern Pacific, and the Texas Pacific. This seemed to be sufficient inducement to persuade the Lesser & Goldman Cotton Company to invest $500,000 in the venture. The firm had already bought $500,000 worth of Plum Bayou Levee District bonds, so it was no stranger to business opportunities in Arkansas. It was at this time that the names of the more prominent people concerned with the MP & G were made known. They were, besides Brown and Henderson, W. K. Ramsey and Mrs. J. W. Brown of Camden; A. C. Ramsey, C. W. Dodson, H. C. Anderson, W. J. Reisinger, T. Lowenburg, J. T. Elder, O. O. Moore, W. W. Wilson, J. H. Wallace, J. L. Skillern, and James Skillern, all of Nashville; W. E. Barkman, R. E. Major, and R. B. F. Key of Arkadelphia; J. L. Cooper of Malvern; and H. L. Remmel of Little Rock.

The railroad was saved the added expense of installing a communication line of its own when the Nashville Telephone Company completed a line to Ashdown and established an office in the Frisco depot. The MP & G decided to lease these lines and build its own later.

A route survey was made to Paris, Texas, and the folks there pitched in to help extend it to some point on the Gulf of Mexico.

The surveyors proceeded south a few miles and called a halt at the little town of Ferrell. Time passed, the survey stakes rotted in the ground, and nothing more was heard of running the rails to Paris.

There was enough interest in tapping the new diamond fields to the north and west of Nashville that five Murfreesboro citizens came to Nashville on January 8, 1908, to talk with railroad officials: J. C. Pinnix, C. B. Owens, C. A. Kizzia, C. A. Kelley, and J. N. Riley. They met with president W. W. Brown, superintendent C. W. Dodson, and traffic manager A. C. Ramsey.

No details of the meeting were made public, but there was probably only a bit of sparring and talk in generalities, with no definite commitments from either side. The visitors said they were very hopeful that the railroad would come to their town and that a public meeting would be held in the near future at Murfreesboro so that a report could be made to the railroad officials by January 21, when the annual meeting of the stockholders would be held.

While this dickering was going on, superintendent Dodson was informed that doctors had definitely diagnosed two cases of smallpox at White Cliffs. In the early days of this century, smallpox was a highly dreaded disease because it was capable of going on a rampage and annihilating entire communities. Dodson acted immediately by forbidding any train to stop at White Cliffs until the doctors reported there was no danger. The action was effective, for no cases were reported at any other near-by area settlement.

Business was very good on the MP & G. Two locomotives were running regularly on the main line, and another was kept busy trundling log trains out of the woods to sidings at strategic points along the main line.

On the morning of March 3, 1908, contractor E. A. Williams was seen beside the track at Nashville, carefully and deliberately scratching furrows in the ground with a pointed stick. Some curious citizens stopped to watch a few minutes, then asked what was going on. He told them he was marking the outline of a new passenger and freight depot. It was going to be a one-story frame structure, thirty-two feet wide and sixty-six feet long. He was also planning to grade up a roadbed for a storage track, just south of the main line near the depot, where the passenger equipment could be stored and trains could be made up.

A few days later, the spring rains came. Rain fell day after day. The new roadbed became soggy and soft. The creeks rose until they ran bankfull. Still the rains came.

Little River rose by the hour. Muddy waters swished and hissed along the crumbling banks and swirled angrily around the pile bents of the railroad bridge. One bent near the east bank quivered as a floating tree collided with it. The tree turned as the rushing waters fought to carry it past this barrier and on downstream. The heavy root growth swung into the swift current, then wrapped its tentacles about a second bent. It was only a matter of minutes until debris, riding the crest of the flood, began to accumulate, forming a dam.

The tremendous force of the flood proved to be a worthy adversary. The bridge piling gave way, and twelve spans fell, sank beneath the flood, and were swept away. When the unruly waters finally subsided, there was a 400-foot gap in the bridge. Only an 80-foot section was left standing. The rampaging Little River had put the MP & G completely out of business.

Company officials decided to profit from their sad experience. Early in April, they met in Nashville with representatives of bridge contractors from Kansas City, St. Louis, and Chicago. The Kansas City Bridge Company was awarded a contract to build a 400-foot steel bridge across Little River. It was to be strong enough to withstand any future flood.

The railroad company had a contract with Uncle Sam to deliver mail to Ashdown, and the mail had to move. The story was told that at each end of the open gap across the river temporary supports were erected. Rails were spliced together with bolts and fishplates, and soon a continuous line of twin rails spanned the gap, 200 feet of them swinging free, with nothing under them but air and water. A small Chevrolet mail truck was fitted with flanged wheels, and the sacks of mail were stowed aboard. The little four-wheel mail train slowly inched its way out onto sagging rails. After what must have seemed an eternity, the venturesome vehicle rolled away toward Ashdown with its precious cargo. It also was reported that the mail sacks were taken across the river by boat, then wheeled seven miles into Ashdown aboard a motorcar.

Joe Wilson, owner of the Wilson Engineering Company at Texarkana, was a novice at the time of the flood. He was given the task of assisting the surveying engineer in setting grade stakes to govern the excavation work required to remove the muck of a large landslide which had covered the track near the west bank. The chief set up his transit, and he and Joe began driving a line of stakes for the excavation crew to follow. Joe scooped up an armload of stakes and began a laborious struggle up the soft mud-slide. Partway up the slope, he heard a coughing, grunting sound above the wheezing of his own laboring lungs. Glancing up, he suddenly froze. Disputing his passage was a wild razorback boar, ivory tusks curling upward from its lower jaw well above its snout and red eyes glinting. Prudently Joe backtracked. After a while, the boar made a triumphant retreat into the forest with inherent arrogance.

A bit of disappointing news was received in the spring of 1908: the cement plant at White Cliffs was in receivership and had been ordered sold to the highest bidder on May 7 unless full operation were resumed. All officials of the company had gone to Kansas City in an effort to procure between $75,000 and $100,000 to salvage the plant. The deposits of limestone were rich and extensive and there was a fairly good market for cement, but the plant's equipment was obsolete and in rather poor condition. This made it very difficult for the company to compete with other concerns equipped with more modern facilities. Closing the plant would mean a loss of revenue for the railroad.

There was seldom a dull moment in the life of the MP & G. On a bright spring day in May, 1908, the southbound passenger train pulled out of Nashville right on the advertised. There was a most satisfactory crowd of passengers, and all was well with the world. The engine rocked and swayed just enough to keep the crew from taking a nap.

A few miles south of Nashville, the train swept around a curve, and the hogger saw three horses a short distance ahead, grazing along the track. His left hand reached for the cord swaying just above his head. Hauling down on it, he let the whistle blast out its raucous warning. This startled the three horses. They tossed their heads high, snorted, and stampeded—directly in front of the engine, along the ends of the ties and across the trestle. The hogger big-holed the brakes, and the little train bucked and jumped as the brakeshoes grabbed at the wheels.

Two horses made it across, but the third stumbled, almost fell, and then its feet dropped between the ties, blocking the trestle. It struggled furiously, but was held fast, snorting and whistling through flared nostrils. As the terrified animal fought the confining prison of the trestle, just as furiously did the engineer fight to halt the train. It bucked to a stop just as the pilot reached the end of the trestle. The hogger and his fireman, weak and trembling with relief, climbed shakily to the ground. An animal of that size was guaranteed to wreck a train. Employees and passengers would surely end up in the creek beneath the trestle.

It soon was determined that the trapped animal was more frightened than injured, though bruises and lost hide were abundantly evident. The train crew and several scared and shaken passengers came up to survey the damage. A handsaw was found after a few minutes of rummaging through the baggage compartment of the combine. Several timbers of the trestle were cut through, and the frightened horse finally was freed. The train was delayed two hours.

The business prospects of the MP & G had brightened considerably by the time summer arrived. The fourth locomotive came in and was promptly assigned to work-train service. Two carloads of steel had arrived at Nashville for use in constructing the new bridge at White Cliffs, and officials had ordered begun the survey for extending the rails toward Murfreesboro and the Pike County diamond fields.

The survey was put in charge of civil engineer Buchanan from Little Rock. His crew began driving stakes in front of the new brick Garner Hotel, crossed Mine Creek near the Nashville Lumber Company mill, then turned north through the fairgrounds (this portion later was relocated to give a better grade with less cut and fill). The first camp was set up about five miles northwest of Nashville.

While staking out the right-of-way and securing permission from property owners to cross their land, Buchanan's crew arrived at the home of one very cantankerous settler. They found the bearded old fellow sitting on the front porch of a rough-hewn log cabin. A gun leaned against the wall beside him. No infernal, smoke-belching railroad was going across his place!

The surveyors decided not to dispute the authority of a smoothbore squirrel rifle, so back to camp they went. A bit of inquiry revealed that several years earlier, the settler had caught up with a man whom he thought was wanted by the sheriff. He proceeded to clamp a chain around the man's leg and secure him to a stump in the front yard at his cabin. Making a casual trip to town, he found his suspicions confirmed: there was a five-hundred-dollar reward for the fugitive, dead or alive. Returning home not quite so casually, the settler came to the spot where the fellow was chained to the stump, contemplating his bad run of luck, which had now come to a sudden end. The old fellow decided there was always a chance his prisoner would escape before they got back to town, so, to protect his "investment," he put a rifle ball through the fugitive's head, draped his body across a pack mule, took him to town, and collected.

It would be the height of stupidity to try to drive survey stakes across that man's property. There was only one thing to do. The chief engineer backtracked to the point where his line approached the settler's boundary and set up his transit. He instructed his rodman to go around this particular piece of land and come down the opposite boundary. When the latter appeared at the far side of the clearing, the engineer was able to establish the desired point and proceed with his survey. The crew entered the Murfreesboro city limits at noon on July 12, 1908. Oh, yes, the court ruled in favor of the railroad and the rails crossed the old settler's farm.

The contract for clearing the entire route was awarded to Charles Kilgore, who also got the contract for furnishing all of the bridge piling. Grading work was the responsibility of W. V. Murphy, who hired several subcontractors to lend a hand. The grading was fairly simple, since the profile followed the contour of the rolling countryside as closely as possible. The only real difficulty came when the line approached the Little Missouri River, where a cut through an abrupt swell just south of the river was required to put the rails thirty-seven feet below the top of the ridge. This task was given to W. H. Dennison, who had young Joe Wilson working for him.

One day while inspecting a portion of the cut, an engineer by the name of McClure found what appeared to be a piece of pottery buried in the mud. He dug around it, lifted it out, and carefully cleaned away the clinging muck. It was an Indian water bottle, such as was customarily buried with its owner. After cleaning the bottle, McClure could see there was something wadded up inside it. Taking a small forked twig, he carefully extracted a well-preserved human scalp with a heavy growth of auburn hair attached. The gruesome discovery was presented to superintendent Dodson.

Joe Wilson recalls that as the cut grew deeper, it became muddier, since only a small amount of water was required to make the reddish clay very soft and spongy. The mules, pulling and tugging at the heavily loaded Fresno slips, began to sink into the quagmire. The drivers cajoled, cursed, and whipped, but the mules just sank a little deeper. Finally, one team after another balked and lay down in the mud; if they were going to sink in the mud, it might as well be while they were resting. One of the men went to a near-by logging camp and borrowed some oxen which were being used to snake logs out of the woods. Back at the cut, an ox team was driven up to one of the mules which had laid down on the job and a trace chain was attached to the ox yoke. Mr. Mule was dragged out of the way, the ox team was hitched to the scraper, and work continued.

The construction crew of the Kansas City Bridge Company, responsible for the new span across Little River at White Cliffs, was excavating to set the piers on a firm foundation. During the afternoon of July 20, 1908, the tools struck an object which wasn't solid enough to support a bridge but which impeded progress. Digging around it for a while, the men discovered it was the hulk of a steamboat, sunk many years earlier when there was quite a lot of river traffic. It didn't take long for them to decide it wasn't worth raising, so it was dynamited out of the way.

Meanwhile, at Nashville, there was another meeting of railroad officials and a group from Murfreesboro. The people of Murfreesboro wanted a railroad badly enough to make a cash donation of fifteen thousand dollars and to provide right-of-way from where the rails crossed the Pike County line all the way to Murfreesboro. In addition, there would be a gift of land for a depot site and room for a marshaling yard, all not to exceed ten acres inside the town limits. In return, the railroad promised to have trains running to Murfreesboro within eighteen months.

While negotiations were going on, the grading crews were busy, a bridge gang was spanning the Little Missouri River, and a railroad crew was driving trestle piling across Mine Creek at Nashville. The first rail was spiked down on December 14, 1908. Water tanks were to be built at Little River, Nashville, and Murfreesboro, with pumps operated by gasoline engines.

The MP & G made arrangements with the Prescott & Northwestern to install a crossing where the rails met near Tokio. The MP & G had also purchased the extensive McMahon Gravel Pits in the vicinity of Highland, a short distance north of Tokio Junction, and the P & NW agreed to permit MP & G trains to use its track to the gravel pits. The crossing was completed and switches installed to give access to the P & NW by February 22, 1909, and gravel trains began running immediately to supply the Kansas City Southern with ballasting gravel. The Hope Brick Works bought two hundred carloads. This extra business really put a strain on the four MP & G engines, so, early in March, master mechanic J. B. Steward went to Hattiesburg, Mississippi, to inspect an engine which the Gulf & Ship Island had put up for sale.

The morning of Sunday, April 12, 1909, dawned bright and clear. The MP & G auditor, W. J. Peppard, and a Mr. Mills from the Nashville Lumber Company decided it was a perfect day for a ride over the new road toward Murfreesboro, so they went down to the depot and fired up one of the gasoline motorcars. Thumping over the crossing diamond at the Arkansas & Louisiana track, the car rumbled across the Mine Creek bridge, slowed for the crossing of the wagon road to Prescott, and then they were out of town. Letting the car putt-putt along lazily, they gave themselves up to the enjoyment of a beautiful spring day.

Entering the deep cut at the Little Missouri River, Peppard shut the engine off and let the car roll to a stop. The men spent nearly all morning inspecting the uncompleted new steel bridge and climbing to the top of the cut. When they were ready to leave, they discovered that the engine of the motorcar refused to start. Pulling and tugging at the starter cord proved futile, and putting the car in gear and pushing it along the track was a waste of strength. Giving up in disgust, they were forced to leave the gas buggy and borrow one of the old "armstrong" hand-pumped cars.

Alternately bending and straightening, they pumped the handle up and down, up and down. The miles passed slowly, and sweat stained their white shirts. As it approached Nashville, the track was on a descending grade. Happily taking advantage of this, the weary travelers ducked clear of the up-and-down flailing of the handle with which they had been laboring for so many miles. With the cool breeze drying their sweat-stained shirts, they were enjoying the free ride.

Just before they reached the wagon road to Prescott, Mills noticed that the free-wheeling car was rapidly approaching a switch, the points of which had been left lined for a spur track. With a startled yell, he joined the birds. The speeding car struck the open switch and lurched through the turnout and onto the spur track. Peppard was thrown clear and plowed up several yards of newly placed gravel ballast, luckily missing the rails and the ends of the ties. Mills was pretty well shaken up, but Peppard didn't fare so well. His white shirt, Sunday trousers, and a large area of skin were rather badly treated by the gravel ballast; fortunately, no bones were broken. The experience satisfied these fellows' desire to ride handcars.

Another group of citizens from points along the route from Ashdown to Nashville decided they, too, wanted to see what the new piece of railroad looked like, but they went about it in a more prosaic manner, commonplace as it may seem when compared to the Mills-Peppard adventure. They traveled aboard six passenger coaches loaded to the platforms.

The train left Ashdown early on the morning of May 7, stopping every two or three miles to welcome aboard a few more eager excursionists. They were well supplied with food in wicker picnic baskets, a great variety of fishing tackle, and several box cameras. Before the train reached Nashville, it was evident that all the folks who wanted to make the trip would never be able to crowd into the coaches. Another train was called to accommodate the overflow crowd. They left Nashville at 12:30 P.M.

Groups of happy, hungry travelers gathered in the shade beneath convenient newly leafed trees for the spreading of a picnic lunch. Privacy-seeking young couples strolled nonchalantly along the river, passing the eager Nimrods casting fish lures into the placid, blue-green waters. Several venturesome young daredevils made their way out onto the steel framework of the bridge reaching almost to the opposite bank of the Little Missouri. Such was a day in the unhurried era of innocence on a shortline railroad in Arkansas.

The Kansas City Bridge Company put the finishing touches to the Little Missouri structure on May 25, 1909, and the gandy dancers took advantage of good weather to spike down the rails. A festive spirit was evident among the crews, and tracklaying progressed rapidly. On June 4, 1909, the first train entered Murfreesboro in the warm glow of an afternoon sun, and a new MP & G time card was issued, effective June 5:

Pass *No. 1*	Mixed *No. 3*		Pass *No. 2*	Mixed *No. 4*
5:00 A	3:00 P	Lv. Murfreesboro Ar.	9:10 P	12:00 A
5:43 A	4:00 P	Ar. Nashville Ar.	8:27 P	11:00 A
7:00 A	6:15 P	Ar. Ashdown Lv.	7:10 P	9:00 A

Joe Wilson recalls that after construction was finished, he worked for the railroad in various capacities. There was one day in particular that he is not likely to forget. Joe was working as a brakeman on one of the gravel trains. The Kansas City Southern was extensively ballasting its tracks, and most of the good gravel was coming from the McMahon pits near Highland. It was being delivered in trainload lots by the Memphis, Paris & Gulf to the KCS at Ashdown.

One warm summer day, Joe was helping herd a train of gravel cars to the KCS connection. He had climbed out of the hot confines of the caboose, made his way up the rear ladder, and was perched on the roof of the crummy. There were eighteen cars of gravel between him and the engine, removing the annoyance of hot cinders dropping down his shirt collar or lodging in one or both eyes.

Sitting ensconced on the swaying crummy roof, Joe was thoroughly enjoying the passing countryside and the pressure of the cooling breeze on his face. Peace and contentment lulled his senses into inattention as the train rolled across the undulating land southwest of Mineral Springs. The first intimation he had that all was not as it should be came when he glanced toward the smoky end of the train and saw several cars of gravel loping off the track in various directions. A well-behaved train just doesn't act like that. By the time Joe fully realized what was happening, it was too late to join the birds.

The car of gravel just ahead of him slewed crosswise of the track, and the leading truck of the galloping crummy reared up and over the vagabond gondola. A very scared young brakie clung to the deck of his wild crummy as it came to a precarious rest atop the upside-down gondola. There was quite a conglomeration of scattered ballast, unattached wheel trucks, and truckless gondolas. The locomotive remained on the track, but everything else had wandered to various and sundry spots along the right-of-way. Joe and the bruised conductor climbed off and out of the crummy and began making their way around the rubble toward the head end. They were near the new town of Paraloma, so the wreck was reported from there.

After a bit of investigation, it was determined that a log train had entered the main line from one of the various spurs with a carelessly secured length of chain dangling from one of its cars. The dragging chain had split a switch, and when the gravel train came along, the switch points opened and cars began leapfrogging in all directions.

Even while the rails were being pushed eastward to Murfreesboro, the Memphis, Paris & Gulf was feeling growing pains. In the first week of February, 1909, president Brown and chief engineer Le Manna left Nashville on a scouting survey to find a suitable route into Hot Springs. Two alternate routes were being considered, and the men intended to inspect both thoroughly before returning to town. One line extended from Murfreesboro, by way of Amity, into Hot Springs. The other possibility was to go southeast through Graysonia to Malvern, where connection could be made with the Rock Island. From there, trackage rights could be arranged for access into Hot Springs over the old Hot Springs Railway (the Diamond Jo).

A third route was surveyed north from Murfreesboro to Glenwood by way of Stanley and Kirby, crossing the fourteen-mile Caddo & Choctaw Railroad. The C & C was incorporated April 19, 1907, to build west from Roseboro, headquarters of the Caddo Lumber Company on the Gurdon & Ft. Smith, to logging camps in the woods toward Cooper. The trains hauled saw logs to the large mill at Roseboro. The MP & G survey crew discovered a rugged mountain between Stanley and Kirby, however, and it was finally decided that a line northeast from Murfreesboro to Shawmut on the Gurdon & Ft. Smith would be the most desirable route. The rails of the G & FTS would be available for trackage rights to Glenwood.

Glenwood was the western terminus of the Hot Springs, Glenwood & Western Railroad. In November, 1908, the Thrall & Shay Lumber Mill of Lake Charles, Louisiana, moved a large mill into Glenwood, making a total of three fairly large mills near by employing more than one thousand men. The new mill was to have a daily capacity of 50,000 board feet. The A. L. Clark Lumber Company of Gilmore, Texas, was also moving in a big mill, and there was talk of a railroad into Hot Springs.

The HSG & W was incorporated April 16, 1910, to build from Glenwood, in Pike County, six miles east to Caney, in Montgomery County; the charter was altered as required to extend the road. The first twelve miles were completed and the first train ran on Saturday afternoon, July 3, 1910. There was a huge celebration at Glenwood.

Work was begun July 5 on a ten-mile extension to Pearcy. A. L. Clark Lumber Company, builder of the road, was making plans to extend the rails through Hot Springs and on to Little Rock. The route traversed some of the best timber country in western Arkansas, and Glenwood grew from a village of three hundred to a town of twelve hundred in only six months as a result of the new mills and the railroad. More important, the HSG & W would give the MP & G trackage rights to within eighteen miles of Hot Springs.

The series of events noted above was the deciding factor in locating the MP & G route into Hot Springs. With so much established, it was almost certain that MP & G trains would roll to the City of Vapors. MP & G officials had already approached Hot Springs citizens, who were enthusiastic about the idea. In fact, they were so enthusiastic that they agreed to make a cash bonus of $100,000 to the MP & G and to donate six miles of right-of-way from the Ouachita River into town. They would also render as much assistance as possible in securing right-of-way to the heart of town.

In August, 1909, superintendent Dodson, secretary J. W. Bishop, and H. C. Anderson, assistant manager of the Nashville Lumber Company, journeyed to Hot Springs for a meeting with some of the businessmen's organizations. When they arrived, they learned that three members of the Hot Springs Executive Committee were out of town. The MP & G men, asked to return in about sixty days, were assured the deal would be closed.

Feeling certain the road was facing prosperous days, MP & G officials bought two new locomotives in July, making a total of eight. The railroad was only forty-two miles long that summer, but it had one engine for each five and one-half miles of track, and additional engines were to be purchased soon to accommodate rapidly increasing business.

W. J. Covington of Nashville had a cousin, Mrs. J. A. Covington, who lived in Pike County near the diamond fields. Fifty-seven years old in 1909, she had never ridden on a train; in fact, she had never *seen* a train. Girding up her courage, she went to Murfreesboro, bought herself a ticket to Nashville, and bravely climbed aboard. Recalling the trip, she said she had enjoyed it immensely, although she had to admit she was a mite apprehensive when the train rolled out onto a the big steel bridge high above the Little Missouri River. All in all, it was a most rewarding experience.

On August 20, 1909, W. W. Brown officially announced at Nashville that the MP & G was going to build into Hot Springs from Murfreesboro. About a week later, secretary Bishop and MP & G route-locating engineer Cravens left Nashville to inspect the proposed extension from Ashdown to Paris, Texas. They also talked to people along the way about donations of cash and right-of-way. Never overlook a good thing!

Meanwhile, it was announced that mail service was being inaugurated September 6 between Nashville and Murfreesboro. The mail was already being delivered from Nashville to Ashdown, but only by means of sealed pouches. A few towns between Nashville and Murfreesboro had rural routes radiating from them, so a clerk was required aboard the railroad mail car to sort and unload mail for these towns. He would make one round trip a day from Ashdown, going north on the eleven o'clock morning train and returning on the four o'clock evening train.

Bishop and Cravens had returned from their goodwill tour, and the latter was dispatched with a corps of sixteen men to make a survey of the most desirable route to Terrell, Texas, located south of Paris on the Texas & Pacific into Dallas. The survey crossed the Red River into Texas at the Laynesport Ferry near the Oklahoma line. The Dallas Chamber of Commerce had promised to finance extension of the road to the Gulf of Mexico if the MP & G would build to the Red River and construct a bridge there. The promise soon faded, however, and the rails never got beyond Ashdown.

Bishop was then sent out on another safari, this time to look for a desirable route to Memphis, as was indicated in the company's corporate title. He investigated various towns east of Murfreesboro to determine the degree of their interest in obtaining a railroad, among them Pine Bluff, De Witt, Marianna, and Helena.

In view of the proposed extension, superintendent Dodson was asked whether he intended to absorb the Arkadelphia Lumber Company's railroad. He replied that nothing definite had been decided but that the road extended in the right direction and was in good condition. There was a good possibility, he said, that it would be acquired.

The pike in question was another of the countless roads built by flourishing lumber companies. It had a name whose length rivaled the length of its rails—Ultima Thule, Arkadelphia & Mississippi River Railway—which extended south from the east bank of the Washita (now Ouachita) River to Dalark. At Daleville, on the east bank of the river opposite Arkadelphia, was a large Arkadelphia Lumber Company mill. The railroad was established June 11, 1883. From a point on the Texas & St. Louis (now the Cotton Belt) at or near Fordyce, in Dallas County, it extended, via Princeton and Arkadelphia, to Ultima Thule in Sevier County, a distance of about 140 miles. It was to be financed by a $1,500,000 stock issue. The name was changed to Ultima Thule, Arkadelphia & Mississippi Railroad in December, 1887. Nothing much seems to have developed in its ambition to furnish competition for Jay Gould's Texas & St. Louis.

The owners of the Arkadelphia Lumber Company also built a thirty-mile road west from Arkadelphia to a connection with the Gurdon & Ft. Smith at Graysonia. Called the Antoine Valley, it was incorporated April 20, 1907. The Ultima Thule and the Antoine Valley were the roads to which Bishop had referred when he spoke of absorbing the Arkadelphia Lumber Company's railroad.

February 12, 1910, came on Saturday, and the weather had been rather decent for a change. The MP & G roadmaster cranked up his little gasoline-engine motorcar at Nashville for a reconnaissance trip toward Murfreesboro. Any damage to the roadbed during the winter would require attention before the spring rains set in. He went into the operator's office to check on any trains in the area. Luckily, there were none on the track, for the motorcar was feeling frisky in the early spring sunshine. It kicked itself into gear and took off up the track, swung around a curve, crossed Mine Creek bridge, and attacked the upgrade east of town, its little engine sputtering happily. With a clear track and a full tank of gasoline, a jaunt of unbridled joy was in the offing. Around the many curves, up and down the numerous grades, the car rolled freely.

A crowd of employees gathered quickly when they heard the car taking off by itself. There were quite a few predictions of how far it would run if left alone, plus all manner of suggestions on how to stop the runaway.

Superintendent Dodson had the operator telegraph his counterpart at Bingen to tell him there was a maverick motorcar coming his way. The latter hurried down to the west end of the passing track and opened the switch. The speeder covered the four miles in just a few minutes, and the brass pounder rejoiced as he watched it head through the switch onto the siding. He had it trapped. Like many a wild mustang before it, however, the car didn't stay trapped long. It romped along the siding, split the switch at the far end, and derisively continued its dash.

The chagrined operator at Bingen dot-dashed this embarrassing story to superintendent Dodson. Then the agent at Tokio Junction, another four miles up the road, where the MP & G crossed the rails of the Prescott & Northwestern, announced that superintendent Richey of the Iron Mountain and superintendent Bemis of the P & NW were riding another motorcar somewhere between Murfreesboro and Tokio Junction.

Dodson decided the foolishness had gone far enough. Someone could get hurt, perhaps killed. He ordered the operator at Tokio to stop the car—or else. A section foreman was called, and when he learned what was going on, he said he would capture the runaway. Going out to the main line, he fastened a heavy piece of timber across the rails and sat down to wait. Soon he heard the putt-putt coming along at a good clip. He watched anxiously as the car approached. The piece of timber proved to be an effective derail, and the wild machine hit the roadbed. It wasn't badly damaged and, when placed back on the rails, was run docilely back to Nashville under its own power.

During the month of February, 1910, officials of the MP & G

repeatedly visited several towns in eastern Arkansas concerning the proposed route of the extension toward Memphis. It was the opinion of most speculators that the survey would follow the earlier line of the Ultima Thule, Arkadelphia & Mississippi west from Arkadelphia. The crossing of the Rock Island would be at either Carthage or Leola, and the road would then head directly for Pine Bluff.

Meanwhile, the Hot Springs, Glenwood & Western was getting up a head of steam. The corporation had been legally formed by A. L. Clark of Dallas, Texas; J. N. Jones of Tyler, Texas; and J. A. Bonner, W. E. Mayher, C. T. Crosby, and S. W. Pryor of Glenwood, Arkansas.

On May 17, 1910, the stockholders of the MP & G held their annual meeting at Nashville. They increased the capital-stock funding of the railroad to $6,260,000 in order to finance the eastern extension. At the same time, the corporate name was changed to Memphis, Dallas & Gulf, or, as many were wont to call it, the "Mud, Dirt & Gravel."

The new MD & G assumed control of the Antoine Valley Railroad and the Ultima Thule, Arkadelphia & Mississippi on June 1, 1910. It operated these roads separately while making the required public announcement and other legal arrangements. Then, on October 6, 1910, W. E. Grayson and N. W. McLeod, secretary and vice president, respectively, of the two smaller roads, and J. W. Bishop and W. W. Brown of the MD & G legally ratified the purchase and consolidation of the three roads. Conductor J. A. Couch was assigned to the Arkadelphia Division and would have charge of the train there until the connecting link was built.

The preliminary survey of the route between Murfreesboro and Graysonia, on the Gurdon & Ft. Smith, was completed in late July, 1910, and the field crews returned to Murfreesboro to begin the final alignment location. Construction of this portion was to begin just as quickly as possible because the Graysonia and Nashville lumber companies were very anxious to have a direct connection between their mills. A new time card was set up for the Memphis, Dallas & Gulf, effective July 20:

Read Down					*Read Up*		
No. 1 Daily *Ex. Sun.*	No. 3 Daily *Ex. Sun.*	No. 5 Sun. *Only**			No. 2 Daily *Ex. Sun.*	No. 4 Daily *Ex. Sun.*	No.6 Sun. *Only**
9:30 A	3:00 P	4:00 P	Lv. Murfreesboro	Ar	9:00 A	2:48 P	10:03 A
10:05 A	3:20 P	4:20 P	Ar. Tokio	Ar.	8:25 A	2:25 P	9:40 A
10:30 A	3:41 P	4:41 P	Ar. Nashville	Ar.	7:55 A	2:04 P	9:19 A
12:01 P	5:00 P	6:00 P	Ar. Ashdown	Lv.	6:30 A	12:45 P	8:00 A

* Morning train connects with northbound KCS at Ashdown.
* Afternoon train connects with southbound KCS at Ashdown.

One Sunday afternoon in early August, engineer Couch opened the throttle of his hog, and train No. 5 rolled out of Murfreesboro right on the advertised. With a light train on her drawbar, the engine loped along nicely, crossing the P & NW track at Tokio with a minute to spare. Clattering across the diamond, No. 5 crested a slight rise and headed for Bingen.

A couple of miles past the station, the hogger poked his head from the cab window, unconsciously adjusting to the pitching and swaying of the engine. Left hand draped slack across the throttle lever, he leaned out as far as he comfortably could, trying to catch a cool breath of air. Heat waves shimmered along the track ahead. These sometimes cause optical illusions, but the figure of a man walking across the crosstie ends just outside the rail was no illusion.

The hogger, instantly alert, reached for the whistle cord just above his head, loosing several blasts from the quill. Whether or not it was heat waves playing tricks, he didn't know, but he thought he saw the man look back. He felt a sharp, momentary sting of anger because of the utter foolishness people are prone to display. A few anxious seconds later, the hoghead grabbed the whistle cord and held it down as the distance between his engine's pilot and the plodding figure grew shorter and shorter. Then anger gave way to dismay as he realized the man wasn't trying to step out of the way.

A gauntleted left hand instinctively turned loose the whistle lanyard and reached for the shiny brass handle of the brake valve. Couch wiped the clock and slammed the throttle shut, knowing it was a useless gesture. As brakeshoes grabbed at steel wheels, the train bucked. The hogger was on his feet, gripping the throttle lever as tightly as the shoes gripped the wheels, staring helplessly through the glass of the front window. The slanting side of the pilot struck the man, throwing him away from the grinding wheels. The train jerked to a stop, and the crew rushed to the crumpled figure.

It was a young man. His left foot and lower leg were badly mangled, and he was unconscious. They quickly placed him in the baggage compartment of the combine, and hogger Couch rolled into Nashville in record time. The injured fellow was taken to the office of Drs. Daly and Garner, physicians for the railroad. Examination disclosed internal chest injuries and a fractured skull. The left foot was so badly crushed it had to be amputated.

Two hours later, a woman and two men hurried into the office to inquire about the injured man. They proved to be his mother and brothers. Residents of Kilgore, they had been visiting in the Bradford Crossing community and were on their way home. They identified the victim as Leonard Buckley, twenty years old and completely deaf. And, they said, his mind had not fully developed.

Mrs. Alice Buckley and two of her sons were traveling in a wagon. Leonard was walking as far as Nashville because he wanted to visit a man who lived there. He was following the railroad because it afforded a shorter route than the wagon road. When the folks in the wagon called at the Nashville man's house and learned that Leonard hadn't arrived, they began to search for him, ending up at the doctor's office. Leonard died a few minutes later without regaining consciousness.

August, 1910, seemed to be a jinx as far as the Memphis, Dallas & Gulf was concerned. On the morning of Saturday, August 20, the regular conductor of the log train didn't feel too well, so he reported he was unable to make the run that morning. Because of the close association of the MD & G and the Graysonia-Nashville Lumber Company, the railroad decided to make a conductor of the engine hostler at the lumber mill. So it was that J. R. Whitesell had the honor of being a freight-train conductor.

Down the main stem a ways, the brakie flipped the switch and headed the low-wheeled hog down a spur toward a logging camp deep in the woods. Here the engine was run around a wye and turned. Dropping a pin through the link of the head car, the crew started for the mill with a string of loaded log cars. The brakie, using a pick handle for a brake club, climbed aboard the end car while the new conductor rode the engine cab.

As they approached the main line, Whitesell knew the brakie would need a little help in setting a few binders, since there were no air brakes on the log cars. J. R. climbed from the cab and across the coal gates to the top of the tender. He jumped from the back of the engine tender toward the top log of the first car.

There was a scream as J. R. slipped and fell between the tender and the car. By the time the brakie and the hogger stopped the train and found the conductor caught beneath one of the cars, there was nothing they could do for him. There was a large hole in his side, and his back and neck were broken.

Whitesell's battered body was brought into Nashville immediately, and funeral services were arranged so that he could be buried the same day (because of the hot weather and the condition of the body). J. R., who was 35 years old, his wife, and their two children had recently moved to Nashville from Roseboro, where he was employed in the logging business.

On October 6, 1910, the Memphis, Dallas & Gulf and the Prescott & Northwestern reached an agreement whereby they would operate trains over each other's tracks. It proved to be an advantage to the folks at Nashville. Because of a change in the train schedule of the St. Louis, Iron Mountain & Southern, mail which had arrived at Nashville from Hope at noon via the Arkansas & Louisiana wasn't reaching town until 5:45 P.M. This prevented businessmen from answering their correspondence until the following day. Martin Walsh, passenger and freight agent of the MD & G, took a petition signed by the businessmen of Nashville to Fort Worth, Texas, to talk with a Mr. Gaines, who was superintendent of mail service in the southern Arkansas area. Walsh explained that since the MD & G and the P & NW had inaugurated joint service, mail from Prescott could reach Nashville at 12:30 P.M. As a result of the meeting, two letters arrived from Fort Worth:

Ft. Worth, Texas
Oct. 10, 1910
Mr. C. C. Henderson, v.p.
MD & G R.R.
Nashville, Ark.

Sir:

Please refer to your letter of October 6th, calling attention to the new time card effective on the MD & G railroad on October 9th. In response to your suggestion that mail for Nashville and Murfreesboro, and from these points, be routed over your line, I say that full advantage will be taken of the schedule offered by your company in dispatching mail. We will publish for the use of railway postal clerks and postmasters the change in time on your line as well as on the P & NW in order that both lines may be used to advance the dispatch of mail.

Respectfully,
W. L. Cate,
Acting Sup't.

Ft. Worth, Texas
October 10, 1910
Postmaster
Nashville, Ark.

Sir:

Hereafter clerks on the Little Rock to Ft. Worth train No. 5 will make pouch for your office, forwarding from Prescott daily. Pouch will leave on P & NW No. 1 daily except Sunday and will be delivered to MD & G train No. 5 at Tokio. On Sundays will go forward from Prescott on P & NW train No. 7, reaching MD & G train No. 5 at Tokio.

You will dispatch pouch labeled Little Rock and Ft. Smith, forwarding daily except Sunday by MD & G train No. 6. This pouch will be delivered at Tokio to P & NW train No. 2. On Sunday pouch will leave Nashville by MD & G train No. 8 and will be given to P & NW train No. 8 at Tokio.

Respectfully,
W. L. Cate,
Acting Sup't.

On Monday morning, November 7, 1910, an MD & G log train was on its way to the mill at Nashville. Approaching one of the rolling land swells, the eagle eye pulled the throttle lever back and dropped the Johnson bar toward the front of its quadrant. The little hog hit the grade with her stack barking. Part of the bed of coals dancing on the grates was lifted out through the stack. The result was a spectacular fire extending along the north side of the track from Mineral Springs almost to Nashville.

When the fire was reported, general superintendent Dodson assembled a firefighting crew and accompanied it to help combat the destruction. The heaviest losses were sustained by Mrs. Puckett, Squire Dennis, Bowden Young, Mid Bandy, and J. P. Exall. Fences on nearly all property near the railroad were burned. Fencing on Exall's place escaped, but the flames ate their way across his pasture.

When 1911 rolled around, business on the passenger trains of the Memphis, Dallas & Gulf had increased beyond all expectations. Traffic was so heavy and stops so frequent that it was impossible for the conductor to operate his train as it should be run and collect tickets and cash fares at the same time. To give him relief, young Joe Broadnax was put to work as a train auditor.

There was trouble in the deep cut at the west approach of the bridge across the Little Missouri River. The backslopes of the excavation had begun to slide after being exposed to the rains for a while, and the roadmaster often had to dispatch a crew to remove mud which had covered the rails. To remedy the situation, the slopes were cut back and made flatter. This widened the cut to one hundred feet and lowered the track grade ten feet, which made a much more desirable approach from the west. But it required removing eighty-five thousand cubic yards of earth—quite a bite for shovels and Fresno slips. The dirt was used in filling long wooden trestles at the Little Missouri and seven other locations. The whole thing was done in the winter, before the spring rains of 1911. There was no need to interrupt service, which was ideal, for on the fifteenth of February, the MD & G would begin running a mixed train in addition to the regular passenger run, giving double daily passenger service between Nashville and Murfreesboro.

The eastern extension of the rails began when, on Saturday, March 11, 1911, superintendent Dodson announced that he had awarded a contract to T. H. Sater for building the first mile east from Murfreesboro. Other contracts were being prepared, and there was every intention of heading for Carthage, where the rails of the Rock Island would be crossed.

On March 10, 1911, an important proceeding came up in Pulaski Chancery Court at Little Rock: Arkansas Railroad Commission *versus* the Memphis, Dallas & Gulf Railroad, with William H. Rector, assistant attorney general, representing the commission. The commission had issued an order restraining the railroad from dismantling eleven miles of the southern end of the Ultima Thule, Arkadelphia & Mississippi between Dalark and Sparkman.

Now the MD & G had bought the Ultima Thule because it lay along the proposed extension to the Mississippi River. The eleven-mile portion south of Dalark would be of no particular advantage to this purpose, so all of the timber along that section had been logged out. The track was maintained and an occasional train was run for handling freight, and the railroad was planning to take up the rails and use them on other sections when the Railroad Commission issued its restraining order. The MD & G then brought suit in Chancery Court to enjoin the commission from enforcing the order.

The railroad contended that the commission had no authority to issue such an order, that the order was unreasonable and arbitrary in its demands, and that the order amounted to confiscation of property. The attorney general said that the commission did indeed have the authority to issue the order and that it was reasonable. He also suggested that the proper remedy was for the railroad to take the case before the Circuit Court or, if it were so inclined, take up the rails, violate the order, and set up its plea as a defendant when prosecuted. This was probably what transpired, to the satisfaction of all concerned, for the rails were lifted and no more was heard of the matter.

Contractor Sater started grading the first two-mile section east of Murfreesboro on March 16. The extension was on its way. The rails would go by way of Pine Bluff, De Witt, St. Charles, and Helena. The MD & G was going to become a trunk-line railroad sooner than many had thought.

General manager C. C. Henderson sent superintendent Dodson and chief engineer Van Auken to Graysonia to locate a portion of the line toward Arkadelphia. The company planned to make use of sections of the Antoine Valley between these two points. A crew of graders was already at work between Shawmut and Leard to the west.

Another piece of litigation came up in June. In Clark County Chancery Court, the MD & G secured a decree enjoining the Iron Mountain from interfering with a small plot of land just west of the Iron Mountain depot at Arkadelphia. The MD & G had purchased the land, upon which it proposed to build a depot. The Iron Mountain decided it wanted the land for its own use, possibly for harassment as much as anything. In any case, the Iron Mountain entered a condemnation suit in order to secure the land, stating the MD & G was not in existence in Arkadelphia and therefore had no use for the land. The MD & G withdrew the profile map of its road, which had been filed with the court a week earlier, made corrections on it, and filed it again. This time, the map clearly showed the MD & G entering Arkadelphia from the west and coming down Maddox Branch to the Iron Mountain depot.

The MD & G didn't fare so well in the case involving the death of Leonard Buckley. His mother was awarded a settlement of $2,500. It was easier to pay than to fight it, even though the railroad was not at fault.

There was a bit of speculation during the summer of 1911 by "foreign" roads. W. H. Wylie, general agent for the Wabash, inspected the Mud, Dirt & Gravel for a party of unnamed eastern financiers. A special train was provided for Wylie, who was accompanied by A. C. Ramsey, general traffic manager for the MD & G; J. W. Bishop, secretary and attorney; and E. D. Strong, assistant superintendent. The men also inspected the cement plant at White Cliffs, then looked over the Pike County diamond fields. Wylie never did say why the capitalists were interested in the Arkansas road, and nothing more was heard from them.

Early in June, 1911, the people of Hot Springs began to show renewed interest in the MD & G. Perhaps it was a little applied psychology when MD & G officials seemed disinclined to court the favor of the Hot Springs faction in preference for a route to and beyond Arkadelphia. Be that as it may, a delegation of men from the City of Vapors came to Nashville on Saturday, June 7, to persuade the MD & G to build to their town.

Colonel Sam W. Fordyce, who had ramrodded the Cotton Belt across Arkansas in its early days and who owned quite a lot of property in Hot Springs, was most enthusiastic about the project. He was thoroughly familiar with the railroad business and fully realized the advantage to Hot Springs in having another line compete with the Rock Island and Iron Mountain. There had been rumors of building to Hot Springs from the KCS at Mena, but Colonel Sam said he thought the MD & G's was the only proposition worth considering for securing a railroad from the west. He thought so much of it that he offered to pay one-fifth of the $100,000 cash bonus which had been offered the MD & G.

Moreover, the delegation was as impressed with Nashville and the surrounding area as it was with the railroad. Every man in the group made negotiations to purchase property in or near the city.

The people of Hot Springs had waited long and patiently for another rail outlet. Now the MD & G would give Hot Springs access to the abundant harvests of grain, cotton, and garden produce in southeast Arkansas, things badly needed. And the extra passenger traffic would be profitable, too. A meeting was held in Hot Springs on March 22, and $60,000 in cash was raised as an inducement to the MD & G. That must have been enough because Bishop announced that active construction would begin in a couple of weeks.

While T. H. Sater was busy clearing and grading between Murfreesboro and Shawmut, the MD & G was receiving a very substantial boost in revenue from orders for ballasting gravel from the Iron Mountain, the Kansas City Southern, and the Frisco. One hundred thousand cubic yards were to be delivered to the KCS, and a like amount to the Frisco, while the Iron Mountain would need 75,000 cubic yards. Two gravel trains, in charge of conductors Whatley and Parish, began running September 16. An additional crew would be assigned as soon as engine No. 7 arrived from the repair shop at Nashville. Most of the gravel came from the MD & G's own pit, but some was taken from the Prescott & Northwestern pit north of Tokio.

One October day, the local freight was heading for Nashville with a shirttail full of cars; luckily, it was running about fifteen miles an hour. Just as the engine approached Coulter Creek, the hogger and fireman were almost dumped off their seatboxes. Something seemed to grab the tail end of their little train, trying to stop it immediately, if not sooner. All wheels of the engine tender had left the rails and were chewing their way completely through every crosstie on the trestle. When the bobtailed train stopped, the tender and three cars were resting on the trestle stringers. The engine didn't turn over and no one was hurt, which was a miracle.

A rash of misfortunes occurred along the line during the next few weeks. Late in January, 1912, a freight northbound for Nashville was crossing the Saline River near Paraloma when the engine's headlight burned out and left the engine in complete darkness. After trying in vain to repair the lamp, the crew decided to roll along toward home. The headlight beam didn't really light up so very much of the right-of-way anyhow.

As the train rocked along through the darkness, there was a sudden crash against the pilot. The engine quivered, and the hogger heard a yell from along the right-of-way. He jerked the brake valve in the big hole, and the train bucked to a halt. Taking a hayburner lantern, the engine crew climbed down and began walking back to where they heard the crash.

They soon met two figures stumbling toward them through the night. Holding the flickering lantern aloft, the hogger discovered a couple of familiar faces. They belonged to Roy Millwee and Oscar Reese, who worked for the Nashville Telephone Company. The MD & G used the telephone company's wires to transmit all of its messages. Millwee and Reese had been out repairing a broken wire and were returning to Nashville. No train was expected, so they had no light on the motorcar. The noise of the gasoline engine had prevented the men from hearing the locomotive come up behind them until they barely had time to join the birds before the pilot hit the motorcar. They were more frightened than hurt, which was more than could be said for the little one-lung motorcar. It was tossed into the side door of the crummy, and Reese and Millwee climbed aboard for the ride to town. Never a dull moment on the Mud, Dirt & Gravel.

Tragedy had a near miss in April. The spring rains had fallen heavily, sending the Little Missouri and the Saline rivers on several rampages. North of Tokio the rails crossed a high earth fill between two deep cuts. Floodwaters had backed up against the high embankment until water was nearly twenty feet deep and the embankment was saturated. The southbound passenger train crossed the high fill on a Wednesday morning, and its passage caused sufficient vibration of the embankment to allow a trickle of water to ooze through beneath the track. The trickle rapidly increased, carrying away the fill from under the rails, and there was soon about ten feet of open space under the track. The free-hanging rails were cribbed up with timbers in order to allow passage of the evening varnish run to Murfreesboro. The embankments on the approaches to the Saline were sandbagged to prevent their giving way. It was nip and tuck for a couple of weeks.

An important phase in the development of the MD & G was announced a few days later. Mixed-train service was to be established on the Glenwood Division. In August, 1911, soon after the surge of interest shown by the folks in Hot Springs, the MD & G had purchased the Caddo & Choctaw, running from Roseboro to Cooper, and the Hot Springs, Glenwood & Western between Glenwood and Pearcy, about twenty-one miles.

The train left Nashville April 26, 1912, running over Prescott & Northwestern rails from Tokio to Prescott, then to Gurdon on the Iron Mountain. From there it used Gurdon & Ft. Smith track to Glenwood. The train was in charge of conductor P. D. Whatley, who had moved from Nashville to Glenwood about a week earlier. On the smoky end were eagle eye Fred Jones and ashcat Leslie Olds. Carrying the brake club was a Mr. Hona.

This arrangement left only a fifteen-mile gap from Pearcy to a connection with the Iron Mountain and the Rock Island at Hot Springs. In May, mail service was begun from Roseboro to Pearcy. About six miles of road were being constructed between Murfresboro and Shawmut by contractors Sater and Murphy.

A storm of consternation arose in June, 1912. The Interstate Commerce Commission had met in Washington, D.C., to discuss the rates being charged by what it termed "tap-line railroads" (roads used principally as log haulers for lumber companies). The MD & G and the P & NW were included in this category, which meant their rates for freight and passenger service had to be reduced drastically from the current scale (it was the same as that of the common-carrier roads).

The MD & G instructed its resident attorney in Washington to request that the ICC delay a decision until its case could be presented. He was told to secure a court injunction if necessary, for a tap-line classification would financially ruin the company.

The ICC believed that too much stock in both the railroad and the Graysonia-Nashville Lumber Company was owned by the same men. Further, the ownership of common stock was too closely identified with the interests of the two concerns. In the case of the MD & G, the unconnected portions of the company would be affected more than the main line. The recently purchased Ultima Thule, Arkadelphia & Mississippi; Antoine Valley; Caddo & Choctaw; and Hot Springs, Glenwood & Western were the victims. The main line was fairly diversified in its traffic.

On June 19, Henderson, Bishop, and Martin Walsh, general passenger and freight agent, returned from Washington, where they had explained their position to the ICC. Now they were compelled to wait for a decision to be made.

To complicate the situation further, vice president McLeod had gone to London for the purpose of selling bonds to finance the extension of the road into Hot Springs. If that deal could be consummated right away, the Glenwood Division might be salvaged. Henderson and some of the other officials went to St. Louis to talk with McLeod, who had returned a few days earlier. Brown went on to Chicago August 14 for a conference with a representative of the London syndicate. He was able to close the deal and deliver the bonds.

Meanwhile, the ICC had worked out a proposition which would save the Mud, Dirt & Gravel. N. W. McLeod would separate himself and his St. Louis associates from the railroad by buying the lumber mill and timber lands, while Brown, Henderson, Dodson, and others would retain ownership of the railroad. Henderson, Bishop, and Walsh went to Washington and persuaded the ICC to rescind the order placing the MD & G in the tap-line category so that the Hot Springs extension could be built.

Early in April, 1913, chief engineer W. P. Hart began organizing and equipping a survey crew of fourteen men to establish the final alignment into Hot Springs. He had already made several preliminary surveys and now had only to select and stake the best one.

Another aggravation cropped up April 16 when the MD & G was sued by the Frisco for $6,500. It seems that when the MD & G installed a crossing on the Frisco track at Ashdown, it had failed to provide the proper arrangement of frogs and guard rails. Dan Godbolt, a Frisco switchman, caught his foot in the crossing and lost a foot and a hand to a passing freight car. The Frisco had to pay him $6,500 for injuries, so it was suing the MD & G for the same amount, charging that the MD & G was responsible for Godbolt's injuries. The court ruled that both roads were equally responsible and assessed half the damages to each.

Tracklaying east from Murfreesboro to Shawmut began on May 7, 1913. On the Hot Springs end, contractor McSpadden had a thirty-team outfit at work, and contractor Bush had his sixty-five teams busy clearing and grading. Dirt and stumps were really flying. Several years earlier, some flash-in-the-pan outfit had graded up a roadbed west from Hot Springs nearly to the Ouachita River. The MD & G was rehabilitating this old dump and was getting ready to lay rails on it.

W.W. Wilson, father of Joe Wilson, was given the job of procuring the right-of-way. During the first week, seven miles were donated by people owning property along the route. The attitude of folks between Murfreesboro and Hot Springs seemed very favorable.

Ed Culbreth was given a contract for clearing right-of-way and furnishing ties for the final section of the road from Pearcy to Hot Springs. Engine No. 202 had been put in the shops at Nashville for overhaul, and a combination mail, express, and passenger car was being repainted. The time was drawing near for running trains to Hot Springs.

Early in September, Payne Dooley took his crew of gandy dancers to Glenwood, where they began spiking down rails. Steel for a bridge across the Ouachita had arrived at Nashville and was receiving a good coat of paint. All piers were complete and ready for the steel. The company had advertised for thirty-five thousand white oak ties, to be delivered anywhere along the right-of-way between Glenwood and the Ouachita. A fine price of thirty-five cents each was being paid.

Thursday morning, November 20, 1913, the southbound varnish run left Nashville with a triumphant wail from the engine's whistle as she disappeared around the curve. Just about a mile out of town as the fireman was down on the deck wielding his No. 3 scoop, the engine swayed to the left. The hogger jumped off his seatbox when he heard a terrible crashing sound and the brakes went into emergency. At the same time, the hog stumbled to the right, then the right side of the cab disintegrated. She held the rails till the train, which had been running about thirty miles per hour, shuddered to a stop.

The shaken crew climbed out of the shattered cab to discover that the left-hand driver had come off its axle, breaking the main and side rods, which stripped away the air-brake piping. The right-rear driver was also dropped when its axle broke. The loose end of its side rod had flailed the cab away just as the hogger jumped down to the deck. Fortunately, both wheels had rolled down the embankment. If they had dropped between the rails, the entire train would have been wrecked. No one was injured, and another engine was called to drag the crippled train back to town.

The first steel span of the bridge across the Ouachita River was swung into place January 20, 1914. The falsework for the second span was complete, and the company erecting the structure said it would be complete by February 10. After this, it would take only about ten days to lay rails into Hot Springs. On February 25, the Ouachita bridge was finished and a crew of gandy dancers began laying rails.

Bishop and Walsh went to Hot Springs to discuss suitable freight and passenger station facilities. The townspeople and the Arkansas Railroad Commission wanted the Iron Mountain, the

Rock Island, and the Memphis, Dallas & Gulf to combine resources and build a union depot for use by all trains. The venture proved unsuccessful because there wasn't enough level ground in one spot large enough to accommodate the yard and building.

Chief engineer Hart had completed his final survey for locating the line between Murfreesboro and Shawmut by late February, 1914. It was established on a 1 per cent grade, with maximum curves of three degrees; Hart said it was almost as good as the line from Nashville to Ashdown. Rail men from other states said the main line of the MD & G was an exceptionally good piece of engineering. Hart had located it also.

The weather during the spring of 1914 was most unfavorable for railroad work of any kind. Three inches of hail lay on the ground one day in February.

The MD & G made a proposal to the people of Hot Springs in March, and it was declared to be fair and acceptable:

> To the Business Men's League and the Young Men's Chamber of Commerce:
>
> Gentlemen:
>
> Through you we submit the following proposition to the makers of the bonus notes to the Memphis, Dallas & Gulf Railroad.
>
> Notes payable as follows:
>
> FIRST: One third upon completion of road opened to traffic and upon establishment of regular schedule of train service.
>
> SECOND: One third of said amount to be paid on or before six months thereafter.
>
> THIRD: Remainder to be paid on or before 12 months after maturity of first payment.
>
> For the purpose of raising funds to build passenger and freight depots, to cost not less than $15,000 for the passenger station and not less than $5,000 for a freight station at Hot Springs, we propose to the makers of said notes that if they will pay the first two installments in cash on or before March 10, 1914, their notes will be surrendered and cancelled.

By this agreement our company surrenders one third of the amount of the notes. The money is to be paid to a committee comprising the presidents of four banks of Hot Springs and is to be paid out by them upon the architect's estimate of progress of work on the buildings. Any sum in excess of $20,000 realized from the agreement shall be paid over to us at once.

This proposition open to acceptance until and including the 10th day of March 1914.

Very respectfully,
Memphis, Dallas & Gulf Railroad
By C. W. Dodson

A huge celebration was held March 17 in honor of the first train into Hot Springs. A general holiday was declared on that Tuesday, and an elaborate program was prepared. The largest crowd of visitors in history descended on the town. Governor George W. Hayes and Mayor James W. McClendon headed the celebration, and representatives of newspapers from all over Arkansas and from Memphis were present.

A beautifully decorated arch was built to span the track, and a curtain was suspended from the arch. Promptly at 1:30 P.M., Miss Dove Toland of Nashville pulled the cord which withdrew the curtain. As a gleaming locomotive rolled under the arch, Miss Toland christened the road, using water from the world-famous Hot Springs. She was assisted in the ceremony by Mrs. Walter Dodson, the matron of honor. There were numerous speeches by politicians, railroad officials, and many of the notable visitors, as well as parades, auto races, a picnic, and a baseball game. The night was finished off with balls and banquets at the city's leading hotels.

In addition to the freight train, two round-trip varnish runs were established between Hot Springs and Glenwood, a distance of thirty-five miles. Joe Wilson recalls the excursion train which was run to Hot Springs a few days later. A Mogul took nine coaches into town. When the celebration was over, the Mogul wasn't hog enough to lift the train up the westbound grade from the depot. Finally, after much backing and taking up slack, a call was made to Glenwood for a new Baldwin Consolidation. This panting monster was turned and coupled to the pilot of the Mogul.

Now the hoghead of the big Baldwin was somewhat of a practical joker and when the highball came from the brains at the rear, he put on a show for the crowd which had gathered at the depot. Easing the throttle out to take up the slack, he dropped the Johnson bar in the front corner and, leaning out the cab window, began to whip the engine vigorously with a switch while the stack barked and shot up a heavy cloud of smoke. The two iron steeds rolled the train out of town in high style as the crowd cheered.

Not too long after this episode, Joe piloted a new motorcar down the Gurdon & Ft. Smith from Graysonia to Gurdon. The nearest way home to Nashville was down the rails of the Iron Mountain to Hope, then over the Arkansas & Louisiana to Nashville. Asking if the road would be clear long enough for him to reach Hope he was told by the operator that nothing was coming from the south, so Joe rolled his gas buggy out onto the high iron and headed for home, on a foreign road, with no clearance or orders.

He passed Prescott. The little gasoline engine was banging up quite a racket, but running real smooth. Joe said the hair on the back of his neck stood up and his heart was squeezed with fear when he heard the deep-throated chime whistle and the barking exhaust of a locomotive. The road ahead was clear, just as the brass pounder at Gurdon had said it would be. Looking over his shoulder, he saw that the road behind him wasn't clear. He had overlooked the southbound Iron Mountain varnish run No. 4, from Little Rock to Texarkana and points south and west. The brass pounder had handed up a message for the hogger to watch for a motorcar headed south, but Joe didn't know it. There was no time to stop and get his buggy off the rails. No. 4 had come too close before he had heard it above the popping gasoline engine.

There was only one thing to do: he pulled the throttle wide open.

Make no mistake about it, those little gas buggies would run. Joe took off for Hope as fast as his car would run, with No. 4 right behind him, the hogger blowing the chime whistle all the way. Joe didn't know just what he was going to do when he got to Hope if No. 4 didn't have to stop there. The time-card speed from Gurdon to Hope was a little over sixty miles an hour!

Joe approached the station at Hope, with No. 4 still right on his tail and the whistle still shouting. The racket had attracted the attention of a conductor on the Arkansas & Louisiana. When he saw what was happening, he quickly opened the switch of the A & L interchange track. Joe slowed his car enough to sweep through the turnout, his conductor friend closed the switch, and No. 4 was on her way—less than three minutes late. Joe said that was his last trip over the Iron Mountain on a motorcar.

The contract for constructing the passenger and freight stations at Hot Springs was awarded to J. D. Brock on May 13. The cost, not including the plumbing, was $14,174. The plans had been drawn by chief engineer Hart.

By the middle of July, 173 teams of mules and more than 500 men were at work on the division between Murfreesboro and Shawmut. A contract for the building of the last twelve-mile section was awarded to George & Barber, well-known railroad builders from Shreveport, Louisiana, who had a force of more than 100 men to do the work. The tracklaying gangs worked through the month of January, 1915, taking advantage of a good run of weather. Instead of the usual timber trestles, this section was receiving steel trestles installed by the Blodgett Bridge Company. One of these was 100 feet long, another 65 feet, and two were 35 feet, all of them resting on concrete abutments.

Connecting of the MD & G rails with those of the Gurdon & Ft. Smith was made at Shawmut on March 17, 1915. The first train to run from Hot Springs arrived at Nashville at 7:15 P.M. March 18 in charge of conductor Buck Aubry, with master mechanic L. F. Couch at the throttle of engine No. 202. Through service from Hot Springs to Texarkana, over the KCS from Ashdown, was inaugurated March 21.

The Arkansas Railroad Commission again slapped the MD & G in June, 1915, by ordering the road to stop all passenger trains at Roseboro and Amity on the portion of the Gurdon & Ft. Smith over which the MD & G had trackage rights. It also decreed that the G & FS should receive 70 per cent of all revenues received from these stations.

Just when things were beginning to look rosy for the 115-mile Mud, Dirt & Gravel, misfortune struck. With rumblings of World War I coming from Europe, the financial situation was most unstable. In late 1915, W. W. Wilson was advised to dispose of the considerable amount of MD & G stock he had accumulated.

After the war, the MD & G never had a chance to recover. On August 15, 1922, it was sold at public auction in Nashville by receiver Martin Walsh. The former stockholders bought it, and it was reorganized as the Graysonia, Nashville & Ashdown. The Interstate Commerce Commission lent the GN & A $250,000 to continue operations from Ashdown to Shawmut, a distance of only sixty-one miles. Security for this operation took the form of $300,000 in first-mortgage bonds.

The years which followed were evil days for the GN & A, even as they were for railroads everywhere. Henry Ford had begun flooding the country with an avalanche of automobiles, and the family car soon became a nemesis to the passenger train, even as the truck was making inroads in the freight-train monopoly as rapidly as highways could be built.

The new management began to tighten its belt. The timber lands were being cut over, and the remaining logs were going to the mill aboard trucks. The rails between Murfreesboro and Hot Springs were taken up. By 1926, the Murfreesboro-Nashville Southwestern Railway had taken over operations between these two towns, and the GN & A became a 32-mile line from Nashville to Ashdown. The M-NS formed a connecting link between the GN & A and the Prescott & Northwestern.

The Great Depression years dealt the nation a staggering blow, and in 1932 the M-NS was reorganized as the Murfreesboro-Nashville Railway. It struggled along until 1947, when the cards were shuffled again and the Murfreesboro & Nashville Railroad emerged. The entire operation was abandoned in 1952.

The GN & A managed to keep its head above water until the Ideal Cement Company began an extensive operation at Okay, Arkansas. Seeing the advantage of having its own means of transportation, it purchased the railroad in 1927. The venture provided from six hundred to eight hundred cars of freight per month in 1965.

Since Ideal Cement took over, the GN & A has fared rather well. The railroad has always been an integral part of the cement plant's operation. On October 2, 1929, the first trainload of cement left the plant at Okay. There were 125 cars in the train coupled to the drawbar of ten-wheeler No. 2630. Until the emphasis on plant-to-customer transportation sent trucks rolling along the highways, the GN & A handled all of the plant's output. Even in 1954, 40 per cent of its cement production was shipped by rail.

About 75 per cent of the GN & A's business is cement. The remainder is divided among a local bulk-feed processing plant, a knife and scissors plant, and the general businesses of Nashville. Passenger service was discontinued in 1947, but an occasional rail enthusiast is welcome aboard the metal-sheathed crummy.

One steam locomotive came to the GN & A when she was new. Fresh from the shops at Baldwin Locomotive Works, No. 26 arrived in charge of a Baldwin representative in 1926. To demonstrate her ability, a train was made up in the yard at Nashville. It rolled smartly out of town, headed for Ashdown. Just a few miles out, a rail turned, and No. 26, along with a considerable portion of her train, was on the ground. It was not an uncommon occurrence, but the situation was rather embarrassing.

In 1951, steam disappeared from the roster of the GN & A when a 660-horsepower diesel was acquired. Little Mogul No. 26 went to the privately owned tourist road of the Ideal Cement Company, the Nebraska-Kansas Railroad, at Superior, Nebraska. In 1955, it bought the workhorse of the GN & A, 1,000-horsepower diesel No. 55. The engines were numbered for the year in which they were put into service. The entire rolling stock of the GN & A now consists of two diesel locomotives, one crummy, and a home made weed sprayer pulled by a flange-wheeled Chevrolet panel truck of 1947 vintage.

In the late 1940's, the Chevy truck was equipped with flanged wheels and was to be used as an economical experiment in delivering mail and express on a daily round-trip basis between Nashville and Ashdown. Acting as "engineer" was Horace Hedrick of Nashville, who made five stops along the way: Mineral Springs, Paraloma, Schaal, White Cliffs, and Ashdown.

In the early 1960's, the GN & A and the U.S. Army Corps of Engineers reached agreement on efforts to do something about the unpredictable rampages of the Little River through southwest Arkansas. To control water flow in the stream, the Corps of Engineers undertook the construction of a series of dams from Oklahoma to Louisiana along Little and Red rivers.

Millwood Dam, named for the deserted community of Millwood, a few miles east of Ashdown, would inundate approximately 20 miles of the GN & A, the Ideal Cement Company limestone quarry would lie 60 feet below the surface of the lake to be backed up by the dam. The Corps of Engineers agreed to build a 3½-mile levee to protect the quarry and to rebuild the railroad from a point just south of Mineral Springs to Ashdown, with the new rails laid across the face of the dam. The dam was dedicated in December, 1966.

The Graysonia, Nashville & Ashdown rolls along on new rails toward new and prosperous days—a successful Arkansas shortline railroad.

READER RAILROAD (POSSUM TROT LINE)

10

In the latter days of the nineteenth century, a large portion of Ouachita and Nevada counties was covered with lush growths of virgin timber. Giants in these forests towered well over a hundred feet. Just as fragrant blossoms will attract bees, so, too, will forests draw lumberjacks. So it was inevitable that sawmills began to invade Ouachita and Nevada counties.

The St. Louis, Iron Mountain & Southern had extended a tentacle from its main line at Gurdon southeast about thirty miles to Camden on the old Washita (Ouachita) River, making connection with what is now the St. Louis-Southwestern, or Cotton Belt, as it is commonly known. Then, in 1891, the Camden & Alexander Railway pushed its rails from El Dorado northwest into Camden to connect with the Iron Mountain, providing extended service through the vast forest country.

Near the west boundary of Ouachita County a post office was established, called Sayre. It was situated on the Iron Mountain line between Gurdon and Camden. To this tiny hamlet in 1880 came Lee Reader, who erected a mill to convert trees into lumber.

As the forest gradually receded, Reader found it increasingly difficult to keep moving the mill, so the forest was brought to the mill—via flanged wheels on steel rails. The destination of the logging railroad was indeterminate, for there was no pattern to its route: where the felling crews worked, there went the rails. It is entirely possible that the track was built as a narrow-gauge line.

The record of Reader's operation is rather scant and fragmentary. A rather influential man, he prevailed upon the people of Sayre to rename the hamlet in his honor, so it became Reader, Arkansas, situated on the north-south branch of the Iron Mountain and the site of a mill which turned out sixty-five thousand board feet of lumber per day. There is also mention of a Wood & Reader Mill at Curtis, which was probably under the same management as the Reader operation. The plant at Reader was the proud possessor of a little coffee-pot locomotive which had to be assisted over the steeper grades by teams of oxen. The firm gave way to the McVay Lumber Company about 1910. Its mill at Reader burned, and in 1913 the Valley Lumber Company, which was associated with the Stout-Greer outfit at Thornton, took over.

There is record of the Valley Lumber Company's owning three locomotives, Nos. 1, 3, and 6, all 2–4–0's. No. 1 came from Stout-Greer and was formerly No. 1 on the Thornton & Alexander. No. 3 came from the Stout-Greer mill at Lester. No. 6 probably was from the Ruston Machine and Foundry Company at Alexandria. They struggled along until 1924, when the Mansfield Lumber Company bought the Valley outfit.

While the Mansfield Company was busy harvesting trees, it was astute enough to pay attention to the increasing number of oil wells being drilled in southern and southwestern Arkansas. Why would a lumber outfit be interested in oil wells? The answer didn't become evident until several wells were brought in about twenty-five miles south of Reader. It was soon common knowledge that the Waterloo field wasn't the usual type of oil field: some of the crude was so thick it simply refused to be pumped through a pipeline. Tests proved the viscous stuff was 45 per cent pure asphalt!

The Mansfield Company saw a great opportunity and acted to take advantage of it—it chartered the Reader Railroad, reasoning that asphalt was going to be in great demand for a variety of purposes. It was too thick to flow through a pipeline, and in 1925 there were not many good roads in the area nor a large number of trucks to haul it. But it could go to market in tank cars and gondolas on a railroad.

So it was that the Reader Railroad was born on August 10, 1925, because the oil at Waterloo was so thick. The Reader was financed at $325,000 to build and equip slightly more than twenty-two miles of standard-gauge road from Reader southwest to Waterloo. Following along tortuous Cypress Bayou (now known as Caney Creek), 35- to 50-pound rails were laid through the forest, following the contour of the rolling land and running along fills sufficient to raise them above all except the extreme floods of the lowlands. There was also an attempt to extend the Reader's domain from Hope to El Dorado, a little over sixty miles, but this meant intruding into territory of the Missouri Pacific, so the Interstate Commerce Commission put a stop to the grandiose plans in 1927.

The Reader's single locomotive trundled cars between Waterloo and Reader at a profit sufficient to keep black ink on the company's books. Until the days of the Great Depression, that is. A receiver was appointed for a while in 1936; then dividends began to appear in the early 1940's.

In 1956, Mansfield Lumber Company lost its enthusiasm for railroading and decided to undiversify. There was a very good chance the Reader might fade quietly into obsolescence, which it undoubtedly would have if a building-materials merchant at Shreveport, Louisiana, had not learned that it was up for grabs. His wife's grandfather had been instrumental in building the road, which fact made for a sentimental attachment, and the gentleman had a liking for steam locomotives.

So it was that Tom Long, a big man standing well over six feet and possessing a soft Louisiana drawl, came to look over the Reader Railroad. It was in a sad shape, to say the least, and its motive power was even worse. A ten-wheeler, No. 12, originally purchased from the Texas-Mexican Railroad, was drawing her last breath because of bad health in general and a terminal case of boiler trouble in particular. A little Baldwin Prairie type, No. 11, needed a new firebox, which could be remedied at a relatively low cost. She came from the Caddo & Choctaw in the early 1940's. A Mogul switcher, No. 401, having the reputation of a track-buster, was never put back in service. She was a 1905 model Rogers and came to the Reader from the Cotton Belt in 1941. The 401 was scrapped at Reader.

While making a trip over the road aboard a motorcar, Long was almost dumped into Caney Creek when the car hit a bent rail on bridge No. 64. Incidentally, there were 124 such structures in 24 miles, a lot of maintenance on any man's railroad. Thus Long went into business with one sick locomotive, one turkey-wattle-red crummy, and 24 miles of bent, rusty rails.

One of the first requirements was additional motive power, preferably a 75-ton-maximum engine. The realm of internal combustion was considered when it became clearly evident that good hogs were scarce. A 44-ton diesel was being offered practically for the taking, but an engine that small was almost useless on the Reader, whose trains varied greatly. One day there might be two cars and a crummy, but the next might see fifteen or sixteen loads hanging from the hog's drawbar. And rails were often slick with oil around the Waterloo yard. A 70-ton diesel would cost more than fifty thousand dollars, and traction-motor repair would run about ten per cent more. This ridiculous turn of events convinced "Mr. Tom" that the Reader would run with steam hogs or it wouldn't run at all.

After much searching, a 1920-model Baldwin Prairie engine

was located at Keltys, Texas, on the ten-mile Angelina & Neches River road of the San Augustine County Lumber Company. She needed quite a bit of work, but would be good for many miles when put in working order. So it was that No. 108 came to the Reader stable.

The old hogs, No. 12 and No. 401, were scrapped at Reader, and the money was used to help offset the cost of No. 108. She was run into the sheet-metal engine house at Reader, where her cylinders were rebored and her running gear overhauled.

When the 108 went into service, thereby keeping the railroad in business, triple-domed No. 11 took her place over the track pit in the engine house. Her innards were removed and she was completely rebuilt. When she rolled out of the dim, earth-floored engine house, she was in as good condition as when she left the Baldwin shops in 1925. Machinist Jesse Peterson and mechanical officer Kim Byrne had done a masterful job on her. With a fresh coat of black enamel, she glistened in the sun. And when No. 11 rolled twenty-six loaded tank cars of asphalt up Dewoody Hill, her exhaust blasting echoes through the forest, salesmen from diesel-engine firms abandoned the Reader forever. The only thing missing from the picture was the sharp, acrid odor of coal smoke. Since about 80 per cent of Reader's revenue was derived from transporting crude-oil products, it was understandable that its hogs would be oilburners.

To hear once again a barking stack "talk" and to ride the bucking deck of a steam locomotive, I was granted permission by Tom Long to ride with the train and engine crews on a regular run from Reader to Waterloo and back. Perhaps an account of that day will serve best to describe the Nevada County gem.

Reader lies about eighteen miles east of Prescott in southwest Arkansas. From asphalt-surfaced State Highway 24, three miles of well-graveled road lead to the village of eighty-plus inhabitants. Housing Reader Railroad headquarters is a little white depot trimmed in dark green. When the Missouri Pacific abandoned its agency at Reader a few years ago, the budding shortline obtained possession of the depot and remodeled it. Here agent Sallye Moseley reigned supreme.

A short distance from the depot, beside the main line of the Mo Pac and the interchange track, is the unpretentious engine house. The track over its center pit gives access to running gear for maintenance and repair work. The engine house is situated at the edge of a fine forest, and beside it are several huge oaks and pines.

I boarded squat, gleaming Prairie 108. She moved slowly, her exhaust only a whisper as steam and condensate came fogging from open cylinder cocks. Easing along the quarter-mile of track from the engine house to the depot, hogger Nat Turner headed down the interchange track. During the night, about a dozen empty tank cars had been dropped off by the Missouri Pacific. It took only a few minutes for conductor V. W. "Happy" Walker and brakeman C. O. Sykes to line up the tanks, pick up the crimson crummy, check with Sallye Moseley for any phone calls from Berry Asphalt Company at Waterloo, then 108's pilot was pointed south.

This crew had quite an impressive record as shortline railroaders before joining the Reader. Turner, running as hogger while the regular man, W. A. Adams, was off sick, had come from the neighboring Prescott & Northwestern in 1925 when the Reader first began operation. Happy Walker also came to the Reader in 1925 after pulling pins on two logging roads, the Thornton & Alexandria and the Ashley, Drew & Northern. He served for a while on the Rock Island at El Dorado. Fireman C. A. Wheelington was a converted truck driver, and brakie Sykes was a former sawmill worker. A finer group of fellows could not be found anywhere.

Within ten minutes after the highball at the depot, we had literally left behind all signs of civilization. It would have been easy to imagine that we were rolling along through the forest a century earlier. A narrow path had been cut from the wilderness, just wide enough for the embankment and rails. Light rails and an occasional soft spot in the roadbed kept our speed down to about twenty miles per hour, but even then the cab deck still managed to do a fine buck and wing, while the string of tanks did a good bit of rocking and rolling.

Caney Creek is a natural habitat for large colonies of beaver. These mostly tail fellows have the annoying habit of chewing into the roadbed embankment to build their inaccessible lodges. One such mansion was discovered to be more than six feet square when one of the engines almost dropped into it. To discourage such practices, the roadbed was well oiled and sprinkled liberally with ground glass to make it unpalatable. This didn't completely halt the home-building, but it did slow the process down.

Many other creatures of the forest are to be seen on or near the roadbed. Beautiful and graceful deer are frequent visitors. A few special permissions are granted during the deer season to hunt on the Reader right-of-way.

Twelve miles into the heavy forest of Nevada County, the Acorn Lumber Company maintains a large operation at Dills Mill, located at milepost 12.2. Here an empty flat was spotted at the loading platform. and we spent a few leisurely minutes under the shade of a large tree to indulge in a cool drink of water and friendly gossip with some of the mill hands.

With the 108's Nathan chime whistle moaning out a warning, the train was again swallowed up by the forest. About five miles later, a clearing appeared in the forest ahead. Nat Turner eased off a notch on the throttle and let go a couple of blasts on the whistle to announce our arrival at Anthony Switch, where the Long Timber & Pulpwood Company is located. Mr. Tom's family owned the timber and the railroad needed all the extra business it could get, so a post and pole peeling plant was established at Anthony Switch. As the train galloped by, Connie Wheelington kicked off a fifty-pound chunk of ice wrapped in a burlap sack for the mill hands to put in their water cooler.

The forest closed in once more, and while adjusting to the pitch and sway of the deck, I had ample opportunity to savor the nearly forgotten odors of railroading: hot metal, grease and valve

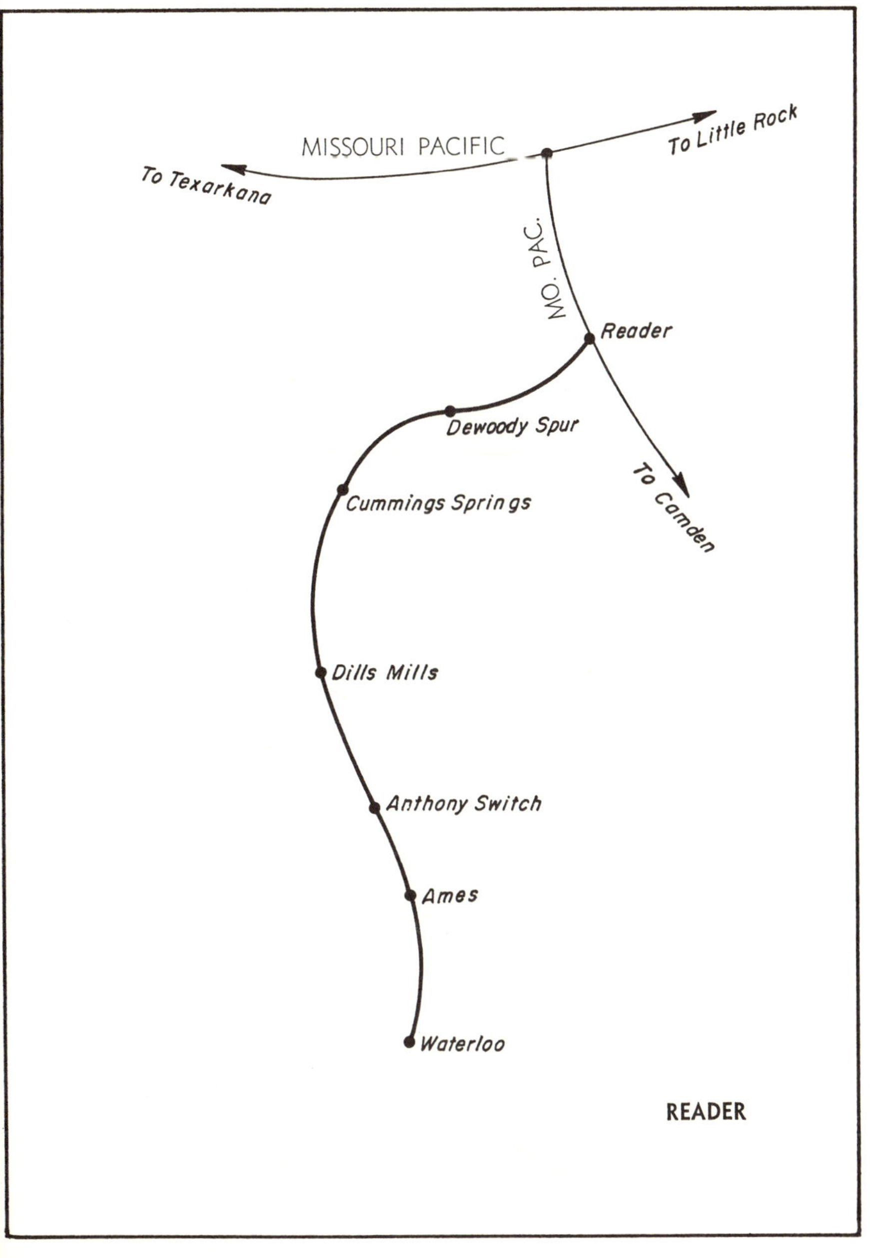
MISSOURI PACIFIC
To Texarkana
To Little Rock
MO. PAC.
Reader
Dewoody Spur
To Camden
Cummings Springs
Dills Mills
Anthony Switch
Ames
Waterloo
READER

oil, and, as the slight wind currents changed, an acrid whiff of burning fuel oil (its odor is faintly similar to that of coal smoke but is not as pungent). The combination of all these is satisfying to the soul of anyone with a love for railroading.

The hogger drew the handle of the train brake valve around and made a ten-pound service reduction. As the slack ran out, he eased the throttle in, made a five-pound reduction, and the 108 came to a stop beside a deep, clear hole of Caney Creek. The fireman climbed down and, from the underframe of the tender, removed about twenty-five feet of four-inch hose, one end of which was attached to the water tank. He tossed the other end into the pool. As the hogger opened the injector slightly, the bypassing steam created a vacuum, drawing water into the tender. Normally, Caney Creek water is so full of salt that it is unfit for boiler use, but at this particular spot, it is a free-flowing spring of clean water.

Leaving the water hole, the 108 loped along for a few miles. Suddenly, the hoghead grabbed the whistle cord and brake valve at the same time. The 108 bucked and jumped to a stop. Just in front of her pilot, a stick rose from between the ties, supporting a piece of red cloth. About ten car lengths ahead, in a slight dip in the track, sat three tank cars. These were coupled to the pilot knuckle and shoved ahead of the train about a mile to the Berry Asphalt Company plant.

Here we learned that a fire had broken out the night before, and the three loaded tank cars were released to roll free down the slight grade of the main line. The improvised flag was put out as a warning. As you can see, there are many unorthodox things to look for in the business of shortline railroading.

A couple of hours of switching had lined up the various plant tracks, and there would be a three-hour delay while we waited for some tank cars to be filled. Had it not been for the fire, these would have been ready to roll. There was a working agreement between Berry Asphalt and the Reader that the train would wait until the current day's production was ready for shipment.

We appreciated our sack lunches, for it was well after dark when we returned to the interchange track at Reader. The 108 was run to the engine house and bedded down. Thus ended a typical day on the triweekly Reader in 1961.

After this thoroughly enjoyed trip and in subsequent correspondence, Tom Long asked for ideas, opinions, and suggestions concerning the Reader's furnishing tourist-passenger accommodations. I like to think I may have played a small part in the decision which brought varnish runs to the unique Reader.

Ever increasing numbers of railroad buffs were learning of the two Prairies and driving considerable distances to see and hear them in action. They were asking permission to sign a release absolving the company of any liability in case of accident for the rare privilege of riding the engine or the crummy. This love affair was generated by the steam locomotives, there was no mistaking that. If a diesel goat were substituted, public interest would melt like the proverbial snowball in Hades. But would people pay to take a nostalgic ride behind a trim little 2–6–2 or give their children the opportunity of doing so for the first time?

My answer to Mr. Tom's question was affirmative, *if* the tourist end of the business were kept in its secondary perspective and *if* the passengers were allowed to see the railroad in its normal state of operation as a freight hauler. Phony circus acts in the setting of the Reader would be incongruous, to say the least. A place to relax was essential for the passengers while the crew was busy with a couple of hours' switching at the asphalt plant in Waterloo, such as a small park, a few picnic tables, and trails for a stroll through the forest. People would seek out a place where they could, even for one short day, enjoy the unhurried pace of an earlier era. They would come and they would pay, but only if the project were sincere.

The Reader decided to accommodate visitors in reasonable comfort, and a search was begun for the necessary equipment. The first good find was the Rambler, a lounge car running on the Kansas City Southern. It was built in 1927 by Pullman as a 36-seat parlor car and was assigned to the New Haven, where it graced the august line consisting of the "candy train," the *Merchants Limited*, as the Taunton. The car was rebuilt by Pullman in 1937 and went into service on the Wabash under the name "Rambler." It finally landed on the KCS in 1953 as No. 500. Now riding Reader rails, it has 14 parlor chairs and 23 lounge seats, as well as a few vending machines. Again the Rambler, it is listed as No. 500.

The next quest was for a good combine. No venerable wooden job with turnbuckle truss rods, please. The Milwaukee proved to be the owner of a suitable vehicle which it had built in 1938 as No. 2708 and which was used in mixed-train service. This flute-sided beauty was purchased by the Reader in 1962 and given the number 501. Soft-drink coolers and vending machines were installed in the baggage compartment.

While these things were being done, an advertising campaign was conducted. News of the Reader spread far and wide as rail fans told of the rare Arkansas jewel. A representative of the Arkansas Publicity and Parks Commission spent a day riding the Reader, and the governer also made an appearance. A brochure promoted the railroad as the "Possum Trot Line," a nickname derived from one of the communities along its route. Possum Trot, Terrapin Neck, Goose Ankle—these aren't figments of the imagination, they really exist. Dave Morgan, editor of *Trains* magazine, came to see the Reader in action. His story was widely read, even in foreign lands. People came, bought tickets, and rode the Possum Trot Line.

Such a royal reception prompted Mr. Tom to begin looking for another steam locomotive, one a little larger than the Prairies he had. Since the acquisition was no emergency, a wide and selective search was begun. Inquiries brought answers from far and wide, but all were in vain. Small park-type engines. Big railbusters.

Broken-down derelicts. Good operating steam locomotives were scarce in America.

A good lead came from within seventy miles of the Reader—right in its own back yard. At Warren, the Bradley Lumber Company's Warren & Saline River had gone diesel and had a 1942 Baldwin consolidation for sale. Mr. Tom, accompanied by chief mechanical officer Kim Byrne, machinist Peterson, conductor Walker, and hogger Adams, went down for a look at 2-8-0 No. 1702.

She was a sad sight. She had been sitting for three years in the weeds on a spur track, a victim of dieseldom, after being retired in 1961. Many miles and many years earlier, she had rolled out of the Baldwin plant at Eddystone, Pennsylvania, in September, 1942, bearing shop No. 64,641 and road No. 1702. The road number was unchanged during her U.S. Army service in World War II. Discharged in 1946, she was sold to the Warren & Saline River.

The inspection team from the Reader conferred with E. J. Anthoni, general manager of the W & SR, then recommended that Mr. Tom buy her. The W & SR had put a good price on her and looked with favor upon the idea of her rehabilitation and continued service in Arkansas.

The 1702 arrived at Reader on July 3, 1964. Her boiler tubes were replaced, as were piston rings, superheater units, brake rigging, driving wheel tires, and even the armrests in the cab. I spent several hours with the engine crew aboard this former GI in 1960 when she was running on the Warren & Saline River. Even then she was spewing almost as much steam from throttle and piston-rod packing as went into her cylinders.

The "doctors" labored with their "patient" for two and one-half months. The European-type buffer plates on her pilot beam, the offset smokebox door, and the blackout storm curtains had already been removed, so the Reader men didn't have to contend with these monstrosities. Even so, theirs was a wearisome task. After the Reader had spent three times what the 1702 was worth as scrap, she was in as good condition as when she left Eddystone in 1942.

In the meantime, while 1702 was in the "hospital" at Reader, Paramount Studio in Hollywood was looking for a steam locomotive of depression-days vintage for use in a movie it was to shoot in the Bay Saint Louis area on the Mississippi Gulf Coast. Paramount officials heard of 1702 and signed a lease with Tom Long for her to appear in *This Property Is Condemned.*

The shopmen at Reader worked sixteen-hour days and seven-day weeks until she was ready to roll, barely meeting the deadline set for them. The 1702 went to Mississippi under her own steam as part of a freight train. She proved her worth by handling up to sixty cars in switching movements and ran easily at seventy miles an hour. She performed nobly before the cameras and returned to Reader proudly waving her smoke plume.

Dave Morgan had promised Mr. Tom that if the 1702 were rebuilt, he would come to Reader and christen her. He kept his promise, and on April 4, 1966, Dave's wife, Margaret, splashed the brightly polished consolidation's pilot with a pint and ten ounces of French champagne. No. 1702 then took her place as the Reader's third steam locomotive in fine running condition, good for many years of service for a railroad which was faithful to steam as the only motive power worth mentioning.

To provide additional service, Mr. Tom purchased two passenger cars from the Rock Island in 1965. They were built by the Standard Steel Car Company as Nos. 2534 and 2549 for use as suburban coaches in commuter service around Chicago. The 2534 was made No. 502 on the Reader and 2549 became No. 503. They will seat one hundred passengers.

LITTLE ROCK, MAUMELLE & WESTERN (NEIMEYER LINE)

11

AT THE TURN OF THE CENTURY, the area west of the Little Rock city limits was virtually untouched timber land. One could travel through pine and hardwood forest about as far as he wished to go toward the Oklahoma border. Arkansas was just beginning to build a reputation as a lumber-producing area in a nation clamoring for building materials. "More lumber" was the cry.

It was heard by A. J. Neimeyer of St. Louis, who came to Little Rock and organized the Neimeyer Lumber Company in November, 1906. Within a few weeks, he had purchased 80,000 acres of land in Pulaski, Perry, and Saline counties. Most of it was originally part of the public lands given the Little Rock & Ft. Smith Railroad by the federal government to assist in its construction (the road is now the Central Division of the Missouri Pacific). The LR & FS was granted 550,000 acres in January, 1858; then, in 1886, following the Civil War, Congress added another 396,000 acres. This gave the Little Rock & Ft. Smith almost 1,000,000 acres, a tidy piece of real estate. Neimeyer was purchasing it in 1906–1907 at $12.50 per acre. It contained enough timber, predominantly pine, he said, to supply his mill for approximately forty years.

Seeing the advantage of such a mill, the Little Rock Business Men's League acquired eighty acres of land, owned by Lewis Roton and Mrs. J. K. Riffel, a couple of miles west of Little Rock on the Nineteenth Street Pike. It was donated to Neimeyer, who promised to build a large lumber mill. The mill and lumber camps in the woods would furnish labor for five hundred men, two hundred of whom would work at the mill. The average wage of the mill hands would be sixteen to twenty dollars per week, or about fifteen thousand dollars per month, most of which would be spent in the Little Rock area. Men at the camps would receive another fifteen thousand dollars each month. These economic facts persuaded the businessmen to make every possible effort to assure that the mill would be built.

Neimeyer also promised to build about seventeen miles of standard-gauge railroad, and the Business Men's League agreed to furnish the right-of-way. It was to be both a logging road and a passenger line. The mill would be its eastern terminus; rails would not be extended into Little Rock. The St. Louis, Iron Mountain & Southern had constructed a branch line from near the present site of the Westinghouse plant to the Arkansas Brick Manufacturing Company, about a half-mile east of the millsite. Traffic would be interchanged between the two roads.

The western end of the Neimeyer road would connect with a railroad whose name was almost as long as its rails—the Fourche River Valley & Indian Territory, a fifteen-mile lumber pike extending west from Bigelow (known as Fourche at that time), on the Rock Island, across Perry County and into Yell County to about seven miles south of Ola. The FRV & IT was chartered August 16, 1905, by the Fourche River Lumber Company, which was owned by Charles Neimeyer, a brother of A. J.

With the Little Rock, Maumelle & Western being granted a

charter in March, 1907, and, when completed, connecting at Bigelow with the Fourche River Valley & Indian Territory, there was speculation that a connection would be made at Ola with the Dardanelle, Ola & Southern, yielding a rail route from Little Rock to Dardanelle on the south side of the Arkansas River. There had also been quite a bit of talk about extending the old Arkansas Central east from Paris to Dardanelle. If it came about, there would be through traffic from Little Rock to Fort Smith, the western terminus of the Arkansas Central. This was almost the identical route proposed in 1901 by the Sawyer & Austin Lumber Company of Pine Bluff. The businessmen of the area showed no interest, however, so the company built the Pine Bluff & Western from Pine Bluff through Sheridan to Benton.

The Neimeyer road was envisioned to extend almost due west through Big Rock Township, cut across the northeast corner of Brodie Township, then run northwest across Owen Township and into Maumelle Township. It was the consensus of businessmen and newspaper editors in the Little Rock area that the only way to get the new railroad was to put up some money and secure right-of-way for it. They estimated it would take $17,000 to buy land for the millsite and right-of-way for the railroad, so a campaign was begun to raise the cash, with $6,050 being received in one day. Subscribers to the fund would not be required to pay anything until January, 1907, when one-fourth of it would be due; the remaining quarters would be due each sixty days thereafter.

A. J. Neimeyer teamed up with Charles C. Rose, Samuel W. Rayburn, A. C. Becker, and E. B. Kinsworthy to form the Little Rock, Maumelle & Western (known as the Neimeyer Line) at an estimated cost of $250,000 to build and equip. One thousand shares of stock had already been subscribed, with Neimeyer owning eight hundred of them.

By January 9, 1907, the preliminary survey had been completed and chief engineer A. J. Hall had a crew in the field establishing the final alignment (the first eighteen miles had already been established). A contract had been negotiated with A. L. Pritchard to furnish ties, and he was busy distributing them along the route surveyed. A few landowners were in dispute with the railroad on the price of land for right-of-way. On January 29, the company asked Sheriff Kavanaugh to serve a notice of condemnation against them. The Circuit Court set the amount of a deposit required from the railroad as payment for the land. Neimeyer was ready to begin building.

Early in April, 1907, there was being circulated around Little Rock a rumor that the Santa Fe was interested in the Neimeyer road. The Santa Fe was supposedly looking for a Gulf outlet at New Orleans, and if the Little Rock, Maumelle & Western were extended through Mena, Arkansas, and into Indian Territory to the Santa Fe, it could become a link in the larger system.

The businessmen and other citizens were rather enthusiastic about the Neimeyer road and subscribed generously to the company's offer of stock to provide the cash necessary for construction. By July, 1907, the rails had crossed Fair Park Boulevard near Thirtieth Street, where they turned north to span Coleman Creek on a wood trestle. Continuing northwest, the route passed Haven of Rest Cemetery and followed Twelfth Street Road (now Rodney Parham Road) to its intersection with Markham Street. Neimeyer said he expected the road to be finished by September, since there were to be no grades steeper than 1 per cent. The huge mill at Little Rock was completed and machinery was being installed. It would have a capacity of one hundred thousand board feet of lumber a day; in the boiler room were eight 125-horsepower boilers. Neimeyer had come down to inspect the mill and see how the tracklaying was progressing. When he had done so, he returned to St. Louis.

During the summer months, the rails were extended westward, stations were established—Becker, Byron, Florence, Pasco, Cairnes, Janice, and Douglas—logging camps were set up, and a determined assault was made upon the dense forests which covered the low, rolling hills. As the timber gave way to whining saws and flashing axes, spur lines were extended from the main road. These temporary branches, roughly constructed, were unsuitable for the solid-frame engines, Baldwin Consolidation Nos. 100 and 101.

The train and engine crews reported for work, performed the required switching at the mill, wheeled the loaded log cars to the millpond, where the logs were dumped, then turned the engine on the wye and headed for end of track with a train of empty skeleton log cars. At the western end, situated in Saline County a few miles north of Paron, the empties were shoved onto a spur track and a train of loads, which had been pulled in the evening before by the Shays from the logging camps, was taken to the mill at Little Rock.

The railroad also did some hauling for other companies. The Clark & Gay operation, located near the Neimeyer mill, used only hardwood for lumber, wagon-wheel hubs, and spokes. And there was a meat-packing firm which used large quantities of hickory for smoking meats. The Neimeyer mill used only pine.

The spur tracks branching off from the main line were mostly prefabricated sections. Rails were spiked to crossties to form panels. These were laid down by a steam loader, and the joints were bolted together. The small cabins in the logging camps were also temporary. They were built with a heavy rod extending upward through the roof. The end of the rod terminated in a loop, and when it came time to move camp, the cabins were skidded near the track, where a steam log loader easily lifted each cabin by its loop and deposited it on a flatcar. Thus everything about the railroad logging operation was temporary except the main line.

The camps were crude and rough in appearance, befitting their temporary status, but all necessities were provided. There was a school which all children in the camp attended regularly. A camp physician was on call at all times, and a hospital was set up to care for injured or sick workers and their families. A company commissary provided employees with all their food requirements. One summer, a few cases of spinal meningitis turned up in one of the camps. The hospital building was skidded a safe distance away to isolate the patients. Two doctors were kept busy. It was touch and go for a while, but only one man died.

To prevent the Little Rock, Maumelle & Western from being classified as only a logging railroad, Neimeyer instituted passenger service on Wednesday morning, October 23, 1907. A gasoline motorcar, seating only ten passengers, would make runs from Little Rock to Maud Junction, eight miles away. The varnish run left Little Rock at nine o'clock each morning and arrived in Maud at 9:30; with an hour layover, it began the return run at 10:30, arriving in Little Rock at eleven o'clock. The afternoon run left Little Rock at three and returned at five. Passengers desiring to make the trip were instructed to board a city streetcar and get off at Thirteenth and Pine Streets. From the end of the car line, it was only a three-quarter-mile walk to the Neimeyer mill.

On such pikes as the Little Rock, Maumelle & Western, serious wrecks were rather scarce because of the slow speed made necessary by the uneven track of fifty- or sixty-pound rail. On the night of May 14, 1908, L. F. Barnes was hoghead on rod engine 100 and Walter Boling was wielding the scoopshovel, trying to keep a decent head of steam in old hog's boiler. This was no child's task, considering the fact that an engine's boiler had to be cleaned and flushed once every week. The supply of water wasn't the best quality in the world.

At about eleven o'clock that night, Barnes and Boling headed onto a spur track at the mill to switch out a few empties. Boling had put a good slug of coal in the firebox of the ten-wheeler and had climbed out onto the pilot footboard to make a coupling with a few skeleton log cars. The track dropped down a steep grade, and as the engine nosed over into it, Barnes reduced his brake-line pressure with the independent valve. The hog hesitated for a moment, then began skating merrily along on dew-wet rails, drivers locked and sliding. Boling, realizing that something was not as it should be, began a mad scramble to get back into the cab and away from the log cars somewhere down the spur, concealed in the enveloping darkness. Barnes joined the birds.

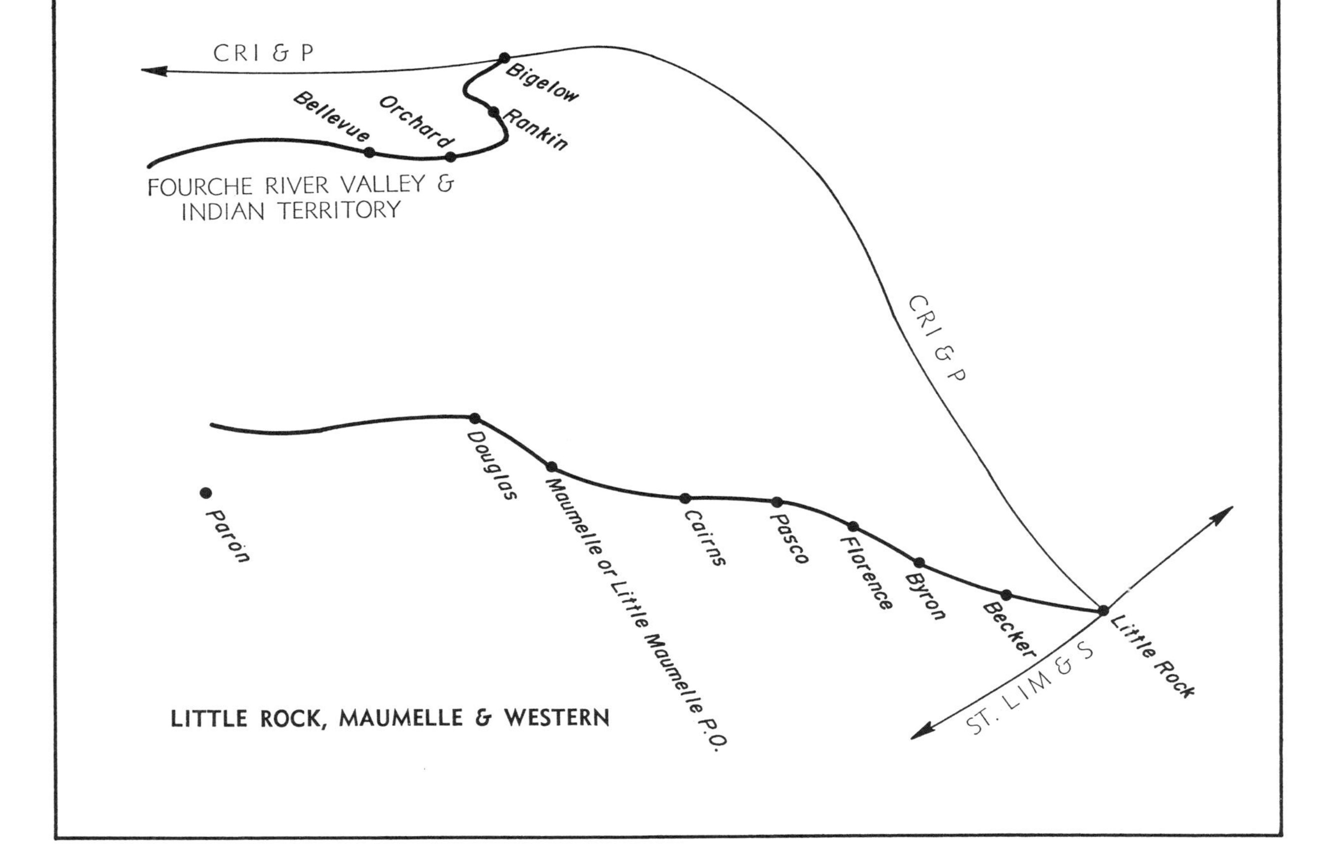
CRI & P
Bigelow
Rankin
Orchard
Bellevue
FOURCHE RIVER VALLEY & INDIAN TERRITORY
CRI & P
Douglas
Maumelle or Little Maumelle P.O.
Cairns
Pasco
Florence
Byron
Becker
Little Rock
ST. LIM & S
Paron
LITTLE ROCK, MAUMELLE & WESTERN

Boling was on the running board along the boiler when the engine pilot found the forward end of the cars. He was tossed end over end to a not-so-gentle landing. There was much crashing and banging for a few seconds, then all was suddenly still and dark. After a few moments of confused searching, the hogger and his scoop-wielder located each other. Barnes was pretty well bruised and his back was severely wrenched. Fireman Boling, considerably battered, spent several days in the hospital. The engine and four cars were on the ground but, strangely enough, were not so badly damaged.

Early in March, 1909, A. J. Neimeyer decided to move his family from St. Louis to a new home in Little Rock so that he could be near the mill and railroad. To make the most of public relations, he invited the members of the Business Men's League to take an excursion over the railroad and inspect its facilities. Quickly accepting the offer, they were favorably impressed by its fourteen-mile length. Viewing the hustle and bustle of the logging camps was a novelty for most of them.

Large quantities of lumber were shipped from the mill over the St. Louis, Iron Mountain & Southern, so the Little Rock, Maumelle & Western was finally extended to Cold Springs, about ten miles west of Ferndale. The logging crews gradually denuded the sharply rolling hills, and it became increasingly difficult to snake the downed logs to railside. Maintenance of equipment was rather expensive, too. There was a small repair shop for the locomotives, but the heavy work, such as turning the wheels, was done by the Iron Mountain.

To supplement the declining revenue from the logging set up, Neimeyer attempted a housing subdivision at Carnes, a station near Little Rock. He cleared the land, then divided it into lots, to be sold to home-builders. He called the place West Little Rock, but for some reason it never was successful.

The boom of World War I began to decline, the demand for lumber was subsiding, and Neimeyer saw the handwriting on the wall. The five Shay engines were disposed of, one to the Glenwood

Lumber Company and another to Ozan-Graysonia Lumber Company at Prescott. Ten-wheeler No. 101, which had cost about fifteen thousand dollars from Baldwin, was sold to the Choctaw Lumber Company for seven thousand dollars in 1921. The Neimeyer Line had lived fourteen years, serving its owners and the public well.

LITTLE ROCK, HOT SPRINGS & TEXAS—LITTLE ROCK & HOT SPRINGS WESTERN

12

By 1900, THE RAILROAD-BUILDING BOOM in central Arkansas had subsided considerably. The Cairo & Fulton had completed a road from Texarkana to Little Rock in 1873, and in 1900, the Choctaw, Oklahoma & Gulf ran a line west from Little Rock into Indian Territory. The latter had been acquired by the Rock Island by 1904. The east-west and north-south roads had been established and were in operation. Even so, the only connection by rail from Little Rock to the Hot Springs National Park area was by way of Malvern on the St. Louis, Iron Mountain & Southern, thence aboard the Hot Springs Railroad, known as the Diamond Jo Line. To many people, travelers and local businessmen as well, this seemed too roundabout and haphazard.

By 1893, businessmen had found the Board of Trade an intolerable institution, so the Commercial League was born. It was determined to bring Little Rock more of everything in order to make the city grow: more factories, more business houses, more railroads, more people.

The movement attracted the attention of Uriah Lott, an industrialist and financier from New York who had migrated to Texas, where he constructed both the San Antonio & Aransas Pass Railroad and the Corpus Christi & Laredo. Lott proposed to Commercial League members that they help finance a railroad from Little Rock to Hot Springs. They were most enthusiastic about the idea, and the folks at Hot Springs viewed the proposition with equal favor, for they believed that competition for the Diamond Jo Line would benefit their town.

The combined action resulted in the Arkansas Legislature's granting a charter to the Little Rock, Hot Springs & Texas Railroad under the direction of Uriah Lott, J. P. Nelson of San Antonio, W. J. Little and Ed Hogaboom of De Witt, and C. Rugg, R. L. Williams, Alf Whittington, J. J. Sumpter, and C. N. Ricks of Hot Springs. The corporation was to be financed by a stock issue of $1,200,000. Brother Lott, an exacting capitalist, soon convinced the cities of Little Rock and Hot Springs that each should contribute $55,000 in cash to acquire terminal facilities and right-of-way within the city limits. Little Rock citizens were persuaded to donate right-of-way for half the distance to Hot Springs. Their $55,000 was to be available by January 10, 1894, if they wanted the railroad built, but the money would not be paid to Brother Lott until it was in operation, which was to be January, 1895. He proposed to lay the sixty miles of track with 60-pound steel rails and white-oak ties.

The Commercial League set up what it called the New Railroad Committee and put solicitors on the trail of every citizen. No effort was spared by anyone in securing the new railroad. Everybody was behind the project. Daily newspaper editorials were filled with glowing praise for the road and its promoters:

> The plan is as solid as the Point of Rocks and the foot of Rock Street, and it will take only $55,000 to do it!

> Build the railroad between this city and Hot Springs and the rest of the world will come to see us.
>
> We must get this road or be listed among the defunct capitals of the United States!
>
> Little Rock will have to fold its arms and wait patiently for the end of the world to come, unless this competing line is built.

By January 5, 1894, the Commercial League was proclaiming in bold newspaper headlines that the cash subscription had risen to $40,507.50. Uriah Lott had spent very little time in Little Rock, merely stopping over on his various trips to New York. On the morning of January 8, he was met at Union Depot by the League's general committee and the committee on right-of-way, the latter reporting that many sites had been offered as a bonus—provided the road would cross the land of the owners. With only two days left until the January 10 deadline, they still lacked $14,492.50. Lott blandly told the committee he hoped they could raise it; if not, there would be no railroad.

When the morning of January 10 rolled around, the exhausted Leaguers came into headquarters for a final report. When all donations were counted, the total was $68,000. They had secured the necessary $55,000, with $13,000 left over for right-of-way. During the hours of jubilation which followed, Colonel J. H. McCarthy, general chairman of the campaign, declined to make a speech. His tongue, he said, was blistered from talking up the subscriptions!

A Little Rock civil engineer remarked that it would take at least one million dollars to build and equip the railroad, since five steel bridges would be required to cross the forks of Saline River and since there would be numerous deep cuts and high fills. Little Rock would be assured a road of such magnitude for the paltry sum of sixty-eight thousand dollars.

A few days later, there circulated a rumor that Lott was actually building a connection between Benton and Hot Springs for the Gould-controlled St. Louis, Iron Mountain & Southern. "Was it only a coincidence that George Gould passed through Little Rock on his way to Hot Springs a few days earlier?" Lott was asked. He vehemently denied the rumor.

By early February, not even one shovelful of earth had been turned. Word was received that people at Hot Springs were asking exorbitant prices for land which Lott needed for depot and terminal sites. He was unable to keep his survey crew in the field at $200 a day, so had called them in and paid them off. All operations were suspended.

Lott reported that the entire cash bonus raised by the folks at Little Rock would be required just to buy right-of-way because of the high price being asked for land. He flatly refused to build from Benton to Little Rock and said the money would be refunded to the Commercial League. Nothing more was heard of the Little Rock, Hot Springs & Texas Railroad. Brother Lott silently stole away.

The failure of their project was a great disappointment to the citizens of Little Rock and Hot Springs. To them railroads and prosperity were inseparable. The more railroads a city had, the more prosperous it was. They had just lost one.

During the spring of 1899, there was a surge of renewed interest in the defunct road. Colonel Sam Fordyce had been out looking at the brush-grown piece of roadbed which had been halfheartedly graded up near Hot Springs. The Colonel, who lived in St. Louis, was no stranger to railroading nor to the people of Arkansas. He had assumed control of the Paramore Narrow Gauge (or the Texas & St. Louis Railway, as it was chartered) in 1881 and successfully pushed it to completion from Texarkana to St. Louis (the route is now known as the Cotton Belt). Sam was born in Senecaville, Ohio, on February 17, 1840. In his thirteenth year, his father and associates built the Central Ohio Railroad, an extension of the Baltimore & Ohio. Because of this, Sam became fascinated with railroading. After the Civil War, he came to Hot Springs to recuperate from his wounds. Here Paramore found him and persuaded him to help build a narrow-gauge road to compete with Gould's St. Louis & Iron Mountain, which it roughly paralleled from Texarkana to St. Louis.

On July 18, 1899, the Arkansas Railroad Commission granted a charter to the Little Rock & Hot Springs Western Railroad to build between the two cities of its corporate title. Capital stock of $1,140,000 was secured by first-mortgage bonds for $1,400,000. Directing the new company were Sam Fordyce, president; John G. Lonsdale, vice president; W. C. Fordyce, assistant to the president; William S. Mitchell, secretary; John M. Moore, general counsel; H. E. Martin, auditor; H. G. Fleming, general superintendent; and F. W. Gregory, general freight and passenger agent.

The new company, aggressive and energetic, was soon known locally as the "Hot Western." The roadbed was quickly graded up, and, strangely enough, no money was asked from the people of Little Rock or Hot Springs. The new outfit seemed to be well financed. A connection was made with the Choctaw, Oklahoma & Gulf at the south edge of Little Rock. The line crossed the St. Louis, Iron Mountain & Southern at Benton and headed west for Hot Springs. On April 10, 1900, the first train was run and the Hot Western was in business.

The new road competed with the Diamond Jo Line at Hot Springs. There was barely enough business there to keep the two lines in operation during 1900, but they kept trains running. Things improved slowly as the months rolled by, but mostly, the year was uneventful.

On July 7, 1906, the eastbound varnish run left Hot Springs at 6:45 A.M., about ten minutes late, with more than one hundred passengers aboard, most of them Negroes returning to Pine Bluff following an excursion to Hot Springs. About nine miles out of the station, hogger Abernathy had the train rolling at a fair clip when, as he rounded a slight curve, he saw a burning trestle a short distance ahead. He wiped the clock and yelled at the tallowpot, Arthur Graham. They joined the birds.

The engine dropped through the flaming bridge, uncoupling

from the three-car train. The first car jerked to a stop, suspended across the abutment of the bridge. Frantic passengers climbed out the windows of the overturned car, most of them unhurt except for cuts from flying glass. It seemed as if the car were waiting for the passengers to climb out, for soon after the last one escaped, it slid into the ravine atop the engine.

Arthur Wilson of Butte, Montana, had three broken ribs, and Dr. J. M. Robinson, a Negro physician from Little Rock, suffered a broken right arm and his body was badly bruised. The engineer and fireman were scratched and bruised from rolling down the steep embankment. Conductor B. B. Jones said it was a miracle no one was killed.

Train No. 6 left Hot Springs for Benton at 5:20 on the evening of July 10, just three days after train No. 2 had run through the burning trestle. As No. 6 rounded a sharp curve where the track crossed Gaines Street in Hot Springs, the hogger heard an engine approaching, its stack briskly barking. He had stopped his train and was attempting to reverse the hog when a lone engine lurched around an opposing curve and rammed the passenger train head on. The front ends of the engines were telescoped, and they both left the rails.

Machinist Stanley had taken a new engine out for a test run and was returning to the machine shop. Because of a difference in the time shown on the watches of Stanley and the varnish hogger, Stanley believed he had plenty of time to clear No. 6. He didn't. Stanley bailed out of the cab and broke an ankle. Conductor Cobb on No. 6 was knocked off his feet and had his shoulders bruised, but none of the passengers were hurt.

The Hot Western seemed to be having more than its fair share of trouble. The engineers and firemen called a strike on September 1, 1906, after negotiations for a pay raise failed. Hoggers were getting $3.50 a day, firemen $2.50 a day. A working day could be considered to be twenty-four hours long, since there was no limit to the number of hours a crew might be required to work. The company had offered the engineers an increase of 25¢ per day in lieu of the 50¢ they had asked, and the firemen would get no increase at all.

The regular 6:30 A.M. train managed to get under way at ten o'clock in charge of a scab fireman named Chaney, who was not competent to run an engine. The regular crew boarded the engine and tried to persuade the men not to leave town. The city police were called, and hoggers J. E. Abernathy and Gus Seamon, along with fireman Arthur Graham, were arrested. The men soon received their raise, and there was no more trouble.

Just three weeks later, the 9:45 A.M. train was nearing Lonsdale, about five miles out of Hot Springs, when the eagle eye spotted a track velocipede with two men aboard. He big-holed the brake valve and watched helplessly as the engine overtook the little three-wheeler. The two men aboard her were so frightened that they froze instead of trying to jump. The engine had almost stopped when the pilot struck the velocipede and tossed it into the ditch. The two men, Andrew Hardin and Ed Richardson, worked with the track gang and lived at Lonsdale. They were not seriously injured and were taken to Hot Springs aboard the train.

Calm marked the winter of 1906. Then on Sunday morning, April 15, 1907, a bridge near Hot Springs was burned. It was suspected that someone was trying to wreck a train for the same bridge had burned eight months earlier. The structure, about 120 feet long, spanned a small, dry creekbed. The morning train from Hot Springs arrived to find the bridge in flames about 6:30. Another train was called from Little Rock, and the passengers walked across the dry creekbed to continue on their way.

In the fall of 1905, a man named William Boling came to the Hot Springs area. He said he was from Capetown, South Africa, and was prospecting in the mountains for a rich mineral claim (gold and silver were to be found in small quantities in the hills west of Hot Springs). He tramped the rough country for two years, not finding a bonanza, but searching persistently. On November 6, 1907, he was walking along the LR & HSW track a few miles east of Hot Springs. When the late-evening varnish run wheeled around one of the many curves, its headlights momentarily revealed the figure of a man plodding along between the rails. The hoghead's frantic action was in vain. Boling was killed.

Late in the evening of December 7, 1907, Sam Tarver and his twelve-year-old son, Payton, were driving a wagon toward home in Benton. They had been working at one of Sam's several lumber yards along the railroad. As they approached Turkey Cut, Sam saw that the railroad trestle was beginning to burn. He jumped out of his wagon, ran to a water barrel placed at the trestle in case of fire, and began tossing water onto the flames with his plug hat. Sam yelled at Payton to tie the team to a near-by tree and run to the home of Robert McAdoo for help.

Mrs. McAdoo gave Payton a bucket so that he could run back and help his father fight the fire while she sent her twelve-year-old daughter, Millie, down the track to flag the evening passenger train from the west. The little girl ran and stumbled a quarter-mile down the track before she heard the sharp exhaust of the engine. When she saw its headlight sweep around a curve, she grabbed a shawl from about her shoulders and began waving it frantically back and forth while standing between the rails. The engineer answered with a double blast from the whistle, and Millie jumped aside as the engine and three cars rushed by. Hogger Allen got the train stopped within a few feet of the burning bridge and, along with the fireman and conductor, helped to fight the flames with a bucket brigade. Millie was an eighteen-carat heroine, and after the excitement was over, hogger Allen, conductor Lommis, and superintendent H. E. Martin promised her that she would receive a Christmas tree covered with presents.

Again rumors were being whispered about that the St. Louis, Iron Mountain & Southern was getting control of the LR & HSW. What the folks didn't know was that the Iron Mountain already controlled three-quarters of the Hot Western's capital stock and that the Choctaw, Oklahoma & Gulf owned the other quarter. The Choctaw had gained control of the new road between Little

Rock and Benton. At 9:00 A.M. on January 24, 1910, a meeting was held in the Hot Western's general offices at Market and Valley streets to convey, sell, and transfer that portion of the road between Benton and Hot Springs to the Iron Mountain.

On February 12, the roundhouse, shop buildings, two locomotives, a baggage car, and a motorcar were burned, completely destroyed. Thus ended the life of the Hot Western. The Iron Mountain became part of the Missouri Pacific in 1917, and the last passenger run was made January 20, 1964. The rails were taken up that summer.

ARKANSAS CENTRAL; PARIS-SUBIACO TRACTION; FT. SMITH, SUBIACO & EASTERN; FT. SMITH, SUBIACO & ROCK ISLAND

13

ARKANSAS CENTRAL is still a little confusing to many Arkansans. The state has had two railroads with that name. Both were operating roads, although one was about twenty years ahead of the other and they were on opposite sides of the state.

The first Arkansas Central was incorporated January 20, 1871, to build from Helena to Little Rock. It was completed from Helena to Clarendon in 1872, and an additional sixty or seventy miles toward Little Rock were being graded and bridges constructed when the Panic of 1873 intervened. On January 1, 1874, the company defaulted in the interest payment on first and second mortgages. Sold on July 22, 1877, the road was reorganized as the Arkansas Midland. In 1901, it was acquired by Jay Gould, who operated it as a subsidiary of his St. Louis, Iron Mountain & Southern. The Iron Mountain was consolidated with the Missouri Pacific in 1917, and a portion is still in operation from Helena to Holly Grove.

The Arkansas Central with which we are concerned here was incorporated April 29, 1897, when the articles were filed in the office of the Arkansas secretary of state. The firm's stated purpose was to build a railroad from Fort Smith to Paris, Arkansas. The incorporators fully intended to build on into Little Rock, but the proposed route had not been selected. The original charter granted permission for construction of any spur tracks deemed necessary by the stockholders.

The Arkansas Central was brought about by the existence of extensive coal deposits lying undeveloped in the area. Arkansas' coal field lies in the Arkansas River Valley between the state's western border and the town of Russellville. It is roughly the shape of an *L*, having its base along the Oklahoma line. It is about thirty-three miles wide, north to south, and sixty miles long. Only in the eastern and western portions of the field are the Hartshorne coal beds found, formed when the southern half of Arkansas was covered by a sea. The Hartshorne sandstone beneath them was formed as the sea gradually became shallower, and the swampy vegetation fell into the water to form the layer of coal now found just above the Hartshorne sandstone. No one vein of coal is continuous over the whole area, and the different beds vary in thickness. The average thickness of the Hartshorne layer is about three feet, and it lies no deeper than 3,200 feet. That part of the layer which lies in Arkansas once contained one and one-quarter billion tons of coal. There is about a 300-year supply left.

The Charleston and Paris coal beds are considered to be of economic importance to Arkansas. The Charleston, with a thickness of more than fourteen inches, covers an area of approximately fifty-two square miles and is low-volatile bituminous rank. The Paris underlies three small areas in Franklin and Logan counties, covering about eighteen square miles and ranging in thickness from fourteen to thirty-two inches. It, too, is a low-volatile bituminous rank, producing very high quality coke. Arkansas coal has been shipped to Colorado, Utah, California, and Texas for use in making coke. Production in Arkansas increased about 100 per cent in 1883 when the Frisco Railroad reached the Hackett-Greenwood area in Sebastian County. Coal became commercially productive when railroad transportation became available.

Now some of the above facts became known to several gentlemen in Indiana and Illinois, two of whom were Charles C. Godman of Chicago and Joseph H. Larimer of Peru, Indiana (a few years later, Godman was to be the prime moving force behind the Dardanelle, Ola & Southern Railroad). They formed the Arkansas Central Railroad with a capital stock of six hundred thousand dollars, half of which they immediately snapped up. Associated with them were Allen G. Tupper of Peru; Virgil V. Beavers of Charleston, Arkansas; John S. Shibley of Paris; and S. P. Day and Wharton Carmall of Fort Smith.

The Arkansas Central was projected to extend from Fort Smith to Little Rock, but only forty-six miles of it (to Paris) were included in the original charter. The remainder would serve those towns which offered the most to the builders. To facilitate the first portion, Paris agreed to donate right-of-way through town, sufficient grounds for a depot, and twenty thousand dollars in cash. Charleston agreed to put up fifteen thousand dollars, and Fort Smith residents pledged the handsome sum of fifty thousand dollars. The Arkansas Central was not a Johnny-come-lately affair. It had been contemplated for more than two years, and Allen G. Tripper, a civil engineer, was engaged to take charge of the field engineers during construction.

Glowing reports were given the folks back in Indiana, possibly to influence them in the matter of investing their money in the Arkansas Central stock. The road was to run through valleys as fertile as any in the world, even the fabulous valley of the Nile. People along the proposed route from Fort Smith to Little Rock, it was pointed out, were compelled to transport their farm produce in wagons anywhere from twenty to fifty miles to a suitable market or means of transportation, so this alone would guarantee enough revenue to make the road a paying proposition. Larimer said he had never met a more hospitable class of people anywhere. He was sufficiently impressed that he moved his family to Fort Smith, a bustling town of eighteen thousand people and the home of former Governor William M. Fishback, who had royally entertained Larimer while he was in town.

About four and one-half miles south of Fort Smith, the rails of the Arkansas Central branched off the St. Louis, Iron Mountain & Southern, which extended to Greenwood. With aggravating slowness, the rails inched their way across the undulating countryside to Barling, Central, Lavaca, and on to Charleston early in 1898. Forty-six miles of sixty-pound rails connected Charleston to Fort Smith via four miles of trackage right over the Iron Mountain.

Difficulties increased for the Arkansas Central during the next year, and on December 29, 1898, it went into receivership. A reorganization was effected by February 9, 1899, and—great surprise—it was learned that Jay Gould's St. Louis, Iron Mountain & Southern now controlled 98.9 per cent of the Arkansas Central's capital stock, which was held by the Mercantile Trust Company of New York. The road's ills seemed to be rather easily cured, and by May 1, 1900, an additional eighteen miles of track had been constructed to reach the coal fields at Paris. With ample transportation available, the mines along the Arkansas Central kept a steady stream of coal trains rolling to Fort Smith and beyond.

In the meantime, Charles Godman had begun construction of the Dardanelle, Ola & Southern, but before even the first segment was in operation, there was a rumor, first heard in January, 1907, that Godman was planning to extend the Arkansas Central the forty-eight miles to Dardanelle. The people there were anxious to have the extension and had raised eighteen thousand dollars to assist Godman in his efforts. For some reason, these plans did not bear fruit.

On February 6, 1908, the Arkansas Railroad Commission granted a charter to the Paris-Subiaco Traction Company for the purpose of building a six-mile electric railroad to connect Paris with the Catholic abbey of the Order of St. Benedict. Colonel Henry Stroup had filed the application with the secretary of state. Associated with him in the venture were D. J. Young, Conrad Elsken, C. J. Dundridge, and Charles J. Jewett. They had capitalized the road at sixty thousand dollars for construction and equipment.

The idea of electricity as motive power for the road was soon dropped. On September 1, 1908, Colonel J. H. Wright, president of the Arkansas Central, announced that the material for the extension had arrived in Paris. Work was to begin at once. Henry Stroup was engaged to supervise the selection of the route, as well as the actual construction work. He started at Paris. By early October, Stroup had begun grading the roadbed, and progress was pleasingly rapid. The new road was completely independent, but an agreeable traffic arrangement had been made with the Arkansas Central.

All six miles of right-of-way had been secured before construction began, and land was acquired near the Subiaco abbey for a townsite (now the city of Subiaco). Grading was very light, and there was a minimum of timber clearing, since the right-of-way passed through land devoted mostly to farms. Ties and steel rails were distributed by a steam locomotive the company had purchased. All grading work was completed and crews began laying steel on March 1, 1909. The final spike was driven and the Paris-Subiaco road was opened to traffic on June 20, 1909. To commemorate the occasion, a spike-driving ceremony was planned for June 30.

At 11:00 A.M., the Right Reverend Ignatius Conrad, O.S.B., closed a solemn ceremony by driving a golden spike into a newly laid tie of the first and only railroad to enter Subiaco. After he had blessed both the railroad and the townsite, the first train arrived, bearing a large delegation of citizens from Fort Smith, including the heads of various departments of the Iron Mountain, the Arkansas Central, and the Frisco. The Benedictine monks celebrated the occasion by holding a banquet at the abbey, which, incidentally, was the second largest in the United States. They were happy to have a direct connection with Fort Smith.

By the latter part of June, plans were being formulated to extend the rails east from the abbey into the rich mining, timber, and farm lands of Logan County. The road now was five miles and forty-six hundred feet long. Still capitalized at sixty thousand dollars, most of its 600 shares of stock were owned by Colonel Henry Stroup and D. J. Young, who had 208 and 240 shares, respectively.

On July 5, 1909, the Paris-Subiaco Traction Company ceased to exist. A reorganization was effected, and the company emerged as the Ft. Smith, Subiaco & Eastern Railroad. It was proposed to extend the rails seven miles north and east from the abbey. To provide the required funds for construction, the capital stock was increased from sixty thousand dollars to one hundred and fifty thousand dollars. The rails were to terminate at a point in the north half of Section 15, where a townsite was platted and named Scranton, in Logan County.

People came to settle on the fertile land, hard-working and industrious people who established homes and put down roots. Many of their descendants, predominantly German, remain there today. Farms were cleared, vineyards begun, dairy herds started. The coal mines expanded extensively, and fine brick depots were constructed at Subiaco and Scranton. At Subiaco, Brother Anthony, one of the monks at the abbey, painted large decorative murals to decorate the station's interior. To express the high hopes of everyone concerned with the railroad, he inscribed across one wall: New York–Subiaco–San Francisco.

On July 31, 1910, the secretary of state granted permission for the Ft. Smith, Subiaco & Eastern to increase the company's capital stock from $150,000 to $500,000 to finance a proposed 23-mile extension to Dardanelle. Here connection would be made with the Dardanelle, Ola & Southern, which tied into the Rock Island at Ola, permitting a direct rail connection between Fort Smith

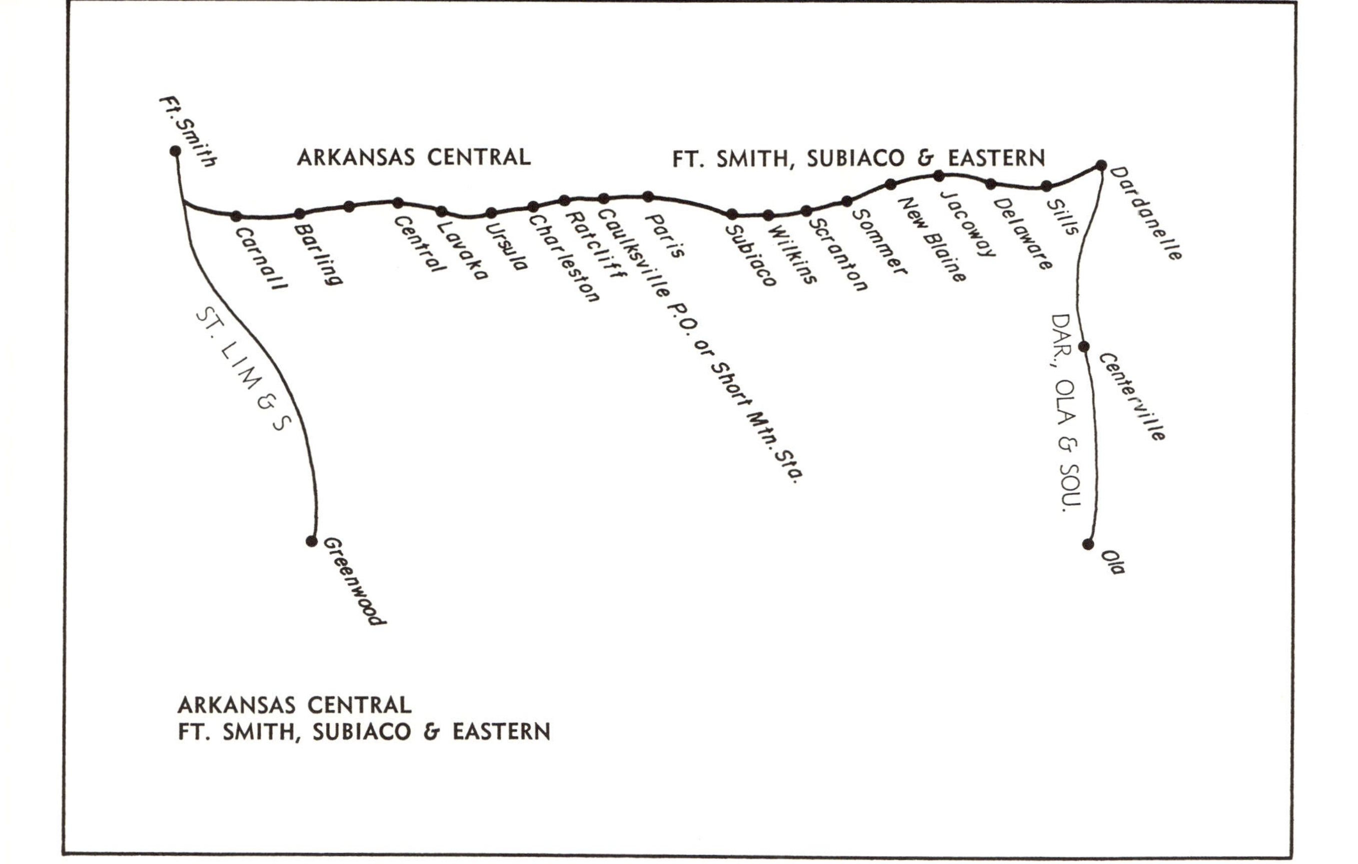

ARKANSAS CENTRAL
FT. SMITH, SUBIACO & EASTERN
Ft. Smith
Carnall
Barling
Central
Lavaka
Ursula
Charleston
Ratcliff
Caulksville P.O. or Short Mtn. Sta.
Paris
Subiaco
Wilkins
Scranton
Sommer
New Blaine
Jacoway
Delaware
Sills
Dardanelle
Centerville
Ola
DAR., OLA & SOU.
ST. LIM & S
Greenwood
ARKANSAS CENTRAL
FT. SMITH, SUBIACO & EASTERN

and Little Rock on the south side of the Arkansas River. The new branch would compete with the Iron Mountain, which roughly paralleled the river on the north.

Tension was building in Europe, and the American financial situation was in a state of flux. By July 12, 1917, the funding of the Ft. Smith, Subiaco & Eastern had reached the staggering figure of $600,000. Abnormal demands for financing in other types of business, as well as the unfavorable attitude of federal commissions and state legislative bodies, had made it virtually impossible for steam railroads to sell bonds.

World War I engulfed America, and the federal government assumed control of the nation's railroads for about six months. Following the Armistice in 1918, the Ft. Smith, Subiaco & Eastern was caught up in the financial upheaval and could not weather the storm. It was sold at a receiver's sale, then reorganized, this time as the Ft. Smith, Subiaco & Rock Island. A charter was granted April 12, 1919.

Work began almost immediately on extending the rails to Dardanelle. Rumor had it that the Rock Island lent a hand in the reorganization, but the larger road denied it. It was known, however, that the shortline had been courting the favors of its interstate neighbor for a couple of years.

Grading began on the Dardanelle end, and good progress was being made early in February, 1920. A large crew began laying steel, and a work train was put on. A new bridge spanned Hayes Creek, and steel rails were laid across it February 23. The crew laid rails four miles beyond the bridge, then began ballasting toward Dardanelle.

To facilitate matters, the citizens of Dardanelle had offered a cash bonus of sixty thousand dollars if a train were operated over the road by May 1. The suggestion that the Rock Island had an interest in the new project was strengthened by the fact that construction had begun at Dardanelle instead of Scranton and the Rock Island had transported the steel and other supplies and had furnished the locomotive and work train. Furthermore, there were enough rails in the yards at Dardanelle to lay ten miles of track.

At 11:50 A.M. on Saturday, April 24, 1920, the first Ft. Smith, Subiaco & Rock Island train rolled into the depot (Iron Mountain) at Fort Smith. Consisting of a locomotive and ten cars, it had left Dardanelle at 6:45 in charge of conductor B. O. Lemoyne. Hogger Ed Skelton, fireman A. M. Goodrick, and brakies Pierce and Kline rounded out the crew. The "bonus train" earned sixty thousand dollars for the company from the folks at Dardanelle.

Many officials from the railroad and the construction company were aboard. They were hailed by enthusiastic crowds at towns along the way: Blaine, Scranton, Subiaco, and Paris. At Scranton, mines and mills set up a screeching din of whistles as church bells tolled news of the train's arrival. Dr. John Newson added to the general uproar by firing into the air what was undoubtedly the largest and noisiest horse pistol ever seen or heard by mortal man.

The noon hour was enjoyably spent at Paris, where Mayor Henry Stroup and many hospitable townspeople saw to it that everyone on the train was provided with a bountiful dinner. The passengers were given special permission by Circuit Clerk of Logan County G. S. Minmyer to visit the hospital, where seventeen victims of a devastating tornado were convalescing. When the train left Paris, Mayor Henry Stroup was aboard.

On September 1, 1920, regular freight and passenger service began, with two westbound and two eastbound trains each day. A test run had been made August 30 to set up the schedule:

PASSENGER TRAIN	—Lv. Ola 6:30 A.M.; ar. Dardanelle 7:15 A.M.; ar. Paris 9:20 A.M.; ar. Fort Smith (Ark. Central) 11:40 A.M.
MIXED TRAIN	—Lv. Ola 11:00 A.M.; ar. Dardanelle 12 NOON; ar. Paris 11:15 P.M.
PASSENGER TRAIN	—Lv. Fort Smith (Ark. Central) 3:30 P.M.; ar. Paris 5:50 P.M.; ar. Dardanelle 7:55 P.M.; ar. Ola 8:40 P.M.

MIXED TRAIN —Lv. Paris 10:00 A.M.; ar. Dardanelle 2:15 P.M.; lv. Dardanelle 2:45 P.M.; ar. Ola 3:45 P.M.

Almost from the beginning, the Ft. Smith, Subiaco & Rock Island began to experience hard times. Production at the coal mines gradually dropped off as the Great Depression descended upon the nation, and then the family automobile appeared. To offset some of the impact, a gasoline-powered doodlebug replaced the steam passenger run. It caught fire and burned. Business went from bad to worse.

The thirty-eight miles of track from Ola to Scranton was taken up in March, 1938. By the latter part of 1948, the track from Scranton to Paris was so deteriorated that spikes would not hold in the Bermuda-grass roadbed; hence trains spent as much time on the ground as they did on the rails. The track looked like a sick, twisted snake.

In April, 1949, the Ft. Smith, Subiaco & Rock Island quietly expired. Tired old ten-wheeler No. 2522 was run onto a spur track and her fire was pulled. Through the years she sat cold and neglected, a victim of fire in her cab (set by vandals), rust, and time. Vandals stripped her of her brass fittings. Finally, in 1966, the city of Paris rescued her, rebuilt and painted her, and placed her in a park. She is there yet, resting out the years.

FAYETTEVILLE & LITTLE ROCK; ST. PAUL BRANCH (FRISCO); BLACK MOUNTAIN & EASTERN; COMBS, CASS & EASTERN

14

THE LAST INDIANS had been driven from the Ozark Mountain region of Arkansas. Soon farms began to appear in the fertile valleys and along the sheltered slopes of the hills. The settlement of Fayetteville became a station on the Butterfield Overland Stage run from Springfield, Missouri, to Fort Smith. Then on May 31, 1881, a man living in Fayetteville spread the exciting news that he had heard the whistle of a locomotive: the Frisco was building through Fayetteville on its way from Pierce City, Missouri, to Fort Smith. The first passenger train rolled into town July 4, 1882.

When the Frisco came to town, a young man named Hugh F. McDanield came with it. He was a construction man and a tie contractor. The railroad had to have ties, hundreds of thousands of them, and McDanield was the man who supplied them. Embryo milling establishments and an abundant supply of timber in Washington and Madison counties attracted his attention. The only thing he needed to make the lumber business a financial success was adequate transportation. Nothing could haul logs and lumber in greater quantities than a railroad, so the only sensible thing to do was build one.

On September 4, 1886, the state granted a charter to the Fayetteville & Little Rock Railroad. Behind the enterprise were Hugh F. McDanield, F. H. Fairbanks, J. S. McDanield, J. F. Mayes, and J. S. Van Hoose, all of Fayetteville; D. B. Elliott of Delaney; J. Pickens of Eversonville, Missouri; J. W. Brown of Brentwood; and B. F. McDanield of Bonner Springs, Kansas. The charter granted them authority to issue capital stock valued at $1,500,000—the estimated cost of building 150 miles of railroad from Fayetteville, in Washington County, by way of St. Paul to the riverboat town of Lewisburg, on the Arkansas River in Conway County near present-day Morrilton. There it would connect with the St. Louis, Iron Mountain & Southern. Hugh McDanield was the real promoter of the venture, and he personally invested $100,000 of his own money in it.

On December 4, 1886, a switch was installed in the Frisco track about a mile south of Fayetteville, and the spot was promptly named Fayette Junction. The railroad was on its way. February, 1887, saw rails laid on raw white-oak ties as far as Powell, twenty-five miles away.

By this time, the Frisco had become interested in the splinter road, particularly its ability to supply needed ties. The Frisco offered to purchase the F & LR, and on February 23, 1887, the transaction was made. The corporate name of Fayetteville & Little Rock was retained, and construction was continued by the parent Frisco.

Powell didn't remain end of track very long. The rails were soon reaching toward Scully, born about 1885 and situated about where State Highway 16 and 23 join today. The rails pushed past Scully and on up the valley a couple of miles to a location nearer timber-cutting operations. Scully refused to be ignored; folks gathered up their worldly goods and migrated to the end of the track. A new townsite was laid out, homes and business houses were built, and the town of St. Paul was born. By recollection of one of the old-timers, the first train rolled into St. Paul on July 4, 1887.

The little town was, of necessity, rather crude in appearance at first. Buildings were rough-hewn but clean new lumber or logs. Streets were ruts cut into the sod by heavy, high-wheeled wagons; they were soft and muddy in the winter months. The railroad installed a heavy turntable to reverse the direction of its engines, and St. Paul was officially declared the terminus of the F & LR in 1887.

Growth began almost immediately. New mills were quickly established to turn out huge quantities of lumber and ties, for which the demand was increasing day by day. People arrived by train, wagon, on horseback, even afoot. The mills were running twenty-four hours a day, and workers were needed badly. St. Paul became a boom town. One of the early tallowpots on the F & LR said: "I sure would like to see what the country around here looks like, but the lumber is piled so high I can't see out the cab window."

Many of the mill owners had names which are still to be found in the area or are well remembered. Among the most prominent were Barron, Phipps, McCoy, Brashears, and Kendrick. General-merchandise stores included Dutton Mercantile, owned by Walter Gilstrap, and the Kendrick store. William E. Bayles (Bales) owned the Old Red Barn Livery Stable. The traveling salesmen who made every settlement, no matter how remote, were regular customers at the Old Red Barn, where they would hire a rig to take them through the winding valleys to country stores and small settlements. Returning to St. Paul, they would put up at the Glendale Hotel, the Coleman House, or perhaps at the Brashears or Stewart hotels for the night, riding the train back to Fayetteville the next morning.

Times were good for everyone around St. Paul in those days. Even small boys could get jobs stacking light lumber, loading freight cars, or driving teams. Everybody who wanted a job had one. The usual hangers-on, always attracted by the smell of money, soon appeared in the vicinity. Gamblers sporting diamond-studded watch fobs and stick pins strolled St. Paul streets, finding plenty of takers. Many homesteads and lumber stakes exchanged hands overnight at the card tables.

Schools were among the first buildings to take shape after homes were finished, and a newspaper was established—the *St. Paul Mountain Air*—owned by E. F. Shinn. Schoolmaster William Hershel Hughes prepared many of his students to take examinations at Huntsville to obtain teaching certificates.

The Fayetteville & Little Rock brought prosperity to St. Paul, and St. Paul gave economic life to the railroad. During 1887, the first year of operation, the McDanield brothers shipped two million dollars' worth of white-oak crossties over the line. This was just one product from one company. Soon new stations were being established: Baldwin, Harris, Elkins, Durham, Thompson, Crosses, Delaney, Patrick, Combs, Brashears, and, later, Dutton and Pettigrew.

Although ties were the prime freight item for the railroad, it was soon hauling bridge timbers, lumber for construction of all kinds, and wagon bows, fellows, hubs, and spokes. J. H. Phipps came to the mountains as a lumberjack, but it wasn't long until he had a mill of his own, turning out wooden parts for wagons. One mill seemed to beget another, and he was soon supplying parts for wagon manufacturers all over the world. In one of his mills was a steam whistle so large that it could be heard thirty-five miles away on a still day.

Into this beehive of activity came big John "Irish" Mulrenin, a robust young man who tipped the scales at more than two hundred pounds. Almost immediately he was offered the job of conductor on the mixed train running the St. Paul branch. Three men had been hired for the job, and each stayed less than a week; some of John's friends were betting he would leave in about the same time. It seems there were quite a few hardfisted characters riding the train to their jobs at the various mills along the road, and they enjoyed harassing the conductor on the way to work or going home. When John heard of the situation, he had some qualms about taking the job, but decided he could quit if things got too rough.

Soon after taking the run John was going through the four coaches, taking up tickets and collecting cash fares, when he came into the head end of the second car. He closed the ill-fitting door, took a couple of steps along the aisle, then stopped. He saw blood trickling from between the seats on the right side. The startled young conductor hurried toward the crimson stain and found a passenger lying on the floor, blood flowing from a wide gash in forehead. There was a jagged hole in the corner of the window beside the seat, and a round iron scale weight lay on the floor. Someone had evidently thrown the missile when the train pulled out of Elkins a few minutes earlier and the incident went unnoticed in the confusion as the train got under way.

One of the passengers quickly wet a bulky handkerchief at the water cooler in the far end of the car and gave it to John, who bathed the man's face. The fellow revived in a moment, and when he clambered back into his seat and saw the devilish scale weight, he made a lunge at the conductor. "Damn ye, ye done it! 'Twas you what hit me with it!" he cried. Two passengers grabbed him and pointed to the hole in the window. Realizing his error, the man apologized to Mulrenin, who continued taking up tickets while a passenger bandaged the injured man's head. Such incidents were common on the St. Paul line.

Business continued to boom, and in 1897, the Fayetteville & Little Rock was extended eastward about twelve miles to Pettigrew, passing through Dutton on the way. Since Pettigrew was to be the permanent terminal, an Armstrong-type turntable was installed. Pettigrew was soon calling itself the "Hardwood Capital of the World," for it had more than a dozen lumber and stave mills. Included were the American Land, Timber & Stave Company; Chess & Wymond; Pekin Cooperage Company; J. M. Bryant Company; Kentucky Stave & Heading Company; and

W. L. Hillyard Stave Company. Phipps Lumber Company, the largest in northwest Arkansas, also had a mill there. The town also had ten general stores, a bank, two drugstores, a number of livery stables, two hotels, several small boardinghouses, and the depot. Two physicians and a dentist had offices in Pettigrew.

Although the lumber mills were the major source of business for the F & LR, they were by no means the only one. Irish Mulrenin said he picked up 125 cars of apples at Elkins during one season, and at one time he spotted ten cars of local merchandise on the team track there. Many times after leaving Fayetteville at about 7:00 A.M., he recalled, it was midnight and after when his train was put away. Occasionally, an extra freight was called to help handle the flood of cars.

In addition to hustling freight, Irish had to put up with some tough characters in the coaches. One fellow in particular, a man named Tucker, had a bad reputation. He lived at St. Paul, and once in a while, he and several other men would go to Pettigrew to drink and play poker while the train crew was busy switching. Tucker had made several trips on the train and had always paid his fare, but he usually had a few insulting remarks to make about it. Irish tells what happened on one occasion:

> We left Pettigrew with about fifty passengers aboard and we were more than halfway back to St. Paul before I came to where Tucker was sitting. I asked for his ticket and he just sat there, saying nothing. Four times I asked for his ticket, then I realized what he was up to.
>
> Before Tucker knew what was going on, I grabbed him by the collar, dragged him down the aisle and out onto the platform at the end of the coach, signaling the engineer for "brakes." I knew we would have to determine who was boss of this train or I would be just another conductor out of a job.
>
> When the train stopped, we dropped to the ground. Passengers swarmed all around us. Tucker charged and I sidestepped, knocking him to the ground. He sprang up and I met him with a hard right to the jaw. Down he went again. He got up cautiously

and I caught him in the right eye, completely closing it. This took all the fight out of him.

After that, we grew to be good friends and I was truly grieved a few years later when he passed away.

Big John said he often avoided trouble by cutting his switching short at Pettigrew and pulling out of town, leaving a bunch of drunks stranded at the depot. Many times on a Friday or Saturday night, he knew the taste of fear. Those rough lumbermen carried everything from iron scale weights to pistols, and they didn't hesitate to use them. Gradually, he convinced them that he had no ill feeling for anyone and soon became friendly with them.

Another local character, a man named Pool, gave conductors trouble, but a different kind. A cattleman, Pool also raised large herds of hogs. Many times when he had loaded a car with cattle and was ready to roll, he would spot an animal which he thought was too young or too poor for shipping. The conductor would have to hold the train while that particular animal was unloaded.

Pool and conductor Mulrenin devised an unusual method of "air-conditioning" cars loaded with hogs. A deep layer of sand was placed on the floor, then well soaked with water. Air moving through the car during the trip evaporated the water and kept the animals cool.

One day Mulrenin discovered he was getting uncomfortably hungry while his crew was switching at St. Paul, so he went across the street to one of the general stores for some cheese and crackers. Talking and joking with the storekeeper while snacking, he forgot the time and his crew finished their switching. The hogger whistled off and the train pulled out of town, headed for Pettigrew. No one missed Irish until the train was pulling into Pettigrew. The crew did the station switching, turned the engine, and picked up the brains on the way back through St. Paul. Irish took quite a ribbing for the next week.

Unusual situations call for unusual action. One day on its return trip to Fayetteville, the train pulled into Elkins, where a woman and her four children were sitting at the depot. It was a little past two o'clock in the afternoon, and she had been there since eleven that morning. She and her children became hungry, so she seated the children on the benches, built a fire in the depot stove, and prepared a meal with supplies from a near-by store. After they had eaten, she cleaned the depot. Irish said she had a real mountain of baggage and insisted that every piece of it be stacked in the coach where she could watch it.

Phipps Lumber Company, the largest such operation in northwest Arkansas, was logging from many thousands of acres in Madison and Franklin counties. The timber land in Franklin County was just as rugged as that in Madison, and it was a mighty rough job getting the logs to the mills. The Phipps brothers therefore decided it would be to their advantage to build a railroad. The one to St. Paul was highly successsful, and perhaps they could do as well.

In January, 1915, the Black Mountain & Eastern Railroad was incorporated through the combined efforts of Ed E. Jeter of Combs, Jesse Phipps of St. Paul, and J. H. Phipps, J. M. Williams, and W. J. Reynolds of Fayetteville. They decided to build a standard-gauge road from a connection with the St. Paul branch at Combs in a southerly direction to or near the little town of Cass, about twenty miles away.

Rails, fishplates, and fastenings were obtained from the Frisco, and the rails were laid over and around the Black Mountain area of the Ozarks. To span the deep gulches reaching up the sides of the rugged mountain slopes, several wood trestles were constructed. Of the timber-bent type, they were more than 125 feet high. The bents were formed on the ground, then tilted to vertical position and secured. There is a report that the grade was so steep at the end of the road that a locomotive couldn't negotiate it with a train of logs, so the individual cars were snaked, one at a time, up the track by ox team to the crest of the grade.

Originally, the road was authorized to issue capital stock amounting to $250,000, and H. B. Shreve, a civil engineer, was

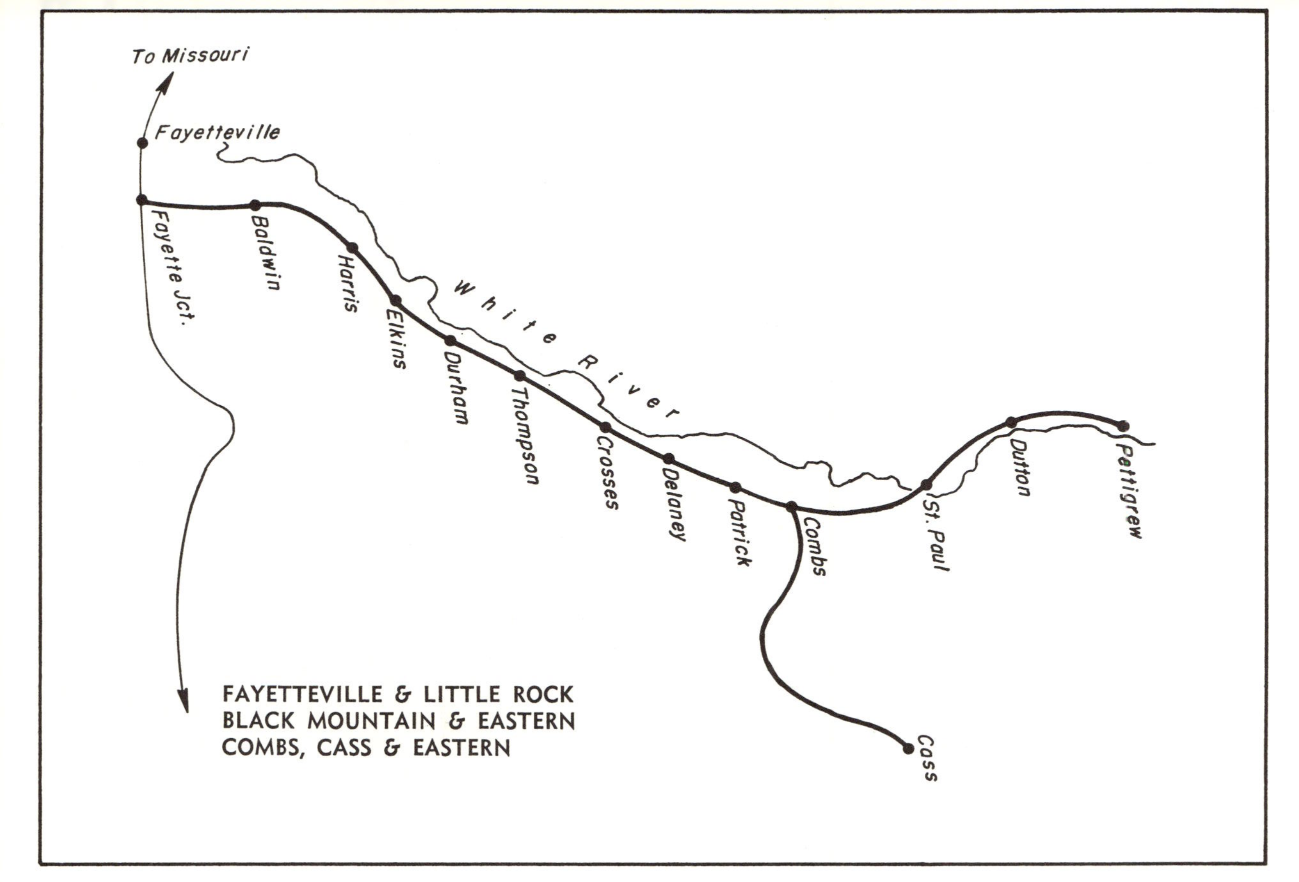
To Missouri
Fayetteville
Fayette Jct.
Baldwin
Harris
Elkins
Durham
Thompson
White River
Crosses
Delaney
Patrick
Combs
St. Paul
Dutton
Pettigrew
Cass
FAYETTEVILLE & LITTLE ROCK
BLACK MOUNTAIN & EASTERN
COMBS, CASS & EASTERN

given the task of surveying and building the BM & E through the mountains. Winding its way through the Black Mountains, a train had to travel about twenty miles to make the twelve miles from Combs to Cass. Even so, the railroad wheeled out logs for millions of board feet of lumber.

On May 13, 1916, application was made to the secretary of state to have the name of the road changed from Black Mountain & Eastern to Combs, Cass & Eastern. Permission to reduce the capital stock from $250,000 to $40,000 was asked on September 7, 1918. The stockholders agreed that the $40,000 capitalization was adequate because that was the actual cost of construction The stock was divided among Jay Fulbright (132 shares), J. H. Phipps (83), and W. J. Reynolds (26).

During its relatively short life, the Combs, Cass & Eastern was an important feeder line for the St. Paul branch and contributed to the prosperity of the area. With the mountains pretty well logged out in the Cass area, the CC & E was abandoned in 1924 or 1926. In the 1930's, its roadbed was again put to use when a car-wagon road was constructed between Combs and Frazier, the only settlement on the CC & E between its two ends. Civilian Conservation Corps (CCC) camp—Camp Frazier—was established at Frazier, and from this headquarters the CCC built roads through the mountains, one running southwest to the White Rock area.

There was a time when the passenger run on the St. Paul branch had more riders than the coaches could accommodate. Many of them readily climbed atop the cars and perched on the clerestory roofs—like so many birds on a roost. Clinging to their swaying perches, they were heading west in 1907 for the opening of the Cherokee Strip.

A most unusual incident for any railroad occurred on the St. Paul. About a mile west of town was a huge whisky distillery, owned and operated under strict jurisdiction by the federal government in about 1904. There were several saloons in the area served by the St. Paul branch, and the distillery supplied their needs. Then came the riotous days of prohibition. Operation of the distillery was discontinued, and it was stored on John Crawford's farm in a large barn. Crawford didn't know what to do with the big copper contraption, so he wrote the government for advice on how to get it removed. Some officials replied that Crawford should send it to Washington. The huge boiler and coil were brought to the depot at St. Paul. When the train rolled in, the efforts of four men were required to lift the contraption into a boxcar. One of them remarked: "I sure do hate to see you go."

Some of the early-day railroaders are still remembered in the hill country. A few of the hoggers were Charlie Vance (who brought the first train into Fayetteville in 1882), Joe Erby, Jim Huff, Joe Leake, Howard Day, Gordy Dakon, Tom Price, and Dolf Rogers. Among the brains were John Mulrenin, Claud Miller, Walter Shultz, and Sam Crabtree. G. W. "Bill" Bivens fired the first locomotive to cross Black Mountain on the way to Cass.

Charles C. Lukas, who, with the help of partner Walter C. Gilstrap, operated general stores in Pettigrew and St. Paul, noticed an unusual amount of traffic coming into Pettigrew. Standing on the front porch of his store, he counted 210 wagons loaded with lumber or ties heading for the railroad. No wonder the area was known as the Hardwood Capital of the World!

Even though no trains were scheduled on the St. Paul branch on Sunday, this was no reason for individual citizens to appropriate the road for their private use. On July 16, 1908, a federal court in Fayetteville issued a temporary restraining order against B. F. Pool, Walter Gilstrap, and John and Paul Gill to prohibit them from traveling from St. Paul to Fayetteville aboard the railroad's velocipede (three-wheel handcar) on Sundays. The railroad petitioned the court to make the injunction permanent.

Inevitably, as in all other sections of America, highways and trucks became more numerous in Arkansas. Roads gradually penetrated the Ozark Mountain region. Timber was being cut over rather extensively, and business was declining on the railroad. By

1934, Irish Mulrenin, instead of commanding four or five coaches of rough, brawling lumberjacks, plus a long string of freight cars, had in his charge one wheezing locomotive and one empty, creaking wooden coach. The maintenance appropriation for the St. Paul branch had been practically eliminated, and weeds and rust were taking their toll.

On May 11, 1926, the stockholders met in person or by proxy in the Frisco office at Fort Smith, and the directors were authorized to dissolve the Fayetteville & Little Rock and to surrender its charter to the state. The Frisco then accepted the road as part of its system.

On July 30, 1937, the decrepit little train made its final run from Pettigrew, and the St. Paul Branch became history. The Frisco Mogul No. 345 which ran on the branch was sold to the the Cassville & Exeter in Missouri, and old boomtowns along its route are now almost ghost towns. The wealth of the area is gone, so is the railroad. Its glory lives only in the fading memories of a few men whose remaining days are numbered.

FT. SMITH AND WESTERN

15

THE FT. SMITH & WESTERN cannot technically be called a short-line Arkansas railroad, since only a little more than a mile of it was on Arkansas soil. However, there was a close relationship between the railroad and the people who were concerned with it. For this reason, and because of that one mile in Arkansas, I include a brief account of it here.

From 1890 to 1920, there was a great surge of development in the coal fields of western Arkansas and eastern Oklahoma. The supply of coal seemed unlimited, and its quality was such that it found a ready market throughout the nation. Some form of bulk transportation was needed, and this could mean only one thing: a railroad.

So it was that the Ft. Smith & Western Railroad Company was granted a charter on January 25, 1899. It was soon discovered that the route proposed by the new company was nearly parallel to the Kansas City Southern's, so a short section of track (about a mile) was laid from the FS & W depot and office on Rogers Avenue in Fort Smith to form a physical connection with the Kansas City Southern. Officials of the two roads worked out an agreement whereby the infant FS & W could operate trains over KCS rails for approximately twenty thousand dollars a year. This would include twenty miles of track extending southwest from Fort Smith across the Poteau River through Spiro to Coal Creek. Thus the FS & W began operation with one mile of rails and two locomotives. The track was laid with used 65-pound rail, and the engines were rebuilt 4–4–0's from the Union Pacific.

During 1901, rails were industriously pushed westward from Coal Creek to McCurtain, a distance of 17.7 miles. This was wild and rough country in those days, infested with outlaws, booze peddlers, and malaria. Business was good, and time was a-wasting. Late in 1902, end of track was established on the south bank of the South Canadian River, another 57.5 miles. During 1903, rails were laid across the river and northwest 69 miles into Lincoln County.

The company had to obtain a charter from what was later to be the state of Oklahoma, so its corporate title became Ft. Smith & Western Railroad Company of Oklahoma. During the early months of 1903, the firm constructed 52 miles of railroad from a connection with the end of track in Lincoln County, Arkansas, into Guthrie, just north of Oklahoma City. On July 3, 1903, the Ft. Smith & Western Railroad of Arkansas purchased 50 miles of track from the Oklahoma company, then, on July 10, bought the remaining two miles, making the Ft. Smith & Western of Arkansas complete for 217 miles from Fort Smith to Guthrie, including the 20 miles of trackage rights over the KCS from Fort Smith to Coal Creek. The road soon gained access to Oklahoma City by trackage agreement with the Missouri, Kansas & Texas (the Katy). The two roads crossed at Fallis, Oklahoma, twenty-two miles southeast of Guthrie, and the Katy agreed to let the FS & W use its track for 33.6 miles into Oklahoma City.

During the next few years, the coal and coke traffic produced considerable revenue. The quality of these products became well known nationwide, and they were in great demand. The Ft. Smith & Western was on its way to a prosperous future. Or was it?

The FS & W was bitten by the expansion bug in the summer of 1906. Its directors were governed by the idea that the more connections they had with larger roads, the more business the Ft. Smith & Western would realize. Therefore, on July 25, 1906, they purchased the 42-mile St. Louis, El Reno & Western, which extended southwest from Guthrie to El Reno, west of Oklahoma City. It was purchased for one million dollars, but the plans being made for its use made that sum seem insignificant. An extension of only sixty miles to the west would provide a physical tie with the fabulous line of Arthur Stillwell—the Kansas City, Mexico & Orient.

At that time, Stillwell had built nearly nine hundred miles of railroad from Kansas City southwest into Texas on his way across Mexico to the port city of Topolobampo, where he would greet ships from the Orient. The road passed through Clinton, about sixty miles west of El Reno, and a connection there would mean a flood of cash into the coffers of the FS & W. The St. Louis, El Reno & Western would be nearly half the tie-in link required, and for only a million bucks. It would be cheap at twice the price, which was probably true for Henry C. Frick, the steel baron from Pittsburgh who owned the FS & W.

In the fall of 1906, a bumper crop of cotton was picked in southern and eastern Oklahoma, most of it destined for textile mills in the East. The Ft. Smith & Western was ideally situated to start this white gold on its long journey, so a cotton train was inaugurated between Guthrie and Fort Smith. It was found that, with careful loading, a flatcar could accommodate fifty bales of cotton, but even at this rate the FS & W had trouble keeping the loading platforms along the route clear.

It was also discovered that bales of cotton made a perfect landing place for sparks shooting from the stack of a locomotive. Now it is almost impossible to extinguish a burning bale of cotton once the fire has worked its way toward the interior of the bale because, after going through a compress, the bale is so dense it is almost waterproof. The only defense is to prevent a fire or barring that, put it out before it can spread. For this reason, the railroad employed additional "firemen" for the cotton train. Each man was given several buckets filled with water and assigned two cars of the precious cargo. His responsibility was to douse water on any suspicious wisp of smoke among the bales.

The desire for expanding operations was not confined to the management of the Ft. Smith & Western. The men who operated the trains were always ready to take advantage of opportunity when it knocked. Sometimes, however, too much of a good thing can be a disadvantage.

On the afternoon of August 9, 1907, the local freight peddler had made its slow and laborious way from Fort Smith to McCurtain, a distance of 38 miles. The train crew dropped off the crummy and went into the depot to see what switching the agent had lined up for them. They never found out. The conductor and the two brakemen were arrested by a deputy United States marshal and charged with importing whisky into the Indian Territory, a federal offense. The deputy searched the train and found 125 pints and 64 quarts of booze concealed in the crummy, whereupon the hapless trio was carted off to the calaboose at Poteau. The tallowpot and the hogger couldn't bring the train in alone, so they wired the main office and waited for a new train crew to be sent out from Fort Smith.

The Ft. Smith and Western knew the frontier in its latter days of violence when law and order were slowly but surely gaining control. No Man's Land was swept clean of outlaws of various types. Comparatively tame years followed, but they were not kind years for the Ft. Smith & Western. Oil and gas fields were beginning to flourish in the Southwest, and their products were quick to replace coal and coke in the realm of fuel and power. This put a drastic drain on the railroad's revenues, especially when the coke ovens were abandoned in 1921.

FORT SMITH AND WESTERN RAILWAY

L. B. BARRY, Jr., Receiver, Fort Smith, Ark.

L. B. BARRY, Jr., Receiver, Fort Smith, Ark.
E. M. WORLEY, Assistant to Receiver, "
WARNER & WARNER, General Counsel, "
W. H. SIMPSON, Auditor, "
J. D. PHELPS, Treasurer, "
A. N. SICARD, Assistant Treasurer, "
E. F. GUTENSOHN, Purchasing Agent, "
B. F. BECKMAN, Chief Engineer, "
J. I. MAILER, Superintendent Motive Power, "
LEWIS T. TUNE, Executive General Agent, St. Louis, Mo.

TRAFFIC

L. L. MOORE, Traffic Manager, Fort Smith, Ark.
F. R. SPURGIN, General Freight Agent, "
C. F. MATLIN, General Agent, } 661 I. W. Hellman Bldg,
ROBT. E. LEWIS, Commercial Agent, } Los Angeles, Cal.
JOS. L. DICKSON, General Agent, 302 Monadnock Building, San Francisco, Cal.
H. W. STIGLER, Gen. Agent, 33 Porter Bldg, Memphis, Tenn.
S. E. GOLDERMAN, Asst. Gen. Fht. Agt., } 918-919 Colcord Bldg.
R. R. STORY, Commercial Agent, } Oklahoma City, Okla.
WALTER MAIER, Commercial, Agent, }
C. P. WILSON, Asst. Gen. Fht. Agt., } 749-750 Marquette Bldg.
GEORGE A. LEU, General Agent, } Chicago, Ill.
G. D. NEUDLING, Jr., Gen. Agt., 417 Fullerton Bldg., St. Louis, Mo.
F. E. WALL, Gen. Agt. 436 Ry. Exchange Bldg, Kansas City, Mo.
B. F. McCOY, Gen. Agent, 1005-1006 Cadillac Square Bldg. Detroit, Mich.
JOHN V. SEVIN, Gen. Agt., 618 Union Trust Bldg. Pittsburgh, Pa.
J. E. WILKINSON General Agent, Fort Smith, Ark.
C. J. CRAFTON, Commercial Agent, "
J. T. KINGSLEY, Traffic Rep., 209 Mills Bldg, Washington, D.C.
H. T. WORTHLEY, Gen. Agent, 601 Kennedy Bldg, Tulsa, Okla.
L. A. POWELL, Gen. Agt., 606 Reynolds Bldg, Winston-Salem, N.C.
C. R. SAWTELL, Commercial Agent, Guthrie, Okla.

GENERAL OFFICES—FORT SMITH, ARK.

CORPORATE OFFICERS

A. C. DUSTIN, President, Cleveland, O.
C. J. CAINON, Assistant to President, Toledo, O.
WALTER C. MERRICK, Treasurer Cleveland, O.
CHARLES FOLLETT, Secretary, Cleveland, O.

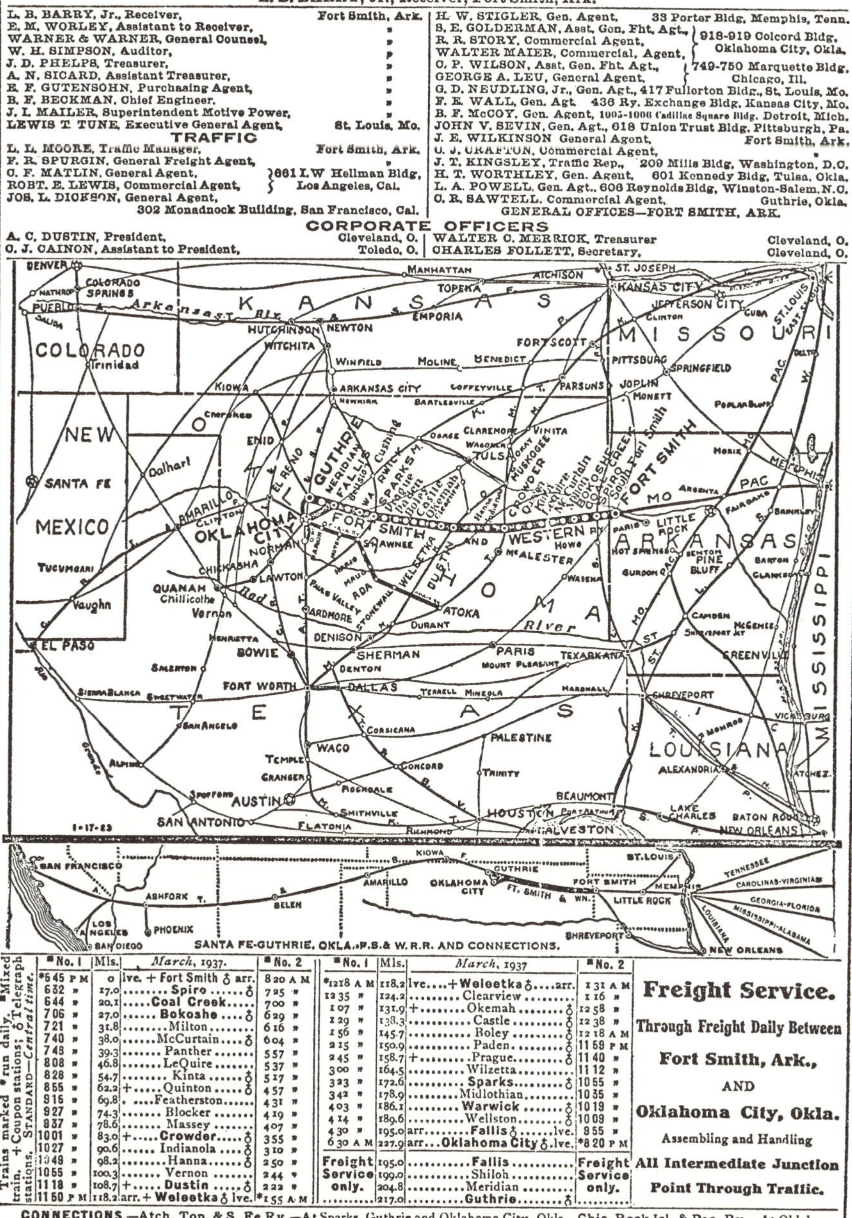

SANTA FE-GUTHRIE, OKLA., F.S. & W. R.R. AND CONNECTIONS.

Trains marked * run daily. ■Mixed train. + Coupon stations; ♁ Telegraph stations. STANDARD—*Central time.*

■No. 1	Mls.	*March*, 1937.	■No. 2
*5 45 P M	0	lve. + Fort Smith ♁ arr.	8 20 A M
6 32 "	17.0	Spiro ♁	7 25 "
6 44 "	20.1	**Coal Creek**	7 00 "
7 06 "	27.0	**Bokoshe** ♁	6 29 "
7 21 "	31.8	Milton	6 16 "
7 40 "	38.0	McCurtain ♁	6 04 "
7 48 "	39.3	Panther	5 57 "
8 08 "	46.8	LeQuire	5 37 "
8 28 "	54.7	Kinta ♁	5 17 "
8 55 "	62.2	+ Quinton ♁	4 57 "
9 15 "	69.8	Featherston	4 31 "
9 27 "	74.3	Blocker	4 19 "
9 37 "	78.6	Massey	4 07 "
10 01 "	83.0	+ **Crowder** ♁	3 55 "
10 27 "	90.6	Indianola ♁	3 10 "
10 49 "	98.2	Hanna ♁	2 50 "
10 55 "	100.3	Vernon	2 44 "
11 18 "	108.7	+ **Dustin** ♁	2 22 "
11 50 P M	118.2	arr. + **Weleetka** ♁ lve.	*1 55 A M

■No. 1	Mls.	*March*, 1937	■No. 2
*12 18 A M	118.2	lve. + **Weleetka** ♁ arr.	1 31 A M
12 35 "	124.2	Clearview	1 16 "
1 07 "	131.9	+ Okemah ♁	12 58 "
1 29 "	138.3	Castle ♁	12 38 "
1 56 "	145.7	Boley ♁	12 18 A M
2 15 "	150.9	Paden ♁	11 59 P M
2 45 "	158.7	+ Prague ♁	11 40 "
3 00 "	164.5	Wilzetta	11 12 "
3 23 "	172.6	**Sparks** ♁	10 55 "
3 42 "	178.9	Midlothian	10 35 "
4 03 "	186.1	**Warwick** ♁	10 19 "
4 14 "	189.6	Wellston ♁	10 09 "
4 30 "	195.0	arr. **Fallis** ♁ lve.	9 55 "
6 30 A M	227.9	arr. **Oklahoma City** ♁ lve.	*8 20 P M
Freight Service only.	195.0	**Fallis**	**Freight Service only.**
	199.0	Shiloh	
	204.8	Meridian	
	217.0	**Guthrie** ♁	

Freight Service.

Through Freight Daily Between

Fort Smith, Ark.,

AND

Oklahoma City, Okla.

Assembling and Handling

All Intermediate Junction Point Through Traffic.

CONNECTIONS.—Atch. Top. & S. Fe Ry.—At Sparks, Guthrie and Oklahoma City, Okla. Chic. Rock Isl. & Pac. Ry.—At Oklahoma City, Okla. Kan. City So. Ry.—At Fort Smith, Ark., Spiro and Coal Creek, Okla. Kan. Okla. & Gulf Ry.—At Dustin, Okla. Mid. Val. R.R.—At Fort Smith, Ark., and Bokoshe, Okla. Oklahoma City-Ada-Atoka Ry.—At Oklahoma City, Okla. Missouri-Kansas-Texas R.R.—At Crowder, Fallis and Oklahoma City, Okla. Missouri Pacific R.R.—At Fort Smith, Ark. Oklahoma Ry. (Interurban).—At Guthrie and Oklahoma City, Okla. St. Louis-San Francisco Ry.—At Fort Smith, Ark., Oklahoma City, Weleetka and Warwick, Okla.

The Ft. Smith & Western was placed in receivership on October 9, 1915 (and was operated until February 1, 1923). Then came reorganization, and the Ft. Smith & Western *Railway* Company was incorporated January 10, 1921. The new outfit acquired the railroad and all property of the former company at a foreclosure sale on January 6, 1923. The road struggled along, gradually losing ground, until June 1, 1931, when the Central United National Bank of Cleveland, Ohio, acting as trustee under the company's first mortgage, brought suit in federal court at Fort Smith to foreclose the mortgage and appoint a receiver. L. B. Barry, Jr., vice president and general manager of the road, was appointed receiver. J. S. Parks was appointed co-receiver on March 23, 1938, and Barry resigned as of June 1, 1938.

Business had fallen off to practically nothing, but the crowning blow came when the Katy refused to renew the trackage rights of the Ft. Smith & Western between Fallis and Oklahoma City. Operations were suspended early in 1939. On July 17, receiver Parks applied to the Interstate Commerce Commission for permission to abandon the entire line. In the application it was stated that in 1932 the FS & W had obtained loans from the Reconstruction Finance Corporation totaling more than $227,000. An additional $136,072 loan was denied in April, 1935. The previous loans matured in March, 1935, and an application for an extension of payment was refused. Receiver Parks was unable to borrow money from any source, and by January, 1939, the FS & W treasury had become so depleted that no rental payments could be made. (This was when the Katy and the KCS cancelled their joint-trackage agreements with the FS & W.) On January 19, 1939, the court having jurisdiction over the receivership issued an order directing the receiver to discontinue operation of the line and proceed immediately to wind up all business affairs of the Ft. Smith & Western. An embargo against all freight shipments was declared.

There had been a first mortgage against the road for $1,500,000 since January 23, 1923, and a second mortgage for $3,744,000 since February 1, 1923. The Central United National Bank was trustee for both. No interest had been paid on the bonds since the date of reorganization except for 1924, 1925, 1926, and 1929. From 1923 to 1938, the FS & W had accrued a deficit of $2,493,-025. By February 28, 1939, it had a debit balance of $3,175,162.

The District Court of the United States for the Western District of Arkansas at Fort Smith directed that the road be sold. The sale was held July 1, 1939, and on July 15, the court accepted a bid from the Schiavone Bonomo Corporation to buy that portion of the road lying between Coal Creek and Meridian, as well as all equipment and rolling stock, for the sum of $345,000. The remaining twelve miles of track into Guthrie went to Commercial Metals Company of Dallas for $14,500.

The physical properties of the FS & W were in pitiful condition. The entire road needed reballasting. No repairs had been made on depot buildings, stock pens, shops, or water tanks in more than fifteen years. A boxcar was being used as a depot at Guthrie. Only temporary repairs had been made on the 190 wooden bridges in the preceding ten years. The bridge across the South Canadian would require $200,000 in repair work.

The Ft. Smith & Western owned 11 locomotives, 122 coal cars, 5 boxcars, 7 cabooses, 3 baggage-mail cars, 7 work cars and a business car at the time of abandonment. The record showed that all of this equipment was obsolete and practically useless for operating purposes.

The receiver exerted every possible effort to operate the road efficiently and economically. Schedules were revised to provide freight service at the most advantageous times for shippers. Rates were reduced on oil and other commodities to meet competition from trucks. Friends of the railroad attempted to show that there was a public need for the resumption of service, but the Interstate Commerce Commission was not convinced, and abandonment was made effective August 17, 1939. The Ft. Smith & Western was sold for junk.

PRESCOTT & NORTHWESTERN

16

LIKE MOST OF THE OTHER SHORTLINE RAILROADS in southern and southwestern Arkansas, the Prescott & Northwestern was born through the efforts of men to develop the beautiful and abundant forests of the region. The few towns of any size in the area during the last years of the nineteenth century were joined by roads of only the poorest type, impassable in the winter months. They were strangled by the lack of communication with neighboring towns and the rest of the state. The little town of Prescott, in Nevada County, was more fortunate in this respect than many settlements in the area, for it was situated on the main line of the St. Louis, Iron Mountain & Southern. Mostly, it was a matter of the railroad's merely passing through on its way somewhere else. The fact that the railroad was there did not generate much enthusiasm among Prescott businessmen. Folks could go down to the depot and watch the trains go through or to climb aboard to go somewhere else. Prescott needed more than this; it needed something which would serve its interests on a more personal basis. Prescott needed its own railroad.

There was much speculation about the best way to construct a road. The only thing produced was conversation. Finally, talk progressed to the point where the state granted a charter to the Prescott & Northwestern on October 16, 1890, with Dr. R. L. Powers as the prime mover behind the project. He had traversed the proposed route early in May with the county surveyor and a civil engineer. They proposed to build from a connection with the St. Louis, Iron Mountain & Southern at Prescott in a northwesterly direction toward Wallaceburg.

Dr. Powers went to Detroit about October 1, and when he returned a couple of weeks later, he assured the people at home that rails and rolling stock had been contracted and would arrive in Prescott as they were needed. He fully expected to have eight miles of the railroad built and a sawmill and a planing mill in operation by Christmas. The mills were to be constructed in the southwest part of town, with a spur track running in from the Iron Mountain. The P & NW would tie into this spur. George Mautz, a local resident, was busy with the survey work.

One morning in late October, Dr. Powers hitched a team of horse to his buggy and invited the editor of the *Nevada County Picayune* to accompany him to the section where the grading was being done. They drove out about three miles and found the construction crew hard at work. There would be relatively little grading along the first eight miles to prepare the road for ties and rails—one or two shallow cuts and a four-foot fill. Dr. Powers declared the embankment would be ready for rails by the first of December. The prosperity of Prescott, he said, was definitely assured.

The forecast for tracklaying was a little optimistic. It was March 2, 1891, before rails were laid far enough into the woods for the first car of logs to reach the mill. Meanwhile, Colonel Ricker and Colonel Kelly of the Iron Mountain had come to Prescott to arrange for construction of the spur track to the mill, and engineer Lewis W. Knight had gone to New York to bring back the first locomotive. He rolled into town on February 16, 1891.

Dr. Powers was putting on a promotional campaign to induce his fellow citizens to subscribe to stock in the railroad. He was very liberal toward those who would help to build it, there being an agreement that any money put up for construction was to be a gift and would incur no obligation on the part of the company's officers. Perhaps this put a damper on the public enthusiasm. At any rate, Powers began issuing paid-up stock certificates for cash donations.

The Bemis & Whitaker mill was being moved from its former base of operation at Ihloe, Texas, to Prescott. Various pieces of machinery were arriving every day and the enterprise was taking shape. W. G. Harrington was selected to act as general manager of the mill, which would have a capacity of sixty thousand board feet a day. The steam drier and planer would furnish finished lumber of first-class quality.

L. W. Knight had returned from New York with the first P & NW engine, and on a Friday morning (even though many people regarded Friday as an unlucky day) in March, 1891, he slowly raised a head of steam in her boiler. The kettle behaved very nicely. She began dragging cars of logs to the completed Bemis & Whitaker mill in April. The firm employed two hundred men, and its annual payroll of one hundred thousand dollars was a much needed boost to the economy of Prescott.

At two o'clock on the afternoon of April 2, 1891, a large crowd gathered at the foot of Front Street in Prescott. Several of the prettiest girls in town were present, along with some young gentlemen to keep them company, and there were some preachers and teachers, a lawyer, a newspaper editor and his wife, and a full complement of young boys. It was a very jolly group that had been invited to the Prescott & Northwestern's first excursion. Benches had been improvised on three flat cars by placing boards across low sawhorses. Amid a chorus of happy cries and with a great deal

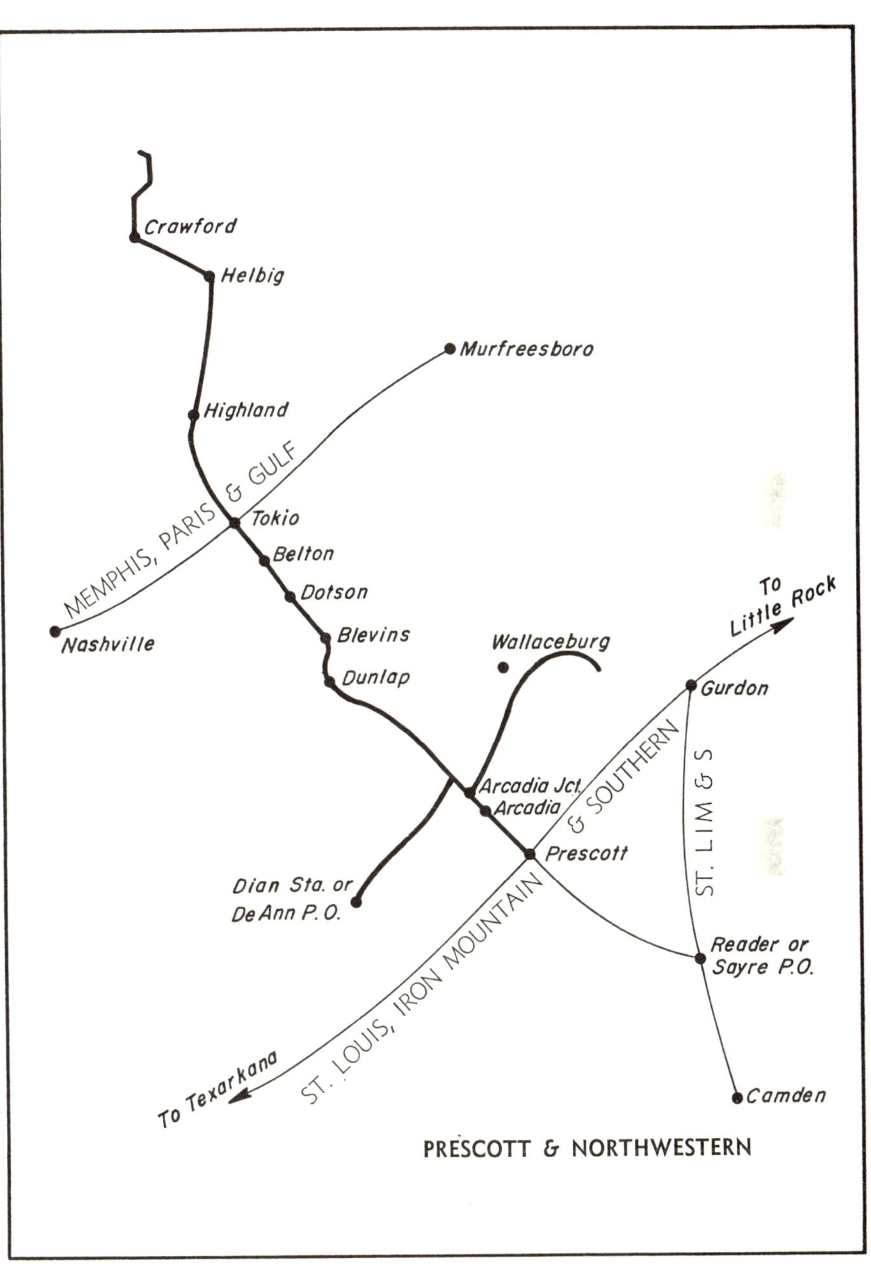
Crawford
Helbig
Murfreesboro
Highland
MEMPHIS, PARIS & GULF
Tokio
Belton
Dotson
Nashville
Blevins
Dunlap
Wallaceburg
To Little Rock
Gurdon
& SOUTHERN
ST. LIM & S
Arcadia Jct.
Arcadia
Prescott
Dian Sta. or
De Ann P.O.
ST. LOUIS, IRON MOUNTAIN
Reader or
Sayre P.O.
To Texarkana
Camden
PRESCOTT & NORTHWESTERN

of whistle talk by hogger Knight, the engine wheeled the merrymakers out of town.

First stop was the Bemis & Whitaker mill, where everyone climbed down for a tour. They saw, many for the first time, huge logs converted into finished lumber by saw and planer. The eagle eye began tolling the engine bell as a signal to climb aboard, and the revelers were on their way again across the swells of Prairie de Ann.

It proved to be a most enjoyable and hilarious trip. Some of the improvised benches collapsed from the motion of the swaying cars, and the passengers found themselves sprawled out on the car floor amid squeals, shouts, bruising bumps, and pretty ankles showing beneath disarranged skirts. There also was the hazard of hot sparks shooting from the stack. Several of the folks had holes burned in their clothing. One gay blade was wearing a new spring straw skimmer. A fat, glowing brand landed on its flat top, smoldered through the straw, and singed the young head beneath. The hat was tossed overboard.

About eight miles out, the train rolled to a stop at Arcadia, a favorite parklike spot that was ideal for picnics. Most of the excursionists took to the woods to gather wild flowers, the season being perfect for violets and daisies. It was a good day for courting, too, and young couples took full advantage of the many foot paths through the forest. A few went down to the post office or to the lumber mill to visit friends. Dr. Powers and several assistants were inspecting track being laid through a deep cut near Arcadia, as well as the grading of a fifteen-foot fill a short distance beyond. Stacks of logs lay beside the right-of-way, awaiting transportation to the mill at Prescott.

The train had been at Arcadia about an hour when its screeching engine whistle brought excursionists scurrying from all directions. The return trip took about twenty-five minutes, the group arriving at Prescott at five o'clock. Many places in the track were quite rough because of continued rains for the past month, but generally, the road was in fair condition.

A spur was extended north from Arcadia to Wallaceburg, passing about a mile east of town and terminating in the forest. Likewise, a branch line was run south and west to Dian (or De Ann Post Office). The road to Wallaceburg was graded nearly all the way by May, 1891. On Monday morning, May 21, track superintendent Henry Hilborn began laying rail beyond Arcadia for an additional seven miles of road.

When tracklaying had been completed beyond Wallaceburg, the P & NW began to haul forty-five to fifty thousand board feet of logs every day. Powers ordered enough new cars to bring the total to seventy-five thousand board feet daily. The rails had penetrated several thousand acres of prime timber land, and this allowed the P & NW to furnish sixty cars to the interchange track with the Iron Mountain during May, 1891.

The summer months of 1891 must have been rather difficult for the lumber mills around Prescott. Dr. Powers obtained a writ of attachment against the Ozan Lumber Company mill at Prescott for nonpayment of a $101,774 debt. The operation had shut down, and other mills were being attached for smaller amounts. A depression and a drop in the market price of lumber were responsible for the trouble. Powers' P & NW was furnishing logs to nearly every mill in the area. In August, when the financial bind was at its worst, the Prescott & Northwestern was valued at $21,807.78 on the tax rolls of Nevada County.

By the latter part of September, most of the difficulties seemed to have been ironed out. The Ozan mill had resumed operation, but Powers was still short of cash. The preceding April 21, he had called upon subscribers of P & NW stock to make a payment of 25 per cent of what they still owed. Now he issued a notice, dated October 21, that the balance of that 25 per cent was due in sixty days and that any stock subscribed for would be forfeited for nonpayment after that date. This brought results, and the P & NW remained solvent.

The pike received a bad name, really through no fault of its own. No saloons were permitted in Prescott—in fact, all of Nevada County was supposedly dry—but there was one in Arcadia, just over the line in Hempstead County. The editor of the *Nevada County Picayune* was in quite a dither about it. He said that with Prescott & Northwestern trains making frequent trips every day and stopping at Arcadia, the situation was every bit as bad as if Prescott had flourishing saloons of its own. There is no record of what remedy, if any, was used to cure this social ill.

To plague the P & NW further, there was a prolonged rainy season in the spring of 1892. This curtailed expansion of rail mileage and at the same time soaked the existing roadbed to the consistency of a sponge. Ties and rails sank beneath the weight of passing trains, and cars of logs began wandering across the right-of-way in all directions. Trains spent more time in the mud than they did on the rails. The mills had to shut down for want of logs. Trouble, it seemed, was ever near for the P & NW, but it continued to struggle along.

During the next few years, Prescott & Northwestern rails continued to creep north and west, connecting several small towns and communities: Dunlap, Blevins, Dotson, Belton, Tokio, Nathan, Helbig. The area was rapidly being developed into what later became known as the "Peach Capital of the World," for its soil was ideally suited to the raising of Elberta peaches.

The P & NW prospered as the communities along its route prospered, but there were also problems to contend with. On June 25, 1906, the mixed train rolled north, right on the advertised. A fruit-tree salesman named John R. Rodgers, who lived at Stephens, boarded at Prescott. The train pulled out of the depot at Belton, and a few moments later the conductor noticed that Rodgers was slumped down in an uncomfortable position. He decided to investigate and discovered that Rodgers was dead. The train was backed up to Belton, and the body was taken to Dr. Dildy's office, where an inquest was held. It was determined that Rodgers had died of a heart attack. He was eighty years old. The body was shipped to Prescott, where it was claimed by a nephew, Hunter Rodgers of Texarkana.

Troubles of one sort or another seemed to favor Dr. Powers' railroad. On the night of October 8, 1907, an extra freight was chuffing along when something went wrong with the engine. The crew decided to head into a passing track in order to work on her. James Attaway, the fireman, climbed down and opened the switch. He stepped back away from the switch stand and over the edge of a trestle twenty-five feet high. He was killed when he landed on the rocks below. The body was brought to Prescott for burial. Attaway left a wife and two children.

Just a month and two days later, an outbound log train of empty cars was rolling along at a pretty good clip when a stray cow wandered onto the track. The hogger set the steam jam brake on the engine and grabbed the whistle cord to call for the train crew to tie down some hand binders, but he knew it was too late for that. Bossy and the little hog met head on. The unfortunate cow was mangled, the engine knocked off the rails. It took the crew most of the next day to rerail her. On the return trip the engine jumped the track. Fireman Charlie Hoyle was killed, and several of the crew were injured.

For a couple of years there had been widespread interest in the area around Elberta (later called Highland Community) as peach-producing country. It looked so promising that the Arkansas Orchard Planting Company set out several thousand acres of peach trees, mostly the Elberta variety, between Murfreesboro and Nashville. Then it began selling orchards to investors from northern states.

The Prescott & Northwestern was not to be the only railroad to tap the peach orchards. An interloper showed up from the west: in February, 1909, the Memphis, Paris & Gulf was given permission to install a crossing diamond in the P & NW track at Tokio. It was on its way to Murfreesboro. Really, there was plenty of peach business for both roads.

Early in November, 1907, as fireman Edgar Woodson was feeding the firebox of an engine heading for Prescott, she left the rails near Arcadia Junction. The train was running about ten miles per hour and Woodson was sure it would stop almost instantly when it hit the ground, but the hog jumped and jerked along for about fifty yards on the ties, then turned over. Woodson was hurt, and he sued the railroad.

It was revealed during the trial that the engine's "blind" drivers were in such bad condition that false flanges had been worn into the face of the rims. These blind drivers gripped the ball of the rails, and the engine was forced onto the ties. The circuit court ruled that if the fireman knew the engine had left the rails and decided to remain in the cab and risk being injured instead of jumping, he was not entitled to damages. Woodson took his case to the Arkansas Supreme Court, which said the railroad was required to furnish its employees with equipment in reasonably good repair. It therefore reversed the lower court's ruling and ordered the payment of damages in July, 1909.

The summer of 1909 wasn't too kind to Dr. Powers' shoestring operation. In July, the road suffered its first wreck in which a passenger was injured. The mixed train had pulled out of the forest onto the open prairie a short distance out of Prescott. It was running about ten miles an hour when the log car immediately ahead of the passenger coach jumped off the rails. The sudden jerk pulled the coach onto the ties, and it rolled over like a playful puppy. A dozen or so passengers were aboard, and one of them, Mrs. Frank Line of Pine Bluff, injured her foot.

There also was a bit of extra revenue that summer to sweeten the cash register of the P & NW and help offset some of the heavy expenses. The Memphis, Paris & Gulf had purchased a rather large deposit of gravel north and east of Tokio, and it paid the P & NW for the privilege of using P & NW track from Tokio to the gravel pits. Gravel was in great demand as track ballast for the MP & G, as well as the Kansas City Southern, and the Hope Brick Works bought about two hundred carloads. In time of need, every little bit helps.

Because of a mixup in train schedules on the St. Louis, Iron Mountain & Southern, mail was arriving at Nashville over the

Arkansas & Louisiana late in the afternoon. Businessmen were unable to reply to letters until the next day. This inconvenience led to the joint operation of trains carrying mail on the Prescott & Northwestern and the Memphis, Dallas & Gulf. The MD & G would operate over P & NW track from Tokio to Prescott, pick up the mail from the Iron Mountain, and head for Nashville. The arrangement began on October 6, 1910.

The spring and summer of 1910 also saw the beginning of plans to extend the P & NW, which was running trains as far north as Helbig. Then one of the directors announced that the road was preparing to lay rails west to De Queen, a move which would connect the P & NW with the Kansas City Southern and give De Queen another rail outlet. Moreover, the KCS could use the P & NW as a bridge road instead of sending freight south from De Queen to Texarkana, thence over the Iron Mountain to Little Rock.

On November 8, 1910, the Prescott & Northwestern made arrangements to operate its passenger trains over the Memphis, Dallas & Gulf as far as Nashville:

TEMPORARY TIME CARD

Daily

NOTE: IRON MOUNTAIN TRAIN NO. 5 ARRIVES PRESCOTT 10:41 A.M.

No. 1 *Read Down*				No. 2 *Read Up*
11:00 AM	Lv.	Prescott	Ar.	4:50 PM
12:10 PM		Tokio		3:00 PM
12:30 PM	Ar.	Nashville	Lv.	2:40 PM
(via MP & G)				(via P & NW)
6:15 PM		Ashdown	Lv.	1:15 PM

When joint service with the MD & G began, the P & NW made an all-out effort to obtain all the business it could possibly get. As an added attraction, it installed free bus service from the P & NW depot and that of the Iron Mountain and would wait until 12:30 P.M. for Iron Mountain train No. 5, its important passenger, mail, and express run.

Plans for expanding the Prescott & Northwestern failed to produce any lasting results, but this didn't prevent their repetition. In September, 1911, citizens in and around Center Point, almost due west of Elberta, met to discuss the possibility of extending the rails in their direction. It was reported that the Bemis family, which now controlled the railroad, had taken options on nearly all land in the Center Point area suitable for peach production. The news inspired confidence that Center Point would become an important railroad town. However, as happens so many times, the plans fell through.

As the spring of 1912 approached, much interest was shown in truck gardening. Until now, such produce had been grown on a personal basis, each farmer planting what he needed for his own use. This year, however, it was to be a feature program for commercial production. Many farmers were planning to try strawberries, and about thirty-five acres were planted near Belton. There also was great promise for a good crop of peanuts. More than three hundred acres were devoted to cantaloupes, and one man had forty acres of tomatoes. Others were setting out sweet potatoes.

The combined acreage of peaches and garden truck in the Highland area would guarantee plenty of work, even for nonresidents, at harvest time. Canneries in the neighborhood would have plenty of business, and the P & NW would haul all of the produce to market. Everyone would profit from the venture. And it was so. On July 18, 1913, a special train of two hundred passengers from Florida rolled over the P & NW to canneries in the Highland area. These people were experienced fruit graders and packers.

Even though prosperity had arrived, at least for a while, misfortune lingered. The Prescott & Northwestern worked out an agreement whereby it could use Memphis, Dallas & Gulf tracks for the operation of log trains from north of Murfreesboro to Tokio. On Monday morning, February 23, 1914, the P & NW rolled out beyond Murfreesboro to one of the Bemis logging camps and picked up several cars. Rufe Louie, the hogger, was backing his train toward Murfreesboro when the engine climbed off the rails about a mile out of town. J. M. Zeal, a Negro mill hand riding the engine, was caught between the cab and tender. His right leg was so badly crushed that it had to be amputated. Will Sanders, a white man who also worked at the mill, was severely crushed at the hips. The Negro fireman, Charles Nelson, was scalded by water and steam from the broken pipes but was not seriously hurt. The hogger was badly bruised about the head and shoulders. Wednesday night, Will Sanders died of internal injuries.

There was a flurry of consternation when the Interstate Commerce Commission included the P & NW in its tap-line ruling, thereby forbidding the road to charge standard rates for freight or passenger transportation. This would just about mean a *coup de grace* for the Prescott & Northwestern. Representatives of the P & NW and the Memphis, Dallas & Gulf called on the ICC repeatedly during the next few months, presenting their pleas in person. A plan was finally worked out whereby the railroad could be divorced from control by the Bemis Lumber Company, and it promptly became an independent corporation.

Following a period of adjustment during which the P & NW had to learn to stand on its own feet and make its own way, it developed into a self-respecting railroad. Its fortune fluctuated, as did those of most other shortlines in the state, going from feast to famine. World War I years were rough and the Great Depression was even worse, but the P & NW survived. In 1967, its operating ratio was 61.36 per cent, compared to 72.13 per cent the preceding year, net income was $31,159 as against $16,389 in 1966. Compared to this, the dividends the road paid were impressive: $3 in 1959, $5 in 1960, and $10 in 1961–65.

Perhaps one reason for the black ink on the ledger was the fact that only one trip a week was made behind the oil-burning 2–6–2 steam locomotive, and this was on Fridays, even into the early days of World War II. During the remainder of the week, service was performed by a gasoline-powered truck, sheathed in sheet metal and facetiously christened the *Elberta Zephyr*. Nevertheless, the P & NW elicited glowing praise, even from Lucius Beebe. He described the Prescott & Northwestern as being almost indescribably beautiful and as operating through the most lyrically beautiful countryside of any shortline in the country.

Will fortune continue to smile upon the Prescott & Northwestern? No one knows. Be that as it may, the P & NW's diminutive trains still sail lazily along over the undulating Prairie de Ann.

APPENDIX A
GOULD SOUTHWESTERN; WARREN, JOHNSONVILLE & SALINE RIVER; WARREN & SALINE RIVER; WARREN & OUACHITA VALLEY; JONESBORO, LAKE CITY & EASTERN; BLYTHEVILLE, LEACHVILLE & ARKANSAS SOUTHERN; DE QUEEN & EASTERN; DONIPHAN, KENSETT & SEARCY

There were many little pikes in Arkansas which flourished for a while, then faded away. Quite a few still exist, although their lives have been rather uneventful, These railroads, about which there is scant information, I have chosen to include here in a separate grouping. Even though they have been more or less secluded and perhaps unknown except in their immediate surroundings, they should not be ignored. The mere fact that they existed is an indication of their importance to the areas of Arkansas they served. Their stories should be preserved.

Gould Southwestern

Star City was an isolated community. Its merchants and citizens were in dire need of communication with the commercial centers of Arkansas, and a railroad was the only practical answer.

So it was that in the spring of 1908, the Gould Southwestern Railroad was incorporated.

On May 1, C. P. Harnwell and several other GSW officials from Gould arrived in Star City to confer with businessmen and other citizens. They agreed to complete the twenty miles of railroad between the two towns as quickly as possible. On the same day, the preliminary survey crew reached Star City, and it was announced that grading of the roadbed would begin in a few days. The pike would connect with the St. Louis, Iron Mountain & Southern at Gould.

By July 18, 1908, a crew of forty men, grading and clearing the right-of-way, had progressed to within ten miles of Star City. Work slowed down considerably during the fall months because most of the crew owned farms and plantations which required attention during the harvest season. By October 15, manager S. G. McClellan had moved his camp of fifty men to the banks of Cane Creek, just two miles from Star City. The roadbed was completed to within two and half miles of town, and one hundred men were at work along the twenty-mile route. McClellan said he expected to have trains running by January 1, 1909.

On January 16, 1909, the first carload of freight rolled into Star City from Gould. Until then, all freight had come by wagon over twenty-seven miles of road, devastating in any but dry seasons, from Pine Bluff. That first car contained wire fencing consigned to J. G. Atkinson; the second was a load of household goods for Cliff Winters. Several small shipments arrived during the week, inaugurating a new era of freighting into Star City. A favorable side effect of the railroad's coming occurred when real estate values began to advance rapidly.

There was no regular schedule for freight movement; a train was run when there was a car or two billed for Star City. Almost immediately, plans were made to extend the rails to Fordyce, in Cleveland County, where connection could be made with the Rock Island and the Cotton Belt. A portion of the right-of-way had already been purchased.

A regular passenger schedule was inaugurated on Sunday, April 25, 1909, with an excursion from Star City to Gould. Some 150 passengers were aboard. There would be one train daily each way, and additional runs would be added as traffic warranted. The train left Star City at 9:30 A.M. and arrived in Gould at 11:30. Leaving Gould at 4:00 P.M., it arrived in Star City at six o'clock. Twenty miles in only two hours!

The Gould Southwestern did not develop into the financial giant its incorporators had hoped for. The planned extension failed to materialize (business did not increase sufficiently to warrant it), and roads were gradually being built through the area. The railroad was put into receivership of Mercantile & Trust Company of Little Rock, with W. H. Roberts in charge. On April 30, 1920, the judge of Chancery Court for the Eastern District of Arkansas ordered the road sold. The court advertised the property for four weeks at Star City, as was required by law, beginning July 9, 1920.

A public bid of $20,000 was made by A. J. Johnson, B. F. McGraw, A. O. Vick, C. E. Fish, R. P. Parker, and D. A. McIntosh. They agreed to assume the interest due on $8,928.85 in receiver's certificates issued by W. H. Roberts. Their bid was accepted.

A stockholders' meeting was held in the office of the Lincoln Abstract Company at Star City on August 13, 1920. As a result, a letter was addressed to the secretary of state requesting that the name of the road be changed from Gould Southwestern Railway to Arkansas Railroad. This was arranged, but the new company wasn't incorporated under Arkansas law until May, 1926, with W. R. Alsobrook as president and general manager, I. A. Chambers as treasurer, and C. E. Fish as secretary. Of the $100,000 in capital stock, Alsobrook owned $99,300.

The change of administration did not help the struggling pike. By the end of 1957, it had a deficit of $24,642—a loss of $24.64 per share of stock. The operating ratio was 185.64 per cent. On December 31, 1957, the Arkansas Railroad became legally idle. During 1958, the Interstate Commerce Commission authorized the road to abandon operations and estimated its salvage value at $96,450. At the end of 1958, the Arkansas Railroad had one employee. The road was abandoned on April 10, 1959.

Warren, Johnsville & Saline River; Warren & Saline River

Practically all of Bradley County was at one time owned by three large lumber companies: the Arkansas Lumber Company, the Bradley Lumber Company, and the Southern Lumber Company. In 1907, the Bradley Lumber Company owned 65,000 acres of timber land, with 60,000 acres of it still virgin forest. At Warren, the firm established its primary mill, which had a capacity of 100,000 board feet of lumber per day and employed about 375 men. Warren was laid out in 1843 as the county seat of Bradley County, a position it still holds.

It followed reasonably that 65,000 acres of forest could not be harvested without the convenience of a railroad, so the Bradley firm began to penetrate its holdings with lines of rails. These were taken up and relaid elsewhere as the area gave way to ax and saw.

The Bradley Lumber Company was owned by two brothers from St. Louis, S. H. and Robert W. Fullerton. These gentlemen decided that a permanent railroad would be a decided advantage to them. Warren was growing rapidly, and smaller towns were springing up as logging camps were established.

The St. Louis, Iron Mountain & Southern served Warren with a branch line off its north–south main line from McDermott. With such a monopoly of service, it is doubtful that the Iron Mountain was in a generous mood when freight rates were set. The Fullerton brothers began to extend a line of rails almost due south from Warren, heading for a connection with the Rock Island at Hermitage, nearly sixteen miles away.

On August 7, 1905, a charter was granted to the Warren, Johnsville & Saline River Railroad. Meanwhile, a five-mile branch was extended to connect Johnsville to the main stem, along which were spurs to various logging camps. These totaled slightly more than fifteen miles—a little less than the main line. The pike had thirty-six miles of track in operation with 56-pound rail at a gauge four feet, eight and one-half inches.

By June 30, 1916, the WJ & SR had accumulated a deficit of $11,767. It was sold to cover a $200,000 first mortgage and was reorganized as the Warren & Saline River Railroad, which was chartered March 25, 1920. By 1961, all of its stock was owned by Potlatch Forests, Inc., and the operating ratio was 110.45 per cent, yielding a deficit of $27,913. By 1963, the ratio had climbed to 121.62 per cent, with a deficit of $38,639. No dividends had been paid since 1957, when a fat $60 per share was declared. The road continues to lose money but trains are still running.

Warren & Ouachita Valley

This sixteen-mile railroad was incorporated and built in 1899 from Warren to Banks by two of the principal lumber companies in Bradley County, the Arkansas Lumber Company and the Southern Lumber Company. The Warren & Ouachita Valley, designed to serve the two firms' large mills at Warren, connected with the Rock Island at Banks, near Moro Bayou. A portion of the track was originally graded as part of the first railroad to receive a charter in Arkansas—the Mississippi, Ouachita & Red River, chartered August 12, 1852.

Passenger service was begun almost as soon as the road was opened. During the depression years, service was rendered by venerable Baldwin ten-wheeler No. 1, three ancient coaches, and a demotorized steel rail-car combine. One of the coaches came from the Dan Patch Railroad and another from the Spokane, Portland & Seattle. The Baldwin 4-6-0 had spoked wheels on the rear truck of the eight-wheeled tender. She is now rolling tourist passengers on a steam-powered tourist road at North Freedom, Wisconsin.

Until World War II, the public roads around Warren left much to be desired. The better ones were graveled. Therefore, one may safely say that the Warren & Ouachita Valley was a real public convenience, even a necessity.

Ownership has since passed to the Rock Island, which owns all 1,500 shares of capital stock (reduced from 3,160 shares in 1933). Between 1908 and 1929 (except for 1918 and 1920), the W & OV paid a dividend every year. The least was $4 in 1919, the largest $15 in 1916–17. No dividends have been paid since 1929. The net income for 1967 was $15,087, and trains still run.

Jonesboro, Lake City & Eastern

In the latter years of the nineteenth century, northeastern Arkansas began to develop, as farming came into its own. The rails of the Kansas City, Ft. Scott & Memphis penetrated the area from the northwest on their way from Kansas City and Springfield to the Mississippi River port of Memphis. On August 23, 1901, the St. Louis–San Francisco (Frisco) executed a long-term lease of the 1,117.50-mile KCFS & M. This put the northeast corner of Arkansas on the route of a major national railroad.

Even so, the valley of the St. Francis River was still more or less isolated from the Frisco. The internal system of roads and highways left much to be desired; in fact, it left practically everything to be desired. As a result, a group of men at Jonesboro conceived of the idea of building a railroad through Craighead and Mississippi counties. It would promote settlement of the area, which contained some of the finest alluvial farm land in Arkansas. This, in turn, would generate business for the railroad, and everyone concerned would benefit.

J. E. Jones, A. L. Krewson, and E. F. Brown, all of Jonesboro, along with D. Kerfoot of Center Hill, incorporated the Jonesboro, Lake City & Eastern Railroad on April 26, 1897, for ninety-nine years. They proposed to build from a point on the Kansas City, Ft. Scott & Memphis (where its tracks crossed Main Street in Jonesboro) eastward through Nettleton to a point on the west bank of the St. Francis River near Lake City. This would give

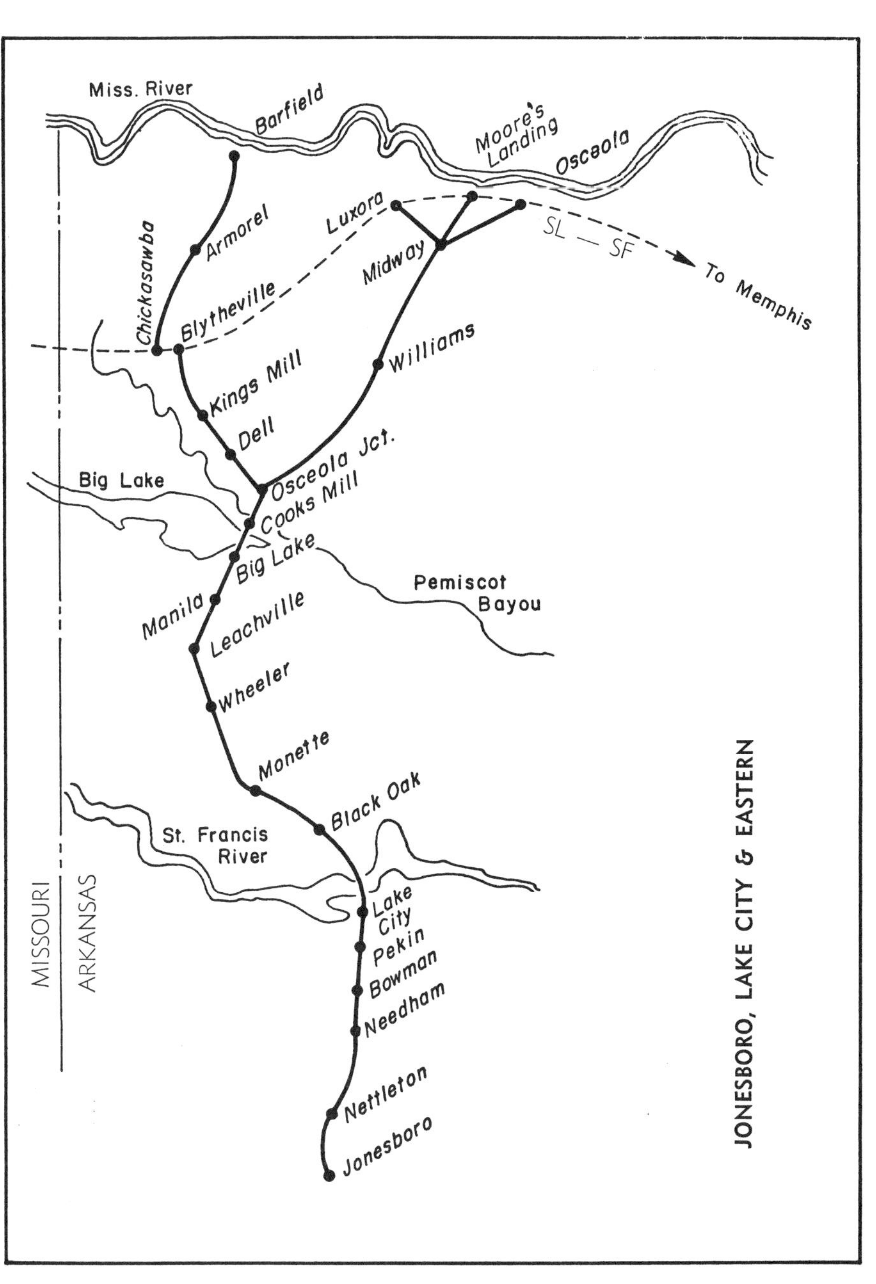

Miss. River
Barfield
Moore's Landing
Oscaola
Luxora
SL — SF
To Memphis
Armorel
Chickasawba
Blytheville
Midway
Williams
Kings Mill
Dell
Osceola Jct.
Cooks Mill
Big Lake
Big Lake
Pemiscot Bayou
Manila
Leachville
Wheeler
Monette
Black Oak
St. Francis River
Lake City
Pekin
Bowman
Needham
Nettleton
Jonesboro
MISSOURI
ARKANSAS
JONESBORO, LAKE CITY & EASTERN

them a railroad about fifteen miles long and a chance to make some money on the sixty-thousand-dollar investment they proposed.

Business was so good that on April 23, 1898, the stockholders met at Jonesboro and requested permission from the Arkansas Railroad Commission to increase the capital stock of the JLC & E from $60,000 to a whopping $250,000. The money was to be used in extending their railroad east across the St. Francis River, thence northeast into Leachville, about fifteen miles.

The venture proved satisfactory, and three years later, on February 7, 1901, the owners decided to take their rails around the southern end of Big Lake and back up to Blytheville. This added another twenty-five miles, making a total of about fifty-five miles of railroad.

On June 24, 1905, the decision was made to push southeast to Luxora and Osceola, and a spur was run a couple of miles east from Luxora to Moore's Landing on the Mississippi River. The Luxora extension left the main road at Osceola Junction, a short distance south of Dell near the south end of Big Lake. The total trackage was now seventy-five miles.

A couple of miles northwest of Blytheville lay the little town of Chickasawba. A shortline, known as Chickasawba Railroad, was incorporated September 20, 1902, to begin in Blytheville at a point on the old St. Louis, Memphis & Southeastern and to extend about ten miles to a point on the Mississippi River. Some of the incorporators were the same men who began the Jonesboro, Lake City & Eastern: A. J. Kerfoot, J. E. Jones, E. F. Brown, and Doswell Brown. Their ten-mile road ended at what is now known as Barfield.

The St. Louis, Memphis & Southeastern was acquired by the Frisco on January 1, 1902. Then on September 7, 1905, the JLC & E absorbed the Chickasawba Railroad. Thus the Jonesboro, Lake City & Eastern gradually expanded to slightly more than ninety-six miles in length from its original fifteen-mile beginning. It rolled along prosaically until January 1, 1950, when it was

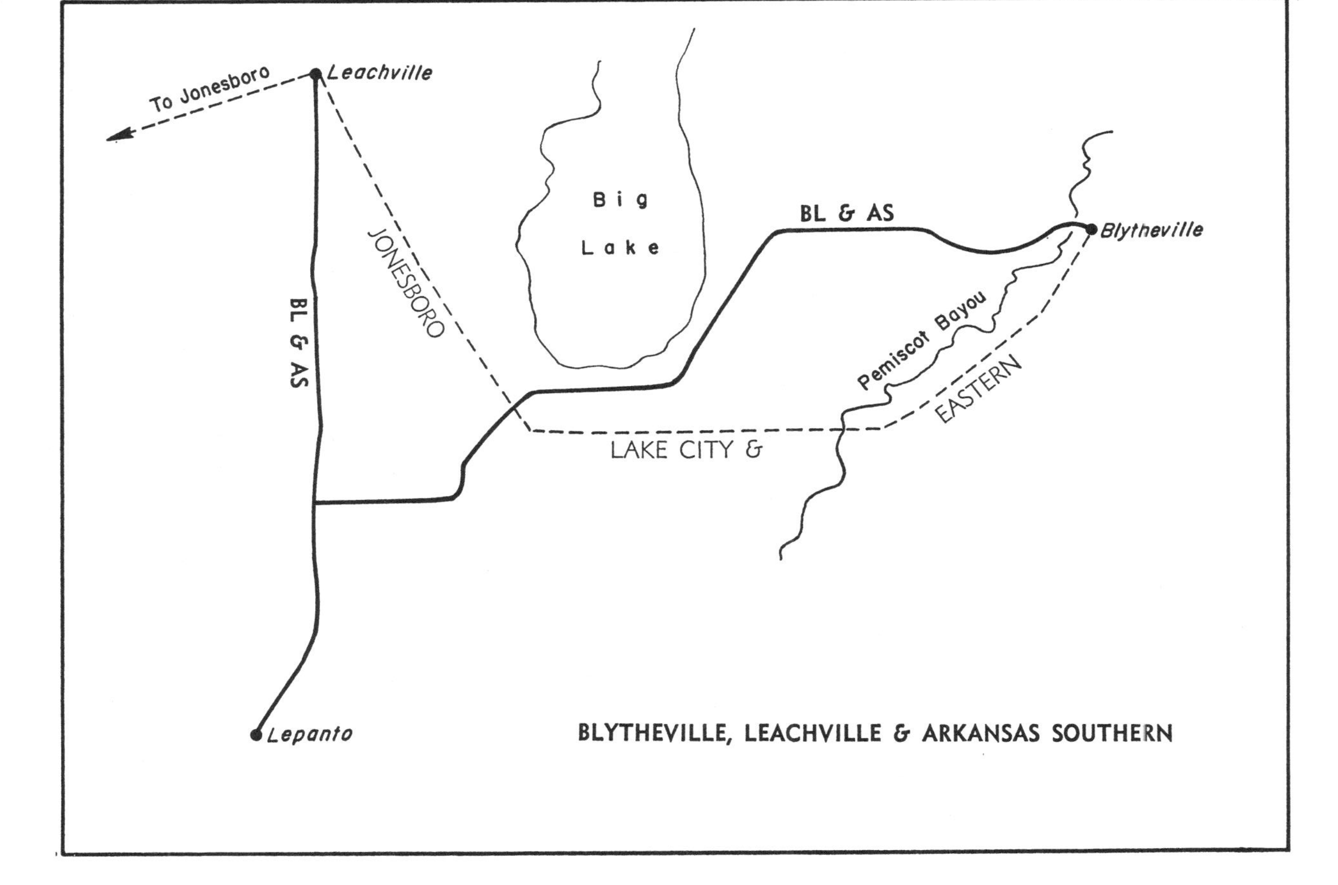
To Jonesboro
Leachville
JONESBORO
Big
Lake
BL & AS
Blytheville
BL & AS
Pemiscot Bayou
LAKE CITY &
EASTERN
Lepanto
BLYTHEVILLE, LEACHVILLE & ARKANSAS SOUTHERN

sold to the Frisco. On August 7, the Jonesboro, Lake City & Eastern was legally dissolved.

Blytheville, Leachville & Arkansas Southern

This northeast Arkansas pike was incorporated April 25, 1908, by A. C. Lange, W. P. Orr, J. R. Hancock, William Wilms, and R. L. McClelland. They proposed to build south and west from Blytheville to a small community known as Glenco and from there to Big Lake. West and slightly south of Big Lake, the line extended to a point in Section 25, Township 14 North, Range 7 East—about where Hancock is situated. Here the rails bent south through Caraway to Lepanto, which was the northern terminus of a Frisco branch from near Tyronza.

The plan would yield about forty miles of track, and it was proposed to run a line north from Hancock to Leachville. The completed road would be about fifty miles long. With a stock issue of $250,000 authorized, the company had no trouble in securing subscriptions for $2,000 a mile, or $100,000. By the time its charter was granted, more than $5,000 had been paid in cash. At Leachville and Blytheville, the line tied into the Jonesboro, Lake City & Eastern. The produce-lumber-hauling BL & AS had little trouble in surviving.

In 1928, the Cotton Belt began what it called the St. Francis Basin Project, the purpose of which was to gain access to the rich and very productive territory of northeast Arkansas. The Frisco had been getting the lion's share of this lucrative business, but now the Cotton Belt stuck a foot in the door by buying up six small railroads already operating in the area and consolidating them. One of these was the Blytheville, Leachville & Arkansas Southern, acquired in 1929 through an exchange of capital stock. On June 21, 1933, the authority of the BL & AS was revoked by proclamation of the governor, and the only portion of it still in use lies between Leachville and Caraway.

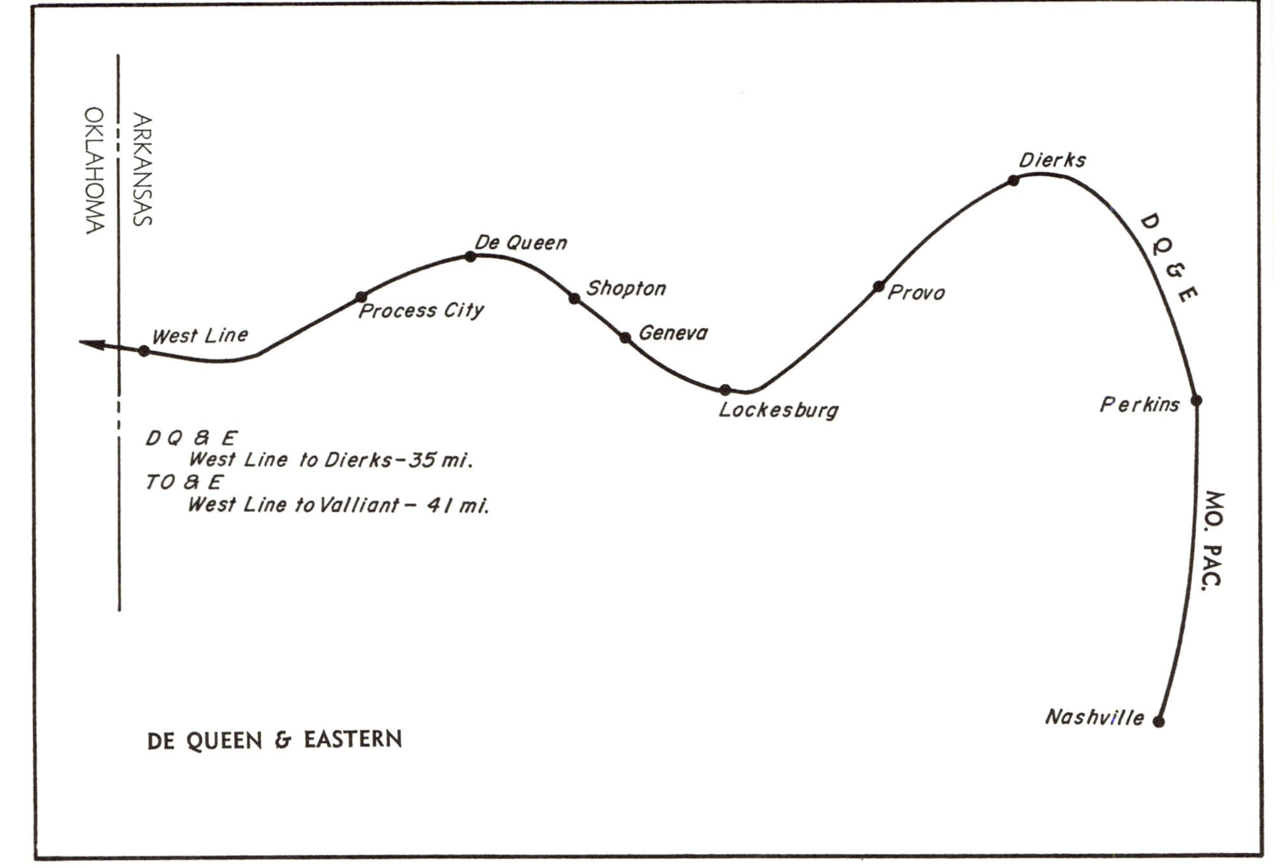

ARKANSAS
OKLAHOMA
West Line
Process City
De Queen
Shopton
Geneva
Lockesburg
Provo
Dierks
D Q & E
Perkins
MO. PAC.
Nashville
D Q & E
West Line to Dierks–35 mi.
TO & E
West Line to Valliant – 41 mi.
DE QUEEN & EASTERN

De Queen & Eastern

Into the lush forest lands of southwest Arkansas in 1900 came four brothers: Henry, Herman, Hans, and Peter Dierks. Having operated several lumber yards in Nebraska, they came to De Queen, where they bought a sawmill and several acres of property. Logs were brought to the mill by teams of mules. Soon the distance became too great for the mules; much too much time was being spent on the way from the forest to mill. Some better means of transportation was mandatory.

On September 22, 1900, the De Queen & Eastern Railroad was incorporated. Hans connected his rails to those of the Kansas City Southern, which passed through De Queen on the way from Kansas City to Texarkana. The Dierks mill now had access to the lumber-hungry markets of the nation. The 60-pound rails were extended east and south through the heavy forest about eleven miles to Lockesburg in 1902, and another town was born.

The Dierks brothers had made good progress since incorporating the Dierks Lumber & Coal Company in 1895. By 1905, their railroad had been pushed north and east another fifteen miles to the newly established town of Dierks (it was the brothers' policy to build towns where they built lumber mills).

Shortly after 1900, they purchased extensive lumber lands in what is now southeast Oklahoma but was then part of Indian Territory. The half-million-acre spread was even more of a wilderness than was western Arkansas. A distinct advantage however, was the fact that lumber was bringing premium prices in the Territory.

The construction of a huge mill at Bismarck (known as Wright City since World War I) initiated the real growth of the Dierks Lumber & Coal Company. To serve their western territory, the brothers decided to build another railroad, and to make it an integrated system, the rails were tied into the De Queen & Eastern at De Queen and extended west. The mill was built in 1910, and on October 21 of that year, Hans Dierks incorporated his second railroad—the Texas, Oklahoma & Eastern—to extend fifty miles from De Queen to Valliant, Oklahoma. The first portion was only eight miles long, running from the mill at Wright City to a connection with the Frisco at Valliant. Another mill was opened at Broken Bow, only twenty-six miles from the Arkansas border, in 1912.

The mill at De Queen burned, and it was decided to build a new one at Dierks, giving the company three large mills. Plans were made to connect the two railroads. The TO & E was extended east, while the DQ & E headed west. The two met at West Line on the Arkansas-Oklahoma border January 5, 1921.

The balance sheets of the two railroads showed a net loss each year until 1948. Passengers and mail were carried almost from the beginning, and these two items caused the consistent deficit. The public service commissions of Arkansas and Oklahoma permitted the TO & E and the DQ & E to discontinue mail and passenger service in 1948. In that same year, the Dierks company opened a large lumber-treating and preserving plant at Process City, about two miles west of De Queen. It helped the bookkeeper to show a profit. Utility poles, fence posts, barn poles, lumber, and railroad ties were treated, and every month saw an extra four hundred cars of freight roll along the De Queen & Eastern.

About 90 per cent of the DQ & E's traffic is generated by the parent owner, but other shippers in the area avail themselves of its service: feed mills, turkey farms, farmers' cooperatives, wholesale grocers, several bulk-oil plants, and some competing wood-products plants.

In 1957, Dierks Forests, Inc., built a fifteen-million-dollar kraft-paper mill at Pine Bluff, locating it near the Arkansas River (the mill would require large quantities of water). Since nearly all of the raw material would come from Dierks pulpwood timber lands in western Arkansas, eastern Oklahoma, and at Mountain Pine, Arkansas (near Hot Springs), the DQ & E would require additional trackage. An agreement was worked out with the Missouri Pacific. The De Queen & Eastern would extend its rails south and east from Dierks, and the Missouri Pacific would come from Nashville.

On the cold, damp morning of January 19, 1957, a spike-driving ceremony was held at Perkins. Presidents Paul J. Neff of the Missouri Pacific and Fred H. Dierks of the De Queen & Eastern were accorded the honor of driving two gold-plated spikes to complete connection of the two roads. It had been planned to drive the spikes with a maul, as was done at Promontory, Utah, on May 10, 1869, when the Central Pacific and the Union Pacific were joined to form the first transcontinental railroad, but plans were revised and a two-thousand-dollar gasoline-powered machine was used instead. The pulpwood and chips could now roll from De Queen to Pine Bluff by way of Nashville, Hope, and Benton on the Missouri Pacific.

The two ceremonial spikes were pulled and given to Neff and Dierks. Engraved gold-plated spikes about three inches long were given to spectators as a souvenir of the occasion. Neff, who began his railroad career as a rodman on a survey crew about the time Hans Dierks incorporated the De Queen & Eastern, remarked: "Spike-driving wasn't this easy when I was doing it for a living."

The point where the two railroads meet consists of the main line, an interchange track on either side, and a painted name board mounted on a metal standard set in a foundation of rocks shaped like a cairn. Each track will hold twenty-five cars. The place was named in honor of Charles E. Perkins, who retired in 1941 as chief traffic officer of the Missouri Pacific. He was formerly vice president of traffic.

The DQ & E was dieselized in 1948, and, along with the TO & E, has an assessed valuation of $2,500,000. The operating ratio for 1967 was 69.04 per cent, yielding a net income of $63,688. Many companies have done much worse.

Doniphan, Kensett & Searcy

In White County is a railroad which has had to struggle to stay

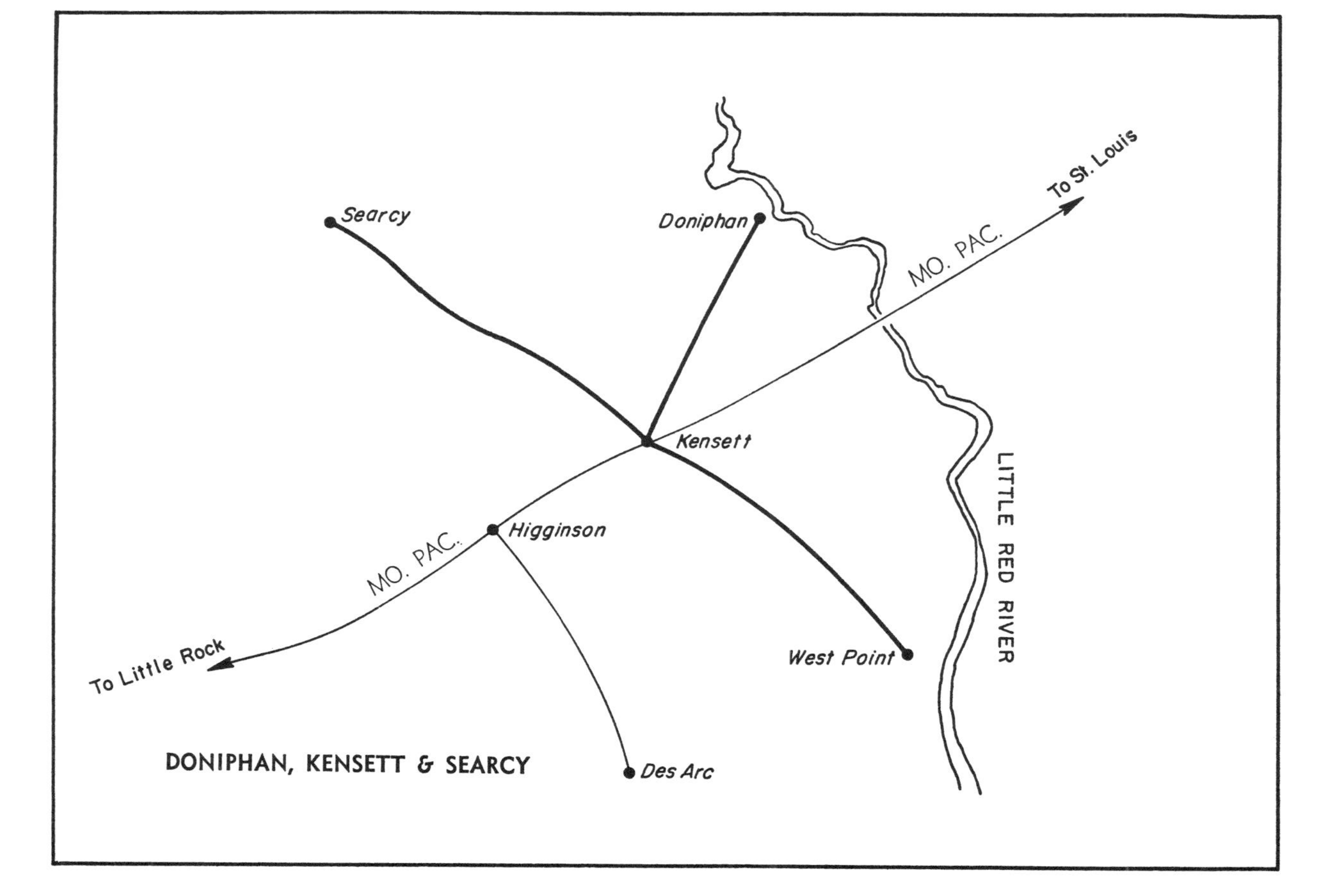
Searcy
Doniphan
To St. Louis
MO. PAC.
Kensett
LITTLE RED RIVER
Higginson
MO. PAC.
To Little Rock
West Point
DONIPHAN, KENSETT & SEARCY
Des Arc

alive. Like many another Arkansas shortline, it was born because a lumber company needed it. The Doniphan Lumber Company had constructed a large mill in the forested foothills of the Ozarks, and the town of Doniphan sprang into existence. During those days of the early 1900's, tax-financed public roads were very scarce in Arkansas, and a railroad was the only dependable means of transportation.

Now it came to pass that the Doniphan, Kensett & Searcy Railroad was incorporated after its organization on March 20, 1906. Instigators of the project were W. H. Horton, H. R. Kilpatrick, E. C. Horton, all from White County, J. J. Cruikshank of Marion County, and C. J. Carter of Jackson County. The state granted them a charter and authorized $45,000 in capital stock to build a railroad from the Doniphan mill, which was approximately on the center line of Section 8, Township 7 North, Range 6 West, in a southerly direction about a mile and a half to the town of Kensett, thence west about five miles to Searcy. This would yield a connection with three fair-size railroads: the St. Louis, Iron Mountain & Southern at Kensett and the Missouri & North Arkansas and the Rock Island at Searcy.

By January, 1907, trains were running from Doniphan to Kensett, pulled by one locomotive, and a new roadbed was being graded from Kensett to Searcy. The company also bought an old tramway which had operated between Kensett and West Point, planning to lay new track on the route and run trains to the old White River port town. The tramway was part of the old Searcy & West Point Railroad.

The DK & S was never a great financial success. Deficits seemed to haunt its ledger sheets. On May 21, 1909, a reorganization was effected, the title was changed from *Railroad* to *Railway*, and the capital stock issue was revised from $45,000 to $100,000. The same names remained on the roster of officers.

The old tramway which operated between Searcy and West Point and whose roadbed was appropriated by the DK & S was a unique sort of operation. Back in 1870, when the route of the

Cairo & Fulton, (later the St. Louis, Iron Mountain & Southern and now the Missouri Pacific) was laid out between Little Rock and the Missouri line, it was learned that the survey would miss Searcy by about four miles. On November 21, 1870, a meeting of the town council was called, and J. C. McCauley, G. F. Baucum, and John Black were appointed as a committee to call on the Cairo & Fulton board of directors. This was done on November 25 at Little Rock, and it was agreed that the survey would be changed if the townspeople would make up the difference in cost, as well as give the C & F a bonus payable in twenty-year bonds bearing 8 per cent interest. The amount of the bonus would be set before the survey crew reached the point where the line would deviate toward Searcy.

On March 14, 1871, the council met again, and the people of Searcy voted 109 to 1 in favor of going into debt for a bonus of twenty thousand dollars to secure the Cairo & Fulton. The road was to be a link in a proposed transcontinental route which lay approximately along the Thirty-fifth Parallel, and being on the route was of utmost importance to any town, large or small. Jesse N. Cypert, a member of the Searcy town council, was an old Civil War buddy of Colonel James H. Morley, chief engineer of the Cairo & Fulton, so it seemed to be almost a lead-pipe cinch that the C & F's rails would pass through Searcy.

The Cairo & Fulton named a bonus figure, which was never made public, but it was so exorbitant that the folks of Searcy refused even to consider it. As an alternative, they decided to build their own railroad and at least be on a branch from the mighty C & F. Thus the Searcy Branch Railroad was formed, with I. M. Moore as president, T. J. Rogers as vice president, P. A. Robertson as secretary, and R. J. Baucum, G. F. Baucum, B. C. Black, L. M. Jones, S. Perry, B. M. Jones, and W. A. Yarnell as directors.

Bid forms for construction were prepared, and the work was advertised. The bid of I. M. Moore and B. C. Black was accepted. They executed a contract to build a wooden railroad for use by one passenger car and one freight car. Horses were to be used as motive power! The contract called for a three-foot-gauge road to be ready for traffic by January 1, 1872. As compensation, they were to receive five thousand dollars in cash and eight thousand dollars in Searcy Branch Railroad bonds, with the payment of bonds to begin in September, 1872. The rails were of white oak, three by five inches, set on edge on crossties two and a half feet apart. A connecting bar, consisting of an iron rod a half-inch in diameter and a piece of white oak two by five inches, was applied at intervals to keep the rails at a constant three-foot gauge.

The wooden pike was a profitable venture, and nineteen hundred dollars was soon raised to ballast the roadbed in order to provide better footing for the four-legged motive power. On January 1, 1874, Ed Faucett and George Chambless leased the road, then subleased it to Black and Wilson.

There was a reorganization on May 4, 1877, and the Searcy & West Point Narrow Gauge Railroad was formed to acquire the tramway from Searcy to Kensett and to extend the rails south and east about four miles to West Point or a navigable point near by on the Little Red River. The project was in charge of W. C. West, J. R. Hardy, and S. G. Tapscott, all of West Point, and Albert G. Ryan and George C. Rumbough of Little Rock.

An unnamed traveler made the trip from Kensett to Searcy in July, 1877, and his account of it was published in the *White County Record* on July 14:

> From Kensett to Searcy connection is made by a wooden tramway, dignified by the name of horse railway. It is very rough, shake-up and jugglety affair; an excellent remedial agent for dyspepsia, but withal a pleasant route of travel and of great convenience to those who wish to transport goods from the depot at the station to town four miles away, or who wish to come out from their bird's nest of a place to journey and see the world. The rolling stock of this road consists of one passenger coach and one freight car. The engines consist of three mules, named respectively, Madam, Muggins, and Hun. We had the pleasure of riding behind Madam,

> a brownish dun-colored animal with a gait like that of an old-clothes peddler, a paint brush tail, and a look of wicked intelligence. Madam is honored by being a passenger engine and is kept in a little better repair than Hun and Muggins, who being compelled to haul freight, feel their humiliation, and when the engineer wishes to attach a tender behind them, let fly their walking beams in a manner which suggests the propriety of putting heavy freight in front of the car and glassware in the rear.
>
> This tramway was built by the city of Searcy, and is owned by that corporation. It cost $16,000 and is leased year after year by the city to the leasee and manager at an average rental of $1,600 a year. The right to run the road and make it earn the manager all that it possibly can is sold at auction on bids. There is some talk of ballasting the track and putting down small T-rails, and putting a light engine with one or two legitimate railroad cars. All this improvement will be made as soon as the people can stand it; for too much improvement at once would send the entire country into convulsions.

There was yet another reorganization, and in January, 1878, the Searcy Branch Railroad Extension was chartered. This outfit was formed by W. A. Yarnell, A. W. Yarnell, Aaron Yarnell, and C. W. Chambless, all of Searcy, and Willshire Riley of Riley's Landing on Little Red River near West Point. They had bought the old road between Searcy and Kensett and rehabilitated it; now they planned to extend it to Riley's Landing or West Point, whichever they might later decide upon (they chose West Point). The route had been surveyed by I. M. Moore in 1876.

Another "locomotive" was purchased and promptly named Kate. Ninas Hardy was engaged to drive Kate, and the two were frequently called upon to run an extra when a dance was being held on a riverboat docked near West Point. Ninas and Kate met every Cairo & Fulton varnish train at Kensett.

From Searcy to Kensett, the track was on a descending grade for about a mile before entering Kensett. Here, at the top of the hill, Ninas would often unhitch old Kate, let his helper ride her into town, and permit his car to coast into Kensett, sometimes attaining the remarkable speed of ten miles per hour. The car's speed was controlled by a length of sapling as Ninas forced one end of it to rub heavily against the ground behind the car. This was known as a "rub brake."

One day on the trip from Kensett to Searcy, Ninas was running a doubleheader (two brawny mules) on an unusually heavy freight car. There was a slight downgrade on the approach to Gin Creek, and as Ninas dropped down toward the bridge, his engines were moving briskly along to stay ahead of the car. A herd of cows came onto the far end of the bridge. There was no chance for Ninas to stop his train. The cows made it across—all but one. The car hit her, knocked her down, and mangled her so badly that she soon died. It was the tramway's only recorded accident.

In January, 1900, George C. Griffith and some other gentlemen built themselves a timber railroad from Higginson, on the St. Louis, Iron Mountain & Southern, to Des Arc, on the White River about twenty-two miles south and east of Higginson. They called it the Des Arc & Northern. Before long, it absorbed the Searcy Branch Railroad and became the Searcy & Des Arc Railroad. The wooden tramway between Searcy and Kensett was abandoned, and the property reverted to the county for nonpayment of taxes. The Rock Island then bought the Searcy & Des Arc and operated it for several years.

The Doniphan, Kensett & Searcy followed the route of the Searcy Branch tramway from Kensett to Searcy. In December, 1931, the DK & S came under the control of the Missouri Pacific, but it still retains its identity and is listed in the *Official Guide of the Railways* along wth the Union Pacific and other little pikes.

APPENDIX B
SHORTLINE RAILROADS IN ARKANSAS IN 1912

This partial list of shortline railroads was compiled by the Arkansas Railroad Commission for the year 1912.

Anderson & Saline River
Arkansas Central
Arkansas, Louisiana & Gulf
Arkansas Midland
Arkansas, Oklahoma & Western
Arkansas Southwestern
Arkansas & Gulf
Arkansas & Louisiana
Bartholomew Valley
Bearden & Ouachita River
Bauxite & Northern
Cache Valley
Caddo & Choctaw
Central of Arkansas
Columbia & Northwestern
Cotton Belt & Northern
Crittenden
Crossett
Dardanelle, Ola & Southern
Dardanelle & Russellville
De Queen & Eastern
Doniphan, Kensett & Searcy
El Dorado & Bastrop
El Dorado & Wesson
Elmore & Southwestern
England & Clear Lake

Fordyce & Princeton
Ft. Smith & Western
Fourche River Valley & Indian Territory
Freeo Valley
Gould Southwestern
Greenfield & Southeastern
Griffon, Magnolia & Western
Gurdon & Ft. Smith Northern
Homan & Southern
Jonesboro, Lake City & Eastern
Kearney & Sheridan
Kendall & Sulphur Springs
L'Anquille River
Lester & Ouachita Valley
Lewisville, Hope & Northern
Little Bay & Hampton
Little River Valley
Little Rock & Hot Springs Western
Little Rock & Monroe
Little Rock, Maumelle & Western
Little Rock, Sheridan & Saline River
Louisiana & Northwest
Luehrman & Western
McMurrain & New London
Malvern & Freeo Valley
Manila & Southwestern
Memphis, Helena & Louisiana
Memphis, Paris & Gulf
Mississippi, Arkansas & Western
Mississippi River, Hamburg & Western
Mississippi Valley & Malvern
Missouri & North Arkansas
Ogamaw & Northwestern
Ouachita Valley
Paragould Southeastern
Paragould & Memphis
Paris-Subiaco Traction
Perla Northern
Pine Bluff, Arkansas River
Pine Bluff & Western
Portland & Southeastern
Prescott & Northwestern
Prescott, Reader & Fordyce
Red River Valley
Rison & Mt. Elba
Rock Island, Arkansas & Louisiana
Round Pond Terminal
Saginaw & Ouachita River
Saline Bayou
Saline River
St. Louis, Kennett & South Eastern
Thornton & Alexandria
Ultima Thule, Arkadelphia & Mississippi
Warren, Johnsville & Saline River
Warren & Ouachita Valley
West Point
Wilmar & Saline Valley
Wyandotte & Southeastern

BIBLIOGRAPHY

Arkansas Democrat, microfilm, Little Rock, Arkansas.

Arkansas Gazette, microfilm, Little Rock, Arkansas.

Beebee, Lucius. Mixed Train Daily, A Book of Short-Line Railroads; Howell-North, Berkeley, California, 1961.

Daily News; Rogers, Arkansas.

Fleming, Howard. Narrow Gauge Railroads of America, ed. Grahame Hardy and Paul Darrell; Grahame Hardy, Oakland, California, 1949.

Gooden, Orville Thrasher. Missouri and North Arkansas Railroad Strike, Studies in History, Economics, and Public Law, ed. by Faculty of Political Science of Columbia University; Columbia University Press, 1926.

Holbrook, Stewart H. Story of American Railroads, Crown Publishers, Inc., 1947.

Interstate Commerce Commission; Finance Docket No. 12365, United States Government Printing Office, 1939.

———, Statistics of Railways In the United States, second annual report, 1889.

Moody, John. Moody's Transportation Manual, Moody's Investors Service, Inc.

Nashville News, Nashville, Arkansas.

Nevada County Picayune, Prescott, Arkansas.

Official Guide of the Railways, National Railway Publication Company, N. Y.

Rayburn, Otto Ernest. Eureka Springs Story; Times-Echo Press, Eureka Springs, Arkansas, 1954.

Robertson, Archie. Slow Train to Yesterday, Somerset Books, Inc., 1945.

Russell, Jesse Lewis. Behind These Ozark Hills, Hobson Book Press, N. Y., 1947.

Vernon, Edward, editor. American Railroad Manual, Vol. II; American Railroad Manual Company, N. Y., 1874.

Young, William S. Short-Line Railroader No. 43; 1960.

INDEX